THE CONCEPT OF FREEDOM

D0196863

THE CONCEPT
OF FREEDOM

by

CHRISTOPHER CAUDWELL

1977
LAWRENCE & WISHART
LONDON

Copyright © the Executors of the estate of C. St. John Sprigg

Studies in a Dying Culture, 1938
Further Studies in a Dying Culture, 1949
The Crisis in Physics, 1939

The 1st, 2nd, 3rd and 5th Studies published in this volume
were first published in 'Studies in a Dying Culture' by Christopher Caudwell, John Lane, The Bodley Head, 1938, and
the 4th and 6th Studies in 'Further Studies in a Dying Culture', John Lane, The Bodley Head, 1949. The five chapters
of 'The Crisis in Physics' are the first five chapters of the
book of that title by Christopher Caudwell, first published
by John Lane, The Bodley Head, in 1939.

This edition 1977

Printed in Great Britain by
The Camelot Press Ltd, Southampton

CONTENTS

PUBLISHER'S NOTE

This volume collects together six of the thirteen essays in Christopher Caudwell's *Studies in a Dying Culture* and *Further Studies*, together with the completed chapters of his *Crisis in Physics*.

The "studies" selected here as the most significant are of "the bourgeois artist", "changing values", "bourgeois illusion", "bourgeois aesthetics" and "bourgeois psychology". The intimate connection of these with the apparently unconnected theme of "the Crisis in Physics" is shown by the fact that the latter might well have been sub-titled, in the same vein, "A Study in Bourgeois Science".

Christopher Caudwell's *Studies* remain the most acute and profound of all the Marxist writing in Britain in the 'thirties, and stand the test of time in the 'seventies. His *Crisis in Physics* was written in the period when the Theory of Relativity, Quantum Theory, and then Heisenburg's Principle of Uncertainty were felt to have shaken the foundations of a long-accepted and seemingly irrefutably established view of the nature of the physical world. Caudwell saw "the crisis in physics" of those days as a crisis in bourgeois ideology.

His book on physics was never completed. The five chapters here reproduced were the only ones fully written up—the rest simply consisted of notes.

"Christopher Caudwell" was the pen-name adopted for his more serious writings by Christopher St John Sprigg, born in Putney in 1907 and killed in action with the International Brigade in Spain in 1937. He had engaged in journalism, in compiling technological textbooks (on aeronautics) and in detective story writing before his interest in Marxism and communism developed in 1934. In the short period from then until his departure to fight against fascism in Spain he produced, under the name of Christopher Caudwell the amazing series of writings, all published posthumously. Living in the East End of London, and putting in his stint of "Party work" there, he had held himself aloof from the "Party intellectuals" of those days. The originality and depth of his ideas, his search for answers and refusal to stay content with any proposed as final, have continued as influence and inspiration ever since *Illusion and Reality* was published just after his death.

We do not have to agree with all Caudwell's pronouncements to appreciate their value. Indeed, he quite evidently did not long continue to agree with all of them himself—since, for example, the rather doctrinaire "psychology" which he introduced into *Illusion and Reality* is already superseded by a more profound critical treatment of the subject in the two "Studies in Bourgeois Psychology" reprinted in this volume.

STUDIES IN A DYING CULTURE

I

D. H. LAWRENCE

A STUDY OF THE BOURGEOIS ARTIST

What is the function of the artist? Any artist such as Lawrence, who aims to be 'more than' an artist, necessarily raises this question. It is supposed to be the teaching of Marxism that art for art's sake is an illusion and that art must be propaganda. This is, however, making the usual bourgeois simplification of a complex matter.

Art is a social function. This is not a Marxist demand, but arises from the very way in which art forms are defined. Only those things are recognised as art forms which have a conscious social function. The phantasies of a dreamer are not art. They only become art when they are given music, forms or words, when they are clothed in socially recognised symbols, and of course in the process there is a modification. The phantasies are modified by the social dress; the language as a whole acquires new associations and context. No chance sounds constitute music, but sounds selected from a socially recognised scale and played on socially developed instruments.

It is not for Marxism therefore to demand that art play a social function or to attack the conception of 'art for art's sake', for art only *is* art, and recognisable as such, in so far as it plays a social function. What is of importance to art, Marxism and society is the question: *What social function is art playing?* This in turn depends on the type of society in which it is secreted.

In bourgeois society social relations are denied in the form of relations between men, and take the form of a relation between man and a thing, a property relation, which, because it is a dominating relation, is believed to make man free. But this is an illusion. The property relation is only a disguise for relations which now become unconscious and therefore anarchic but are still between man and man, and in particular between exploiter and exploited.

The artist in bourgeois culture is asked to do the same thing. He is asked to regard the art work as a finished commodity and the process of art as a relation between himself and the work, which then disappears into the market. There is a further relation between the art work and the buyer, but with this he can hardly be immediately concerned. The whole pressure of bourgeois society is to make him regard the art work as hypostatised and his relation to it as primarily that of a producer for the market.

This will have two results.

(i) The mere fact that he has to earn his living by the sale of the concrete hypostatised entity as a property right—copyright, picture, statue—may drive him to estimate his work as an artist by the market chances which produce a high total return for these property rights. This leads to the commercialisation or vulgarisation of art.

(ii) But art is not in any case a relation to a thing, it is a relation between men, between artist and audience, and the art work is only like a machine which they must both grasp as part of the process. The commercialisation of art may revolt the sincere artist, but the tragedy is that he revolts against it still within the limitations of bourgeois culture. He attempts to forget the market completely and concentrate on his relation to the art work, which now becomes still further hypostatised as an entity-in-itself. Because the art work is now completely and end-in-itself, and even the market is forgotten, the art process becomes an extremely individualistic relation. The social values inherent in the art form, such as syntax, tradition, rules, technique, form, accepted tonal scale, now seem to have little value, for the art work more and more exists for the individual alone. The art work is necessarily always the product of a tension between old conscious social formulations—the art 'form'—and new individual experience made conscious—the art 'content' or the artist's 'message'. This is the synthesis, the specifically hard task of creation. But the hypostatisation of the art work as the goal makes old conscious social formulations less and less important, and individual experience more and more dominating. As a result art becomes more and more formless, personal, and individualistic, culminating in Dadaism, surréalism and 'Steinism'.

Thus bourgeois art disintegrates under the tension of two forces, both arising from the same feature of bourgeois culture. On the one hand there is production for the market—vulgarisation, commercialisation. On the other there is hypostatisation of the art work as the goal of the art process, and the relation between art work and individual as paramount. This necessarily leads to a dissolution of those social values which make the art in question a social relation, and therefore ultimately results in the art work's ceasing to be an art work and becoming a mere private phantasy.

All bourgeois art during the last two centuries shows the steady development of this bifurcation. As long as the social values inherent in an art form are not disintegrated—e.g. up to say 1910—the artist who hypostatises the art form and despises the market can produce good art. After that, it becomes steadily more difficult. Needless to say, the complete acceptance of the market, being a refusal to regard any part of the art process as a social process, is even more incompetent to produce great art. Anything which helps the artist to escape from the bourgeois trap and become conscious of social relations inherent in art, will help to delay the rot. For this reason the novel is the last surviving literary art form in bourgeois culture, for in it, for reasons explained elsewhere, the social relations inherent in the art process are overt. Dorothy Richardson, James Joyce, and Proust, all in different ways are the last blossoms of the bourgeois novel, for with them the novel begins to disappear as an objective study of social relations and becomes a study of the subject's experience in society. It is then only a step for the thing experienced to disappear and, as in Gertrude Stein, for complete 'me-ness' to reign.

It is inevitable that at this stage the conception of the artist as a pure 'artist' must cease to exist. For commercialised art has become intolerably base and negated itself. And equally art for art's sake (that is, the ignoring of the market and concentration on the perfect art work as a goal in itself) has negated itself, for the art form has ceased to exist, and what was art

13

has become private phantasy. It is for this reason that sincere artists, such as Lawrence, Gide, Romain Rolland, Romains and so on, cannot be content with the beautiful art work, but seem to desert the practice of art for social theory and become novelists of ideas, literary prophets and propaganda novelists. They represent the efforts of bourgeois art, exploded into individualistic phantasy and commercialised muck, to become once more a social process and so be reborn. Whether such art is or can be great art is beside the point, since it is inevitably the pre-requisite for art becoming art again, just as it is beside the point whether the transition from bourgeoisdom to communism is itself smooth or happy or beautiful or free, since it is the inevitable step if bourgeois anarchy and misery are to be healed and society to become happy and free.

But what is art as a social process? What is art, not as a mere art work or a means or earning a living, but in itself, the part it plays in society? I have dealt fully with this point elsewhere, and need only briefly recapitulate now.

The personal phantasy or day dream is not art, however beautiful. Nor is the beautiful sunset. Both are only the raw material of art. It is the property of art that it makes mimic pictures of reality which we accept as illusory. We do not suppose the events of a novel really happen, that a landscape shown on a painting can be walked upon—yet it has a measure of reality.

The mimic representation, by the technique appropriate to the art in question, causes the social representation to sweat out of its pores an affective emanation. The emanation is *in* us, *in* our affective reaction with the elements of the representation. Given in the representation are not only the affects, but, simultaneously, their organisation in an affective *attitude* towards the piece of reality symbolised in the mimicry. This affective attitude is bitten in by a general heightening of consciousness and increase in self-value, due to the non-motor nature of the innervations aroused, which seem therefore all to pass into an affective irradiation of consciousness. This affective attitude is not permanent, as is the intellectual attitude towards reality aroused by a cogent scientific argument, but still—because of the mnemenic characteristics of an organism

14

—it remains as an *experience* and must, therefore, in proportion to the amount of conscious poignancy accompanying the experience and the nature of the experience, modify the subject's general attitude towards life itself. This modification tends to make life more interesting to the organism, hence he survival value of art. But viewed from society's standpoint, art is the fashioning of the affective consciousness of its members, the conditioning of their instincts.

Language, simply because it is the most general instrument for communicating views of reality, whether affective or cognitive, has a particularly fluid range of representations of reality. Hence the suppleness and scope of literary art; the novel, the drama, the poem, the short story, and the essay. It can draw upon all the symbolic pictures of reality made by scientific, historical and discursive intellectual processes. Art can only achieve its purpose if the pictures themselves are made simultaneously to produce effect and organisation. Then, even as the artist holds up to us the piece of reality, it seems already glowing with affective colouring.

Reality constitutes for us our environment; and our environment, which is chiefly social, alters continuously—sometimes barely perceptibly, sometimes at dizzy speeds. The socially accepted pictures we make in words of reality cannot change as if they were reflections in a mirror. An object is reflected in a mirror. If the object moves the reflection moves. But in language reality is symbolised in unchanging words which give a false stability and permanence to the object they represent. Thus they instantaneously photograph reality rather than reflect it. This frigid character of language is regrettable but it has its utilitarian purposes. It is probably the only way in which man, with his linear consciousness, can get a grip of fluid reality. Language, as it develops, shows more and more of this false permanence, till we arrive at the Platonic Ideas, Eternal and Perfect Words. Their eternity and perfection are simply the permanence of print and paper. If you coin a word or write a symbol to describe an entity of event, the word will remain 'eternally' unchanged even while the entity has changed and the event is no longer present. This permanence is part of the inescapable nature of symbolism, which is expressed in the rules of logic. It is one of the strange freaks of the human mind that it has supposed that reality must obey the rules of logic, whereas the correct view is that symbolism by its very nature has certain rules, expressed in the laws of logic, and these are nothing to do with the process of reality, but represent the nature of the symbolic process itself.

The artist experiences this discrepancy between language and reality as follows: he has had an intense experience of a rose and wishes to communicate his experience to his fellows in words. He wishes to say, 'I saw a rose'. But 'rose' has a definite social meaning, or group of meanings, and we are to suppose that he has had an experience with the rose which does not correspond to any of society's previous experiences of roses, embodied in the word and its history. His experience of the rose is therefore the negation of the word 'rose', it is 'not-rose' —all that in his experience which is not expressed in the current social meaning of the word 'rose'. He therefore says—'I saw a rose like'—and there follows a metaphor, or there is an adjective—'a heavenly rose', or a euphemism—'I saw a flowery blush', and in each case there is a synthesis, for his new experience has become socially fused into society's old experiences and both have been changed in the process. His own experience has taken colour from all past meanings of the word 'rose', for these will be present in men's minds when they read his poem, and the word 'rose' will have taken colour from his individual experience, for his poem will in future be in men's minds when they encounter the word 'rose'.

But why was the poet's experience different from society's tradition? Because that cross-section of his environment which we call his individual life-experience was different. But if we take all society's art as a whole, i.e. the sum of individual cross-sections, we get on the one hand the whole experience of the environment averaged out, and also the average man, or average genotype. Now the constant genesis of new art must mean that the environment is changing, so that man's individual experiences are changing, and he is constantly finding inherited social conscious formulations inadequate and requiring resynthesis. Thus if art forms remain unchanged and traditional, as in Chinese civilisation, it is evident that the environment—

social relations—are static. If they decay the environment is on the down-grade, as with current bourgeois culture. If they improve, the reverse is the case. But the artist's value is not in *self*-expression. If so, why should he struggle to achieve the synthesis in which old social formulations are fused with his individual experience? Why not disregard social formalities and express himself direct as one does by shouting, leaping, and cries? Because, to begin with, it is the old bourgeois illusion to suppose there is such a thing as pure individual expression. It is not even that the artist nobly forces his self-expression into a social mould for the benefit of society. Both attitudes are simply expressions of the old bourgeois fallacy that man is free in freely giving vent to his instincts. In fact the artist does not express himself in art forms, he finds himself therein. He does not adulterate his free self-expression to make it socially current, he finds free self-expression only in the social relations embodied in art. The value of art to the artist then is this, that it makes him free. It appears to him of value as a self-expression, but in fact is is not the expresion of a self but the discovery of a self. It in the creation of a self. In synthesising experience with society's, in pressing his inner self into the mould of social relations, he not only creates a new mould, a socially valuable product, but he also moulds and creates his own self. The mute inglorious Milton is a fallacy. Miltons are made not born.

The value of art to society is that by it an emotional adaptation is possible. Man's instincts are pressed in art against the altered mould of reality, and by a specific organisation of the emotions thus generated, there is a new attitude, an *adaptation*. All art is produced by this tension between changing social relations and outmoded consciousness. The very reason why new art is created, why the old art does not satisfy either artist or appreciator, is because it seems somehow out of gear with the present. Old art always has meaning for us, because the instincts, the source of the affects, do not change, because a new system of social relations does not exclude but includes the old, and because new art too includes the traditions of the art that has gone before. But it is not enough. We must have new art.

And new art results from tension. This tension takes two forms. (i) One is productive—the evolutionary form. The tension between production relations and productive forces secures the advance of society as a whole, simply by producing in an even more pronounced form the contradiction which was the source of the dynamism. Thus bourgeois culure by continually dissolving the relations between men for relations to a thing, and thus hypostatising the market, procured the growth of industrial capitalism. And, in the sphere of art it produced the increasing individualism which, setn at its best in Shakespeare, was a positive value, but pushed to its limit finally spelt the complete breakdown of art in surréalism, Dadaism and Steinism.

(ii) The tension now becomes revolutionary. For production relations are a brake on productive forces and the tension between them, instead of altering production relations in the direction of giving better outlet to productive forces, has the opposite effect. It drives production relations on still further into negation, increases the tension, and prepares the explosion which will shatter the old production relations and enable them to be rebuilt anew—not arbitrarily, but according to a pattern which will itself be given by the circumstances of the tension. Thus in art the tension between individualism and the increasing complexity and catastrophes of the artist's environment, between the free following of dream and the rude blows of anarchic reality, wakes the artist from his dream and forces him in spite of himself to look at the world, not merely as an artist, but also as a man, as a citizen, as a sociologist. It forces him to be interested in things not strictly germane to art; —politics, economics, science, and philosophy, just as it did during the early bourgeois Renaissance, producing 'all-round men' like Leonardo da Vinci. Whether this is good for art or not is beside the point. Bourgeois art like bourgeois culture is moribund and this process is an inevitable concomitant of the stage preceding art's rebirth. And because of this intervening period, the new art when it emerges will be art more conscious of itself as part of the whole social process, will be *communist* art. This explains why all modern artists of any significance such as Lawrence, Gide, Aragon, dos Passos, Eliot and so on, cannot be content to be 'pure' artist, but must also be prophets, thinkers, philosophers, and politicians, men interested in life and social reality as a whole. They are conscious of having a message. This is the inevitable effect on art of a revolutionary period, and it is not possible to escape from it into 'pure' art, into the ivory tower, for now there is no pure art; that phase is either over or not yet begun.

But at a revolution two paths are possible. So indeed they are in evolution—one can either stay still and be classical, academic and null, or go forward. But at a time of revolution it is not possible to stay still, one must either go forward, or back. To us this choice appears as a choice between Communism and Fascism, either to create the future or to go back to old primitive values, to mythology, racialism, nationalism, hero-worship, and *participation mystique*. This Fascist art is like the regression of the neurotic to a previous level of adaptation.

It is Lawrence's importance as an artist that he was well aware of the fact that the pure artist cannot exist to-day, and that the artist must inevitably be a man hating cash relationships and the market, and profoundly interested in the relations between persons. Moreover, he must be a man not merely profoundly interested in the relations between persons as they are, but interested in changing them, dissatisfied with them as they are, and wanting newer and fuller values in personal relationships.

But it is Lawrence's final tragedy that his solution was ultimately Fascist and not Communist. It was regressive. Lawrence wanted us to return to the past, to the 'Mother'. He sees human discontent as the yearning of the solar plexus for the umbilical connexion, and he demands the substitution for sharp sexual love of the unconscious fleshy identification of foetus with mother. All this was symbolic of regression, of neurosis, of the return to the primitive.

Lawrence felt that the Europe of to-day was moribund; and he turned therefore to other forms of existence, in Mexico, Etruria and Sicily, where he found or thought he found systems of social relations in which life flowed more easily and more meaningfully. The life of bourgeois Europe seemed to him permeated with possessiveness and rationalising, so that it had got out of gear with the simple needs of the body. In a thousand forms he repeats this indictment of a civilisation which consciously *and just because it is conscious*—sins against the instinctive currents which are man's primal source of energy. It is a mistake to suppose that Lawrence preaches the gospel of sex. Bourgeois Europe has had its bellyful of sex, and a sex cult would not now attract the interest and emotional support which Lawrence's teaching received. Lawrence's gospel was purely sociological. Even sex was too conscious for him.

'Anybody who calls my novel (Lady Chatterley's Lover) a dirty sexual novel, is a liar. It's not even a sexual novel: it's a phallic. Sex is a thing that exists in the head, its reactions are cerebral, and its processes mental. Whereas the phallic reality is warm and spontaneous——'

Again he wrote:

'What ails me is the absolute frustration of my primitive societal instinct ... I think societal instinct much deeper than the sex instinct—and societal repression much more devastating. There is no repression of the sexual individual comparable to the repression of the societal man in me, by the individual ego, my own and everybody's else's. I am weary even of my own individuality, and simply nauseated by other people's.'

One more analysis by him of the evil in bourgeois culture: (In the Cornish people)—

'the old race is still revealed, a race which believed in the darkness, in magic, and in the magic transcendency of one man over another which is fascinating. Also there is left some of the old sensuousness of the darkness and warmth and passionateness of the blood, sudden, incalculable. Whereas they are like insects, gone cold, living only for money, for *dirt*. They are foul in this. They ought to die.'

Now here is a clear artistic, i.e. *emotional*, analysis of the decay of bourgeois social relations. They live for money, the societal instinct is repressed, even the sex relations have become cold and infected. Survivals of barbaric social relations between men (the 'magic transcendency' of man over man) stand out as valuable in a culture where these relations have become relations between man and a thing, *man and dirt.*

But Lawrence does not look for a cause in social relations themselves, but in man's consciousness of them. The solution of the individual's needs is then plainly to be found in a return to instinctive living. But how are we to return to instinctive living? By casting off consciousness; we must return along the path we have come. But intellectualism consists in this, that we give either linguistically, plastically, or mentally, a symbolic projection to portions of reality, and consciousness or thinking consists simply in shuffling these images or verbal products. If therefore we are to cast off intellectualism and consciousness we must abandon all symbolism and rationalisation *tout court,* we must *be,* and no longer think, even in images. Yet on the contrary Lawrence again and again *consciously* formulates his creed in intellectual terms or terms of imagery. But this is self-contradiction, for how can we be led intellectually and consciously *back* from consciousness? It is our consciousness that Lawrence attempts to extend and heighten even at the moment he urges us to abandon it.

Consciousness can only be abandoned in action, and the first action of Fascism is the crushing of culture and the burning of the books. It is impossible therefore for an artist and thinker to be a consistent Fascist. He can only be like Lawrence, a self-contradictory one, who appeals to the consciousness of men to abandon consciousness.

There is a confusion here due to equating consciousness with thinking and unconsciousness with feeling. This is wrong. Both are conscious. No one ever had or could have an unconscious affect or emotion. Feeling indeed is what makes the unconscious memory traces conscious, and heats them into thoughts. All of us, in times of deep feeling, whether artistic or emotional feeling, are aware of heightened consciousness almost like a white light in us so intense and clear is it. But Lawrence never clearly saw this, and constantly equates unconsciousness with feeling and consciousness with intellect. For example:

21

'My great religion is a belief in the blood, in the flesh, as being wiser than the intellect. We can go wrong in our minds. But what our blood feels and believes and says is always true. The intellect is only a bit and a bridle. What do I care about knowledge? All I want is to answer to my blood, direct, without fumbling intervention of mind, or moral, or what not. I conceive a man's body as a kind of flame, like a candle flame forever upright and yet flowing: and the intellect is just the light that is shed on the things around, coming God knows how from out of practically nowhere, and being *itself,* whatever there is around it that lights up. We have got so ridiculously mindful, that we never know that we ourselves are anything—we think there are only the objects we shine upon. And there the poor flame goes on burning ignored, to produce this light. And instead of chasing the mystery in the fugitive, half-lighted things outside us, we ought to look at ourselves and say, "My God, I am myself!" That is why I like to live in Italy. The people are so unconscious. They only feel and want, they don't know. We know too much. No, we only *think* we know such a lot. A flame isn't a flame because it lights up two, or twenty objects on a table. It's a flame because it is itself. And we have forgotten ourselves.'

Feeling and thinking play into each other's hands and heighten each other. Man feels more deeply than the slug because he thinks more. Why did Lawrence make this error of supposing them essentially exclusive, and equate feeling with unconsciousness? Once again, the answer is in the nature of current society. All feeling and all thinking must contain something of each other to form part of consciousness at all. But it is possible to distinguish certain conscious phenomena as chiefly feeling, or vice versa. 'Pure' feelings, any more than 'pure' thoughts, do not exist at all, since the first would be a mere instinctive tendency, the second nothing but a mnemenic trace. Both would be unconscious and evidenced therefore only in behaviour. Lawrence might mean that feeling has wilted under modern conditions and that we must expand the feeling basis of our consciousness.

We know this of feelings (and affects generally) that they

come into consciousness associated with innate responses or—more loosely—that they seem to be born of the modification, by experience and in action of the 'instincts'. Instinct going out in unmodified action, in mechanical response to a stimulus, is without *feeling*, it is pure automatism. Only when it becomes modified by memory traces or stifled by action does it become conscious and appear as feeling. The more intelligent the animal, the more its behaviour is modifiable by experience, the more feeling it displays. This extra display of feeling is *because* it is more intelligent, more conscious, less swayed by heredity, more subject to personal experience. Modification of innate responses by experience simply implies that previous behaviour leaves a mnemenic trace on the neurones, chiefly of the cortex. These when innervated produce a new pattern, whose modification takes in the cortical sphere the form of thoughts and, in the visceral and thalamic sphere, the form of feelings or emotional dynamism. The different proportion of the components decides whether we call them thoughts or feelings. Even the simplest thought is irradiated with affect, and even the simplest emotion is accompanied by a thought, not necessarily verbalised but of some such character as 'I am hurt', or 'A pain'. It is because thought and feeling arise from the same modification of innate responses, by experience, that the growth of intelligence, i.e. of the *capacity* for modification of behaviour by experience, is accompanied by a steadily increasing emotional complexity, richness, and deepness. It is plain that the growth of civilisation in *homo sapiens* has been accompanied by a steady increase in sensibility to pain and pleasure. This is the famous 'sensitiveness' of civilised man, the 'luxury' of high cultures, which is also manifested in their art and their vocabulary. Primitive peoples on the other hand show a marked deficiency in their sensibility, not only to refined emotions but even the cruder ones. The extremely erotic character of savage dances is not due, as some observers naïvely suppose, to the emotional erethism of the natives, but to the reverse, that in them the erotic impulses, owing to their deficient sensibility, can only be aroused by violent stimulation, whereas a slight stimulus will set off the hair-trigger emotions of civilised people. The same phenomenon is shown in pri-

23

mitive insensibility to pain. Consequently if we are to return down the path we have come from, back to primitiveness, to the blood, to the flesh, it is not only to less and cruder thought but also to less and cruder feeling, to a lessened consciousness in which feeling and thought, precisely because they are less rich and complex, will be more intimately mingled, until finally, as they both blend completely and become one, they vanish and nothing is left but unconscious *behaviour*. But how can this goal be of value to an artist, save on condition he denies himself the very law of his being? Art is not unconscious behaviour, it is conscious feeling.

It is, however, possible to broaden feeling without altering thought or losing consciousness, by altering the ratio between them in modern civilisation. That is precisely the purpose of art, for the artist makes use always of just those verbal or pictorial images of reality which are more charged with feeling than cognition, and he organises them in such a way that the affects re-inforce each other and fuse to a glowing mass. Consequently, he who believes that at all costs the feeling element must be broadened in presentday consciousness, must preach and secure, not the contraction of all consciousness, but the widening of feeling consciousness. This is art's mission. Art is the technique of affective manipulation in relation to reality. Lawrence was doing what I suppose him to have wished to do, just when he was artist pure and simple, sensitively recording the spirit of a place or the emotions of real people—in his early work. In proportion as he became a prophet, preaching a gospel intellectually, he departed from that goal.

How did he come to make first the initial *sortie* in favour of feeling, and then the contradictory error, deserting art for preaching? He came to the first conclusion because feeling is impoverished by modern bourgeois culure. Social relations, by ceasing to be between man and man and adhering to a thing, become emptied of tenderness. Man feels himself deprived of love. His whole instinct revolts against this. He feels a vast maladaption to his environment. Lawrence perceives this clearly when he talks about the repression of the societal instinct.

But things have gone so far that no tinkering with social relations, no adaptation of the instincts to the environment by means of art, will cure this. Social relations themselves must be rebuilt. The artist is bound for the sake of his integrity to become thinker and revolutionary. Lawrence therefore was bound not to be content with pure art, with widening feeling consciousness in the old circle. He had to try and recast social relations and proceed to a solution. But there is only one revolutionary solution. Social relations must be altered, not so as to contract consciousness but so as to widen it. The higher feeling must be found, not in a lower but as always in a higher level of culture.

Naturally consciousness seems in bourgeois culture now, as in all periods of decay, full of defects with which being struggles, and this seems like unconsciousness crippled by consciousness. Those defects in bourgeois social relations all arise from the cash nexus which replaces all other social ties, so that society seems held together, not by mutual love or tenderness or obligation, but simply by profit. Money makes the bourgeois world go round and this means that selfishness is the hinge on which bourgeois society turns, for money is a dominating relation to an owned thing. This commercialisation of all social relations invades the most intimate of emotions, and the relations of the sexes are affected by the differing economic situations of man and woman. The notion of private property, aggravated by its importance and overwhelming power in bourgeois relations, extends to love itself. Because economic relations in capitalism are simply each man struggling for himself in the impersonal market, the world seems torn apart with the black forces of envy, covetousness and hate, which mix with and make ambivalent even the most 'altruistic' emotions.

But it is simplifying the drama to make it a struggle between contemporary consciousness and old being. It is a conflict between production relations and productive powers, between the contemporary formulations of consciousness, and all the possibilities of future being including consciousness latent in society and struggling to be released from their bonds. Bourgeois defects are implicit in bourgeois civilisation and therefore in bourgeois consciousness. Hence man wants to turn against the intellect, for it seems that the intellect is his enemy, and indeed it is, if by intellect we mean the bourgeois intellect. But it can only be fought with intellect. To deny intellect is to assist the forces of conservatism. In hundreds of diverse forms we see to-day the useless European revolt against intellectualism.

In any civilisation the rôle of consciousness is to modify instinctive responses so that they flow smoothly into the mill of social relations and turn it. Instinct not money really turns the social mill, though in the bourgeois world instinctive relations can only operate along the money channel. Hence when social relations come to be a brake on society's forces, there is felt a conflict between the social relations and the instincts. It seems as if the feelings were out of gear, as if the world was uncomfortable and hurt the feelings and repressed them. It seems as if the instincts, and the feelings, those products of the instincts, were being penalised by the environment, and that, therefore, the instincts and feelings must be 'given their due', must be exalted even if it means breaking up and abandoning the civilised environment for a more primitive one. To-day this exaltation of the instincts is seen in all demands for a return to deeper 'feeling', as with Lawrence, and in all worships of unconscious 'mentation', as with the surréalists, Hemingways, and Fascists. In individuals this mechanism is infantile regression, seen in its pathological form in the neuroses.

Now these mechanisms involve the discovery of a real defect. Social being *is* held back by social consciousness; the instincts *are* thwarted and the feelings *are* made poor by the environment. But the remedy is wrong. The neurotic cannot, as we know, be cured by infantile regression. All it does for him is to secure him unconsciousness and take from him painful thoughts, at the price of a lowering of consciousness and an impoverishing of values. Civilisation cannot be cured by going back along the path to the primitive, it can only become at a lower level more unconscious of its decay. Just as the neurotic's return to childhood solutions of problems is unhealthier than childhood, so a civilisation's return to a primitive solution is unhealthier than primitive life itself. The very history between makes such solutions unreal. To the primitive these problems have never existed. To the regressive they have existed but he has repressed them. It is into the wilderness these people would lead us. They preach, not new vigour, but old decadence.

What then is the cure? We know that both in the case of the neurotic and the civilisation, the cure is a more strenuous and creative act than the invalid's relapse into the womb of that unconsciousness from which we emerged. Our task is to be performed, not in an air heavy and fetid with mysteries and dead symbolism like that of a cavern used for old obscene rites, but in the open air.

We are not to return to the old but it is into the new we must go; and the new does not exist, we must bring it into being. The child would love to return to the womb, but it must become adult and face the strenuous and bracing tasks of life. We are not to abandon consciousness but to expand it, to deepen and purge feeling and break up and recast thought, and this new consciousness does not exist in any thing's keeping, either Mexicans or Yogis or the 'blood', but we must make it ourselves. In this struggle with reality in which instincts, feeling and thought all partake and interact, the instincts themselves will be changed, and emerging in consciousness as new thought and new feeling, will once again feel themselves in harmony with the new environment they have created. Social relations must be changed so that love returns to the earth and man is not only wiser but more full of emotion. This is not a task which one prophet can perform in one Gospel, but since the whole fabric of social relations is to be changed, every human being must in some sort participate in the change, be either for it or against it, and be victorious if he is for it and be defeated if he is against it.

Why did Lawrence, faced with the problem, fail of a solution? He failed because while hating bourgeois culture he never succeeded in escaping from its limitations. Here in him, too, we see the same old lie. Man is 'free' in so far as his 'free' instincts, the 'blood', the 'flesh', are given an outlet. Man is free not through but *in spite of* social relations.

If one believes this—which, as we have seen, is the deepest and most ineradicable bourgeois illusion, all others are built on this—one must, if one is hurt by bourgeois social relations, see security and freedom only in casting them off, and returning to a primitive state with less 'constraints'. One must necessarily believe freedom and happiness can be found by one's own individual action. One will not believe freedom and happiness can only be found through social relations, by co-operating with others to change them, but there is always something one can do, fly to Mexico, find the right woman or the right friends, and so discover salvation. One will never see the truth, that one can only find salvation for oneself by finding it for all others at the same time.

Lawrence therefore could never escape from this essential selfishness—not a petty selfishness but the selfishness which is the pattern of bourgeois culture and is revealed in pacifism, Protestantism, and all varieties of salvation obtained by individual action. The world to which Lawrence wished to return is not really the world of primitives, who are in fact bound by more rigid relations than those of bourgeois Europe. It is the old bourgeois pastoral heaven of the 'natural man' born everywhere in chains, which does not exist. It does not exist because it is self-contradictory, and because it is self-contradictory the bourgeois world in striving for it more clearly produces the opposite, as in moving towards an object in a mirror we move away from the real object. Lawrence's gospel therefore only forms part of the self-destructive element in bourgeois culture.

Lawrence for all his gifts suffered from the old *petit bourgeois* errors. Like Wells, he strove to climb upwards into the world of bourgeois culture; being more artistic than Wells and born in a later era, it could not be the security and power of that already sick class that appealed to him. It was their cultural values. He succeeded in entering that world and drinking deeply of all its tremendous intellectual and aesthetic riches, only to find them riches turning into dust. The shock of that disillusion, added to the pain endured in that climb, filled him finally with a hatred for bourgeois values. He could criticise them relentlessly and bitterly, but he could provide no solution for the whole set of his life; all that long difficult climb of his into the bourgeois sunshine ensured that he remained a bourgeois. His was always bourgeois culture, conscious of its decay, criticising itself and with no solution except to go back to a time when things were different and so undo all the development that had brought bourgeois culture to this pass.

Had he been born later, had that sunlit world never appealed to him so irresistibly, he might have seen that it was the proletariat—to whom he was so near at the start of his climb— that was the dynamic force of the future. Not only would he then have had a standpoint outside bourgeois culture from which to criticise it, but from that position he would have been able to find the true solution—in the future, not the past. But Lawrence remained to the end a man incapable of that subordination of self to others, of co-operation, of solidarity as a class, which is the characteristic of the proletariat. He remained the individualist, the bourgeois revolutionary angrily working out his own salvation, critical of all, alone in possession of grace. He rid himself of every bourgeois illusion but the important one. He saw finally neither the world nor himself as it really was. He saw the march of events as a bourgeois tragedy, which is true but unimportant. The important thing, which was absolutely closed to him, was that it was also a proletarian renaissance.

Everywhere to-day will be found the conscious or unconscious followers of Lawrence—the pacifists, the snug little hedonists, the conscientious sexualists, the well-meaning Liberals, the idealists, all seeking the impossible solution, salvation through the free act of the individual will amid decay and disaster. They may find a temporary solution, a momentary happiness, although I judge Lawrence to have found neither. But it is of its nature unstable, for external events to which they have regressively adjusted themselves, beget incessantly new horrors and undreamed-of disasters. What avails such pinchbeck constructs during the screaming horror of a war? One may stop one's ears and hide oneself in Cornwall like Lawrence, but the cry of millions of one's suffering fellow-humans reaches one's ears and tortures one. And, the war at last survived, there come new horrors. The eating disintegration of the slump. Nazism outpouring a flood of barbarism and horror. And what next? Armaments piling up like an accumulating catastrophe, mass neurosis, nations like mad dogs. All this seems gratuitous, horrible, cosmic to such people, unaware of the causes. How can the bourgeois still pretend to be

free, to find salvation individually? Only by sinking himself
in still cruder illusions, by denying art, science, emotion,, even
ultimately life itself. Humanism, the creation of bourgeois culture, finally separates from it. Against the sky stands Capitalism without a rag to cover it, naked in its terror. And humanism, leaving it, or rather, forcibly thrust aside, must either
pass into the ranks of the proletariat or, going quietly into a
corner, cut its throat. Lawrence did not live to face this final
issue, which would necessarily make straw of his philosophy
and his teaching.

II

LOVE

The natural human failing is to suppose nothing changes, that ideas are eternal, and that what is denoted by a word is as changeless and invariant as the word. Wisdom consists chiefly in learning that those vague gestures towards parts of reality, gestures we call concepts, not only cannot describe the thing indicated, but cannot even point to the same thing, only to something *divers et ondoyant* flashing to our interested eyes in the process of becoming. The dog subsumes all small running things under the concept 'prey'. He does not utter it as a word, but still shows the unvarying nature of his concept by a stereotyped action of pursuit. We can see his foolishness, for we have divided 'prey' into rabbits, rats, and cats, even perhaps into individual cats with different habits. But at a higher level of reference we make the same kind of mistake.

We tend to think, for example, that love is something definite and quite clear. If we are romantic poets, novelists or film-goers, we are in danger of picturing it as a kind of Paradisial pit into which we fall. There is no doubt about it, either we are over the edge and deep in, or safe outside it. To the instinct psychologist love is an innate response, i.e. a clearly defined behaviour pattern set off by certain stimuli, just as an automatic model is set going by putting a penny in the slot. To the psychoanalyst, love is a quantity of psychic energy, called libido, as limited and homogenous as a pound of suet, which is parcelled by repressions and inhibition into various channels, returns on itself, is transferred, cathexed and displaced, but is still visualised as the same consistent suet.

But 'love'—unless we are to restrict the word to a specialised behaviour pattern dependent on the particular institutions of matrimony and property of our period of history—is

31

man's name for the emotional element in social relations. All languages and usages seem to agree in this. I love, *j'aime*, are expressions which may be used both for sexual and social emotions. The Freudian has an explanation for this, which we shall examine in a moment. If our definition of love is correct, it is true that love makes the world go round. But it would be rather truer to say that society going round as it does, makes love what it is. This is one of those relations like that of knowing and being, which can only be understood in a dialectical manner. Thought guides action, yet it is action which gives birth to consciousness, and so the two separate, struggle, and return on each other, and therefore perpetually develop. Just as human life is being mingled with knowing, society is economic production mingled with love. This seems crude and even ludicrous to anyone accustomed to think of love as ethereal and in the soul, and economic production as base and earthly. But we love with our bodies and we eat and labour with our bodies, and deep love between two persons is generally distinguished from more transient forms of it by this test, that the two want to live together and thereafter function as one economic unit of society. As between the two, we know from biology that love, in its sexual form, appears before social economic production. But we also know that economic production in its primary individual form of metabolism, necessarily appears before love, for it is the essence of life. In the primitive cell metabolism exists before love has come into being. The cells at first multiply by fission, as a kind of surplus anabolism, and do not come together either in colonies (social behaviour) or fused in pairs for propagation (sexual behaviour). But because metabolism in the very dawn of life's history precedes the relation of love, it does not follow that love is a chance iridescence on life's surface. Metabolism, in the yet not fully understood affinity it demands among its protein molecules, already contains at a material level the rudiments of what men came to name Eros. Love must be implicit in matter.

Both popular and philosophic thought has recognised these deep foundations of love. Popular thought has given the same name to the affective tie that binds man and woman sexually, man and man in friendship,, and parents and child in family relationships. A king's love for his people, a disciple's love for his teacher, an animal's love for its young and its master, have all been included in the one category in spite of obvious differences. It is no accident that all the great religions which have moved men's minds have spoken so much of love. Religions always drew their value and their power from their symbolisation of unconscious social relations, and, since social relations are mediated by love, it is always about love that religion is essentially talking when it utters fantasies about God, salvation, Heaven, Hell and grace. The mystics' claim *God is love*, and the hymn of St. Paul to love, are accurate statements of the valuable common content of all religions which in the past have been social forces. The Trinity, the cherubim, the Holy Souls in Purgatory, and the Communion of the Saints do not exist, and it did not really matter to men whether they existed, for in the past men have been content with Yahweh and Sheol, Buddha and Nirvana, Baal and Gilgamesh. What does matter to men is the emotional element in social relations, which these myths symbolise, and which makes man in each generation what he is. This emotion is not separate from but springs out of the economic basis of these relations, which thus determine religion. Man's quality in each age is determined by his emotional and technological relations, and these are not separate but part of the one social process.

The Freudian position is that all emotional relations are simply variations of sexual love, cheated of their aim. That is why men call all varieties of tender relations 'love', because they are simply modified sexuality or diverted libido. Tenderness is inhibited sexuality. Although this view is attractive as a simplification, it is based on confused thinking. It assumes that there is a clear goal, sexual intercourse, and any love that does not achieve this goal is in some sense thwarted. This, however, presupposes something with this goal clearly in mind, and unless we believe in a god of love, this can only be the lover. But by definition the psyche whose inhibited sexuality is supposed to become love, is unconscious of the real goal. Take the example of infantile sexuality, an important part of Freud's theory of love. How can infantile affections be thwarted sexual love? On the one hand the infant, with no experience of sexual intercourse, cannot desire it consciously, and he cannot desire it unconsciously, i.e. somatically, because he has not the organs or reflexes for achieving sexual intercourse. Without the appropriate reflexes, sexual intercourse cannot exist for the unconscious. Its love therefore is of another kind—childish love. It is true that childish love is associated with zones many of which afterwards become sexually erotic, but that is only to say that man is material, that he has a body, and that this is used for contacts with other bodies. His contacts with other members of the world must be real physical contacts—mainly tactile when he is an infant, afterwards also visual and aural. Childish love is not thwarted sexual love, for the child neither knows sexual intercourse as an aim, nor is capable of it. It is childish love. That childish love is later to become sexual love is a truism. 'Thwarting' begs the question. Suppose, instead, Freud had said that infantile love was 'modified' adult love. We should at once have seen the fallacy. On the contrary it is adult sexual love which is 'modified' infantile love. It includes the more primitive behaviour pattern, but, as Freud admits, integrates it in a much more elaborate and powerful new system, due to the coming into being of the reflexes associated with sexual intercourse, the secondary sexual hormone, and all the qualitative changes in psychic orientation and content associated with puberty. Therefore Freud is standing love's development on its head. It would be precisely as accurate to regard the baby's body as a thwarted or inhibiter adult body, as to regard the baby's affective life as that of a 'polymorphous perverse' adult.

In the same way the relation of a parent to an infant is not sexual love thwarted or inhibited. Sexual love is a behaviour-response, including a desire for sexual intercourse, evoked by certain stimuli. The infant is not a stimulus for this. It is very doubtful if the infant is primarily the stimulus for instinctive parental love at all. The phenomenon of 'false pregnancy' among bitches seems to prove the reverse. These animals develop after heat, in certain circumstances, maternal behaviour and emotion, without having become actually pregnant. To suppose that their maternal love is thwarted sexual love to-

wards a non-existent puppy is to make psychology a comic
opera. The parental love behaviour patterns varies widely
from the sexual.

Again, the normal relations of friendship between persons
of the same sex, in all their variety, from lasting and intimate
friendship to a tenderness we feel for someone we have never
seen merely because he is a fellow-countryman or a fellow-
creature in distress, form a group of distinctive behaviour-
patterns. It is unscientific to regard these as kinds of thwarted
or inhibited sexual love. Indeed, to do so robs the quite clear
concept of sexual perversion of any meaning. In homosexuality
or zoophily the sexual behaviour-emotion pattern is directed to
abnormal objects, and is necessarily modified thereby. But if
all tenderness for persons of one's own sex or animals, is simply
the sexual pattern of behaviour modified by the novel circumstances, what is the difference? How can we distinguish between friendship and perversion? The error is due to a mis-
understanding of what the instinct really is. An instinct is a
certain innate behaviour-pattern or chain of reflexes, conditioned or modified by experience. The word 'love', as common-
ly used, includes such modified behaviour-patterns as delight
in other peoples' presence, sensibility to one person rather than
another, generosity towards them, desire to see them, and various other forms of affectionate behaviour which psychologists can only describe aridly and formally. It includes also
the desire for sexual intercourse. Only behaviour-patterns of
which this last is a component should be called sexual love,
and to suppose that all the other forms of friendliness contain
a suppressed desire for sexual intercourse, which is roughly the
Freudian position, is to adopt the plan of the White Knight—

> to dye one's whiskers green.
> And then to use so large a fan
> That they will not be seen.

Man, like all animals, is a creature whose innate behaviour-
patterns are modified by experience, usually for 'the better',
that is, so as to deal more expertly with reality. This process
is called learning. We learn with our love responses as with

others. To call this process inhibition or repression inverts the process of evolution.

Of course, sexual and friendly behaviour responses are very closely connected, and each pattern contains component parts common to both. But since one body, with one central nervous system, is common to all of one organism's behaviour, it is obvious that all its behaviour-patterns must contain a large number of common components. Running may, for example, in any animal, figure as part of sexual behaviour or as part of self-preservation (fear) behaviour. It does not follow that one instinct is the other, modified, repressed or inhibited.

As soon as we rid our mind of mythological entities of these separate instincts, like distinct souls, planted in the animal or human breast, we will be clearer on this point.

In 'the instincts', the savage soul—the little manikin dwelling in the marionette body and pulling the strings—has returned to psychology. With Freud this manikin, under the name of libido or eternal Eros, figures in the strangest way as a kind of symbolisation of bourgeois conceptions of liberty, like Rousseau's natural man. The unfortunate libido is exploited and oppressed and chained in the cruellest way by the structure of society and in its torments gives birth to all sociological and ideological phenomena. All this is simply a return to the old 'natural philosophy' conception of an indwelling vital force, with eternal desires and aims of its own.

This conception leads Freud to suppose that whatever a thing becomes, it remains the same thing inhibited or sublimated. This is to deny change. If soil becomes a rose, it is not just soil inhibited and sublimated. It is certainly still composed of the same elements, but it is also a rose, with its own character and qualities and laws. Even here Freud makes another error. If what is derived from a thing is nothing but that thing, we should not say social relations are nothing but sexual relations; we should say that sexual love is nothing but social relations. In evolution primitive social relations precede primitive sexual relations if the following considerations are correct:

It is generally supposed that ontogenesis corresponds on the whole to phylogenesis. Before the infant achieves sexual love, it first experiences the simple metabolic relation between mother and foetus, in which sexual love cannot be said to enter, for here there are no erotogenous zones. This is an economic relation between mother and child. The next step is infantile love, with erotogenous zones but not distinctively sexual behaviour. Finally, in the crisis of adolescence, the distinctive sexual reflexes appear. It will be argued that the sexual congress of ovum and spermatozoon precedes these stages. But these are protozoic relations, and man is metazoic. In the metazoa, sexual relations come after the simpler social relations of genesis and nurture.

In any case the same holds good of protozoa. The precedent condition of the congress of ovum and spermatozoon is the production of ova and spermatozoa. This is an asexual process and is part of the internal asexual economy of the cells of the body, bound together in a metabolism which is plainly economic. The relations of the primary sex cells are therefore asexual before they are sexual. But this is so with all protozoa, even those that do not become metazoa. Asexual relations between them always precede sexual, which grow out of them as a kind of late differentiation. Indeed this must plainly be the case. Before multiplication can proceed by sexual congress, there must be multiplication by fission, for you cannot, mathematically, get many out of one by fusion. Fission must come first, and fission demands a surplus anabolism which of itself implies a primitive economic basis. These considerations show clearly that, on the 'nothing but' basis, sexual love is *nothing but* social relations. But, of course, the 'nothing but' reduction is invalid. Sexual love is in mankind *something more* than the innate response that produces fusion between male and female cells. Social relations in humanity are something more than the metabolism that coordinates the cells of a metazoan, or a volvex colony. Passionate love and social altruism are the results of long periods of historical change, and the change is real, it is not just the old eternal entities wearing masks. But like a modern Parmenides, the instinct psychologist seems reluctant to recognise the reality of 'becoming'.

The simpler relations between cells, as evidenced in the ordinary metazoan body or the aggregations of asexual protozoa known as colonies, are primitive social or economic relations and form the basis from which human society's productive relations and forces have flowered. But it does not follow that they are the 'same thing' carried out in different media. They are what they are, subject to their own distinctive laws. What the individual body has in common with society is this: the relations between the cells of the human body are economic, there is division of labour, central control, exchange of products, and so forth. The one subordinates its interests, when required, to the whole. As in all socio-economic relations, the cells achieve more in unison than they do separately. But the body is subject to biological, society to sociological laws.

The sexual cells appear on the scene at puberty, when the metazoan body has been a social entity for some time. Sexuality is therefore a kind of luxury, appearing at a late date, as a special modification of social-economic relations. *Sexual love is a modified economic relation.* Altruism, for example, is not, when exhibited socially, the result of an identification of one's self with the loved one, and therefore a special form of sexual love, as Freud suggests. Altruism, in its primitive and basic form of the sacrifice of one individual for others, appears long before sexual love, as part of the economic process of metabolism in the cells of the human body, unconnected with sexuality. But conscious altruism in a human being is not just the unconscious 'self-sacrifice' of a white corpuscle. It is a new quality, based on an old quantity. And sexual love is a new quality, differentiated out of the simpler socio-economic relations that preceded it.

Differentiation implies a difference. Although sexual love as a late development of socio-economic relations, gathers up within itself the qualities of its basis, it also contains something distinctively new. Sexual love is not a luxury, existing only for itself, but it returns again into the social relations from which it sprang, making them different to what they were. And, so changed, they in turn feed more richly the new thing rooted in them. Both reflect light on each other, for it is plain that sexual love, basically a chain of simple spinal reflexes, as shown by experiments on decerebrate guinea-pigs, has in humanity attracted to itself a number of economic relations and become enriched by them. The act of sexual intercourse need not involve this interweaving of relations, and in the lower organisms does not. Sexual intercourse need not be intertwined with the relations involved in the rearing of young, as in human family life, nor in the relations involved in earning one's living, keeping house, and making friends, as in human marriage. But because it is so intertwined, it is like a source of warmth irradiating these relations, and these in turn become fuel which feed it and bring about its enrichment and growth. The whole forms an elaborate system, part of the tapestry of society, and the richer pattern resulting from the mutual interweaving indicates that the Freudian conception of social relations as modified sexual love inverts the process of becoming.

The evolution of sexuality was of vital significance in the history of organisms. Primitive metabolic relations, such as those obtaining between the cells of metazoan bodies, are marked by a totalitarian ruthlessness in which the individual, as such, does not exist. The individual cell is completely subordinated to the organism as a whole. This is necessarily the case, because the cell is not yet an individual in its own right, but simply a part of the parent cell which has become differentiated and detached. This involves an almost exact likeness to the parent cell, so that such cells, as long as they continue to be capable of fission, have a kind of immortality, the children being almost exactly the same as the patents. It is also correspondingly difficult for the new to come into being. Generation after generation repeats the same pattern. All defects are reproduced. The parent cell has eaten sour grapes, and therefore the grandchildren's teeth are necessarily set on edge.

The coming of sexuality breaks the stale routine of habit. It is therefore the genesis of individuality within the ambit of society. Something distinctively new now comes into being, because the child will no longer resemble either parent exactly but, by combining a selection of the genes from both, will be someone different from either. Moreover, each child, with a different selection of genes, will be slightly different, and thus bad qualities may be weeded out by natural selection. Not all the children's teeth are set on edge. The range of qualities in the offspring is increased. Some, it is true, will be far worse than the offspring of an asexual patent, for they will unite the defects of both parents, but others will be better, and natural selection will have a wider range of varieties to work on. It is as if good has come into the world by the generation of evil, and if we take seriously the identity of opposites, must not this be the case?

At the same time death has come into the world. Love, the giver of individuality, is also the giver of death, the antithesis of personality. That is why the life-instinct and the death-instinct, Eros and Thanatos, seem so closely united, not as Freud thought because they are specific instincts, but because death defines love. The immortality of primitive cells, secured by simple fission, vanishes when they conjugate and spawn. The parents now live in their children only in a provisional half-hearted manner.

This is a kind of price that life pays for greater difference, for becoming life as we understand it. For greater richness and complexity, hastening the hand of time, we pay the priceless coin of Death. To their children, no longer simple buds of themselves, the individual cells can bequeath more abundant life and greater differentiation but only by sinking half their genetic share in them and giving up their near immortality. Only with this advent of sexual love and real death can one talk about 'personalities' and 'individuals'; other cells are buds. The birth of a new personality demands the death of the old. This 'I' that dies is created by death.

In its appearance, none the less, sexual love is selfish. Sexual cells reject the colonial and social tie of asexual reproduction in favour of an intimate exclusive tie between two of them alone. They are luxurious cells, playing no part in the economic production of the metazoan body. And, similarly, in social life sexual love has a selfish aspect. The lovers turn away from the community; their demand is to be alone, to be by themselves, to enjoy each other. Thus sexual love appears as a dissolving power in society.

The social asexual cell is strictly subordinated to the plan of the organism. It works tirelessly, secreting or vibrating or dying for the good of the community. Beside it the sexual cell seems, in the community, like the selfish hedonist beside the devoted hardworking celibate. The sexual cell is responding with all its being to something which allures merely by the satisfaction it gives to the individual. Love, even in its other-regarding aspect, seems a kind of giant selfishness projected on the beloved. But this is not the whole truth. This same selfish cell brings to birth something which is unknown before—individuality. The cell, temporarily released from the iron plan of organic metabolism by the invention of sexuality, is by this act enriched in behaviour. It is the beginning of that individuation which in man leads to consciousness. The sexual behaviour brings a new pattern into life. On the one hand the sexual cells, ignoring the demands of 'society', are thereby led to enrich and complicate their self-hood. More importantly, this very sexual partnership involves eventually the annihilation of both personalities in the birth of the new individualities, whose characters will be formed from a selection of the genes of both parents, and therefore different from either. The self-sacrificing cell enjoys the possibility of a perpetual immortality as a reward for its self-sacrifice. The sexual cell buys its one brief hour of glorious life for an age without a name, and yet, by that very death and life, it has given rise to the potentialities of individualism.

This, however, is too anthropomorphic a way of looking at it. As long as asexuality prevails, it is not possible to talk about individuality at all. Are the leaves of one tree individual? No, they are part of the one tree. In the same way the cells of the metazoan body are all part of each other though spatially separate. They are formed from each other by simple fission. Therefore neither the question of self-sacrifice nor immortality arises. The asexual cell has no 'self' to sacrifice and immortality is meaningless except in the sense that all matter is immortal. Immortality is meaningless without *personal* immortality, and the asexual cell has no personality.

Immortality is not a superior kind of mortality, a life protracted to infinity, an endless personal survival. It is the primitive state from which both mortality and personality arose. If the concept of life to us is almost meaningless except as the life of an individual, we must say that death gave rise to life; both are aspects of the same movement of differentiation. All craving for immortality, so human and so understandable, is yet a craving for a regression, for a return to primitive unconscious being, to shift off ourselves the heavy responsibilities of consciousness, love and individuality. All conceptions of immortality as endless survivals of personalities walking about in familiar surroundings strike the mind with a strange sense of unreality. The only conceptions of immortality which seem reasonable, even if impossible, are the Buddhist and Hindoo conceptions of immortality as a merging of oneself into the absolute, Nirvana, a beingless primitive sleep. And this is what immortality is, a return to the blind unconscious regression of primitive being, back farther still to the timelessness of immortal matter. Because life, faced with any difficult situation, always tends to wish to relapse to a solution achieved at an earlier stage of development, this concept of immortality makes an appeal to man particularly in periods of inferiority or depression.

This concern with immortality is not so much a fear of death as a special kind of defeatist resignation to it, as in late Egypt and the Oriental mystery cults. A *faint* belief or *complete disbelief* in immortality, so far from begetting a resignation to death, necessarily produces a vigorous dislike of it. All beaten, depressed and terrified people, all slave and expropriated classes, turn to another immortal timeless life for consolation. Biological immortality, splitting into personality and death, generates two opposites which repel each other; the more full and abundant our life, the more we are repelled by death, and this repulsion, so painful, is yet productive of pleasure, for it forces us to cram our now valued lives full of richness and complexity, to seize great armfuls of time and action to achieve and conquer and love and suffer before we die. Death, the negation of life, thus generates it. All spring, all youth, all health yield their peculiar and rich savour just because of this, that they go:

> And at my back I always hear,
> Time's winged chariot hastening near.

Human society is distinguished from the simple metabolic society of somatic cells because it is more than metabolic, it is also individualistic. The individual, apparently opposed to society, yet gives society its inner driving power, and society by its internal development itself brings about the individuation of its units.

Insect society here contrasts with human. There has been a regression to a relative immortality. The workers have all been desexualised. They have lost their individuality and regressed almost to the status of somatic cells. The strange rapport between members of a hive or formicary is not surprising when we think of them as virtually all parts of the one body, daughter cells of the queen. But this same regression and de-individuation produces stagnation as compared with human society. All powers of change and individualism are concentrated in the genetic change of the few sexual members. It is therefore a slow change. Insect societies have almost ceased to live. Immune from the changing and yet living hand of time, they have achieved some of the dull immortality of the diamond.

In human society, however, the endless war between individual and economic relations, between love and metabolism, is the source of endless social advance. Sexuality, because it gave rise to individuality, also helped to give rise to consciousness. Metabolism (or productive forces) changes from age to age, and this change imposes a tension upon production relations. But this strife, extending throughout society, is felt in a characteristic form in the sphere of man's feeling, in his consciousness, for consciousness is basically affective. It is felt as if outside forces in society are starving or thwarting men's emotional lives, as if life is becoming glamourless or cruel. For the production relations are social relations and conscious tenderness is generated in them.

Sexual love itself is continually enriched and changed by economic relations, at the same time as economic relations gain new warmth and complexity from love. To every stage of economic development corresponds a richer, subtler, more sensitive behaviour-pattern associated with sexual love. To bourgeois culture belongs passionate love, to feudal romantic or chivalrous love, and to slave-owning Greek culture Platonic love.

To our generation the association of economic relations with sexual love seems arbitrary, not because our idea of love is too rich but because our notion of economic relations is too bourgeois. Bourgeois civilisation has reduced social relations to the cash nexus. They have become emptied of affection. To a psychologist, the whole world seems suffering from a starvation of love, and this need appears in a compensatory and pathological form as neurosis, hate, perversion, and unrest.

Even to-day, in those few economic relations which still survive in a pre-bourgeois form, we can see tenderness as the essence of the relation. The commodity fetishism which sees in a relation between *men* only a relation between *things* has not yet dried it up. The economic relation of the mother to her foetus, of the child to the parent and *vice versa*, retains its primitive form to show this clearly. We can see fainter traces in the relation of master to pupil, of governess to child, household servant to master or mistress, and the few surviving examples of a feudal relation between master and man.

Where can this tenderness be found in the characteristically bourgeois relations our culture substitutes for them—the relations of capitalist and labourer; hotel servant and guest; company promoter and shareholder; correspondence-course writer and mug? This tenderness, expelled from all other relations, is collected and utilised to-day in a vague mystical manner as the binding force for the one social relation of 'being in the same State'. This is a genuine social relation, that of being in the fabric of coercion exploited by one ruling class, but it is not one which in its named form is likely to produce tenderness. It is therefore necessary to substitute for the naked relation a fictional one—a fictitious 'race', a wonderful happy family, or a dummy King or Leader whose wisdom and statesmanship and character are regarded as semi-divine, even where his position is constitutionally that of a rubber stamp. By this means a powerful '*participation mystique*' is secured. As Fascism and Nazism show, the more violent the exploitation; the more ardent and mythological the patriotism; the more heartless and unemotional the relations, the more the parade of hypocritical feeling. This is characteristic of developed bourgeois relations. In primitive relations among a group, as the researches of anthropologists show, economic production is inextricably interwoven with social affection. Between tribes, between chief and subject, or between different members of a group, the economic relation figures as an exchange of gifts, as a tribute of affection in the literal sense. It is the love that goes with the gifts, which is the giving, is the vital economic thing. Many primitive transactions which to the early bourgeois observer seemed to be bourgeois exchange, that is, the getting of as much as possible for as little as possible, are now, by more searching observers, discovered to be the very opposite, each side trying to embarrass the other by a superfluity of gifts. The Melanesian's pride is found to be in his having contributed more yams than anyone else to his maternal uncle or chief. At the potlatch, the North American Indian demonstrates his social value by impoverishing himself. This conception of economic relation as tender relation, and a fit medium for generosity and altruism, appears in barbaric and even feudal relations. We must not idealise them, or imagine that simple savage tenderness is the same as the more developed, subtle and sophisticated emotion we feel. But it is equally wrong, by wresting and straining the facts, to give a bourgeois cynical interpretation to the different primitive economic relations of agriculture, hunting and land tenure among the primitive African, American and Oceanic races.

In all the distinctive bourgeois relations, it is characteristic that tenderness is completely expelled, because tenderness can only exist between men, and in capitalism all relations appear to be between a man and a commodity.

The relation of the guildsman to his journeyman, the slave-owner to his plantation slave, the lord to his serf, the king to his subjects, was a relation between man and man, and although it was a relation, not of co-operation but of domination and submission, of exploiter and exploited, it was a human relation. It was unpleasantly like the relation of a man and his dog, but at least it was tender. How can even that much consideration enter into the relations of a group of shareholders to the employees of a limited liability company? Or between Indian coolies and British tea drinkers? Or between a bourgeois bureaucracy and the proletariat?

In bourgeois relations the sole recognised legal social relation among adults is the contract, considered as indemnifiable in cash. Nothing can be enforced upon a man but the payment of money; even marriage can be escaped from by a suitable cash compensation. Man is completely free except for the payment of money. That is the overt character of bourgeois relations. Secretly it is different, for society can only be a relation between men, not between man and a thing, not even between man and cash. Bourgeois society thinks that is the relation on which it turns, but, as Marx showed, in bourgeois society it is still a relation between men, between exploiters and exploited. It is the vehicle of a specific type of exploitation. The bourgeois dream is that by substituting this relation to a thing for feudal slave-owning or primitive relations between men, man becomes completely free. But this is an illusion. Since man only becomes free through social relations, this means that the bourgeois shuts his eyes to facts. For conscious planned social relations he substitutes unconscious unplanned social relations which, like all unconscious forces, work blindly and disatrously.

None the less, the bourgeois was determined to believe that the market was the only social relation between man and man. This meant that he must refuse to believe that love was an integral part of a social relation. He repressed this tenderness from his social consciousness. In its final form this becomes the treason of man to his capacity for love, the appearance of love in the form of neurosis, hate, and fantasy, which the psychoanalysts discover everywhere in bourgeois man. In one sense the Married Woman's Property Act was a charter of freedom for women. In another sense it was merely a charter of bourgeois repression, a recognition that the economic relations between husband and wife were no longer tender but merely cash.

In their early stages bourgeois relations, by intensifying individualism, give a special heightening to sexual love. Before they crystallise out as relations to cash, bourgeois social relations simply seem to express man's demand for freedom from obsolete social bonds, and this demand for individuality is then a progressive force. Sexual love now takes on, as clearly seen in art, a special value as the expression *par excellence* of individuality. We have the emergence of that characteristic achievement of bourgeois culture, passionate love, conceived as both romantic and sensual, whereas neither Greek nor mediaeval culture could conceive romantic and sensual love except as exclusive opposites. Passionate love contributes new overtones to feeling and conscious life. Moreover, this remand for individuality was also enriching other forms of love, as long as it was revolutionary and creative. It gave men a new tenderness towards each other, conceived as a tenderness of each other's liberty, of each other's personal worth. Thus bourgeois culture in its springtime gave birth to passionate sexual love, and a tenderness for the 'liberty'—the individual outline—of other members of society. Both these are genuine enrichments, which civilisation cannot now lose.

None the less, the contradiction in bourgeois social relations, that private advantage is common weal, that freedom is sought individually *and* anti-socially, necessarily revealed its nature in due course. Man cannot exist without relations to other men and the bourgeois demand that he should do so merely meant that these relations were disguised as a relation to commodities. As this developing relation produced industrial capitalism and the modern bourgeois State, it sucked the tenderness out of all social relations. Ultimately it even affected sexual love itself, and began to take from it the very enrichments sexual love had derived from tender social relations. Passionate bourgeois love is to-day like a flower which is being stripped of its petals one by one. These petals are the patterns of behaviour derived from bourgeois social relations, which had been transferred to sexual love and been transformed and warmed by it, just as the flower's colourful petals consist of converted green leaves. In the institution of bourgeois marriage, these economic relations—the *individual* family, the *personal* income—were warmed by sexual love into something of nobility. True, bourgeois social relations, even when so transformed, retained some of their ugly untender character. The man too often regards love as similar to a bourgeois property relation, as a relation between a man and a thing and not between man and man. The wife was his property for life. She had to be beautiful to gratify his acquisitive instincts; faithful because a man's property must not alienate itself from him; but he, the owner, can be unfaithful, because he can acquire other property without affecting his present holding. A similar relation imposed itself on the children he had fed and clothed, and therefore paid their wages. They had sold their labour power to him. In Roman slave-owning civilisation, the child's legal position appears as that of slave to the father, and moreover a slave incapable of manumission. But even slavery is a relation between men. These ugly possessive features of bourgeois social relations always gave bourgeois love a selfish jealous undertone, which the bourgeois, despite the researches of anthropology, considers as instinctive and natural. Private property was not invented by bourgeoisdom. It is a potentiality of man's nature, or it could never have appeared in bourgeoisdom. But bourgeoisdom was its flowering, its elevation and the prime motive power of social relations; and the flavour accordingly pervades all bourgeois life.

With the exhaustion of bourgeois social relations, bourgeois passionate love begins also to wither before the economic blast. On the one hand marriage has become increasingly 'expensive'. It must be put off till late life. That marriage—which for bourgeois culture and particularly for the woman had been the most valued pattern of love behaviour—is to-day only a late and specialised variety of it. Children are increasingly expensive, and the tender social relations associated with them more rarely form part of the standard marriage pattern. From these and other causes that elaborate and complex creation, passionate bourgeois love, is more and more being stripped of its corolla and reverting to a primitive form of fugitive sexual intercourse. This, the inevitable consequence of the exhaustion of bourgeois social relations, is denounced as 'Sin', the 'levity of the young', 'the breakdown of the institution of marriage', 'growing promiscuity', the 'result of birth-control', and so on. But all this abuse is beside the point. Passionate bourgeois love really prepared its own death. The same causes which caused its flowering in course of time brought about this withering.

To-day love could prepare an appalling indictment of the wrongs and privations that bourgeois social relations have inflicted upon it. The misery of the world is economic, but that does not mean that it is cash. That is a bourgeois error. Just because relations are economic, they involve the tenderest and most valued feelings of social man. For the satisfaction of all the rich emotional capabilities and social tenderness of which bourgeois relations have deprived him, man turns vainly to religion, hate, patriotism, Fascism, and the sentimentality of films and novels, which paint in imagination loves he cannot experience in life. Because of this he is neurotic, unhappy, sick, liable to the mass-hatreds of war and anti-Semitism, to absurd and yet pathetic royal jubilee or funeral enthusiasms and to mad impossible loyalties to Hitlers and Aryan grandmothers. Because of this life seenms to him empty, stale, and unprofitable. Man delights him not, nor woman neither.

Bourgeois social relations, by transforming in this way all tender relations between men to relations to commodities, prepare their own doom. The threads that bind feudal lord to liege, chief to tribe, patriarch to household slave, father to son, because they are tender are strong. But those that bind shareholder to wage-employee, civil servant to taxpayer, and all men to the impersonal market, because they are merely cash and devoid of tender relations, cannot hold. The chief's laws are understandable. The fiat of a man-god is still a personal and affectionate command. But the laws of supply and demand (their substitute in bourgeois culture) are without any power save blind compulsion. To-day it is as if love and economic relations have gathered at two opposite poles. All the unused tenderness of man's instincts gather at one pole and at the other are economic relations, reduced to bare coercive rights to commodities. This polar segregation is the source of a terrific tension, and will give rise to a vast transformation of bourgeois society. They must, in a revolutionary destruction and construction, return in on each other and fuse in a new synthesis. This is communism.

Thus the forces that produce communism can be viewed from two aspects. From the quantitative aspect, productive forces, which have outgrown bourgeois social relations, burst those fetters. But the fight is fought to an issue in men's consciousness. Man, the individual, feels the outmoding of these relations, their sloughing by reality, as the death of all that is valuable to him. The demand to bring back to consciousness these vanished values appears as hate for the present and love for the new, the dynamic power of revolution. Emotion bursts from the ground in which it has been repressed with all the force of an explosion. The whole structure of society is shattered. This is a revolution.

III

LIBERTY

A STUDY IN BOURGEOIS ILLUSION

Many will have heard a broadcast by H. G. Wells in which (commenting on the Soviet Union) he described it as a 'great experiment which has but half fulfilled its promise', it is still a 'land without mental freedom'. There are also many essays of Bertrand Russell in which this philosopher explains the importance of liberty, how the enjoyment of liberty is the highest and most important goal of man. Fisher claims that the history of Europe during the last two or three centuries is simply the struggle for liberty. Continually and variously by artists, scientists, and philosophers alike, liberty is thus praised and man's right to enjoy it imperiously asserted.

I agree with this. Liberty does seem to me the most important of all generalised goods—such as justice, beauty, truth—that come so easily to our lips. And yet when freedom is discussed a strange thing is to be noticed. These men—artists, careful of words, scientists, investigators of the entities denoted by words, philosophers, scrupulous about the relations between words and entities—never define precisely what they mean by freedom. They seem to assume that it is quite a clear concept, whose definition everyone would agree about.

Yet who does not know that liberty is a concept about whose nature men have quarrelled perhaps more than about any other? The historic disputes concerning predestination, Karma, Free-Will, Moira, salvation by faith or works, determinism, Fate, Kismet, the categorical imperative, sufficient grace, occasionalism, Divine Providence, punishment and responsibility have all been about the nature of man's freedom of will and action. The Greeks, the Romans, the Buddhists, the Mahomedans, the Catholics, the Jansenists, and the Calvinists, have each had different ideas of liberty. Why, then, do all these

51

bourgeois intellectuals assume that liberty is a clear concept, understood in the same way by all their hearers, and therefore needing no definition? Russell, for example, has spent his life finding a really satisfactory definition of number and even now it is disputed whether he has been successful. I can find in his writings no clear definition of what he means by liberty. Yet most people would have supposed that men are far more in agreement as to what is meant by a number, than what is meant by liberty.

This indefinite use of the word can only mean either that they believe the meaning of the word invariant in history or that they use it in the contemporary bourgeois. sense. If they believe the meaning invariant, it is strange that men have disputed so often about freedom. These inellectuals must surely be incapable of such a blunder. They must mean liberty as men in their situation experience it. That is, they must mean by liberty to have no more restrictions imposed on them than they endure at that time. They do not—these Oxford dons or successful writers—want, for example, the restrictions of Fascism, that is quite clear. That would not be liberty. But at present, thank God, they are reasonably free.

Now this conception of liberty is superficial, for not all their countrymen are in the same situation. A, an intellectual with a good education, in possession of a modest income, with not too uncongenial friends, unable to afford a yacht, which he would like, but at least able to go to the winter sports, considers this (more or less) freedom. He would like that yacht, but still—he can write against Communism or Fascism or the existing system. Let us for the moment grant that A is free. I propose to analyse this statement more deeply in a moment, and show that it is partial. But let us for the moment grant that A enjoys liberty.

Is B free? B is the sweated non-union shop-assistant of Houndsditch, working seven days of the week. He knows nothing of art, science, or philosophy. He has no culture except a few absurd prejudices, his elementary school education saw to that. He believes in the superiority of the English race, the King's wisdom and loving-kindness to his subjects, the real existence of God, the Devil, Hell, and Sin, and the wickedness of sexual intercourse unless palliated by marriage. His knowledge of world events is derived from the *News of the World*, on other days he has no time to read the papers. He believes that when he dies he will (with luck) enter into eternal bliss. At present, however, his greatest dread is that, by displeasing his employer in some trifle, he may become unemployed.

B's trouble is plainly lack of leisure in which to cultivate freedom. C does not suffer from this. He is an unemployed middle-aged man. He is free for 24 hours a day. He is free to go anywhere—in the streets and parks, and in the museums. He is allowed to think of anything—the Einstein theory, the Frege definition of classes, or the doctrine of the Immaculate Conception. Regrettably enough, he does none of these things. He quarrels with his wife, who calls him a good-for-nothing waster, and with his children, who because of the means test have to pay his rent, and with his former friends, because they can enjoy pleasures he cannot afford. Fortunately he is free to remove himself from existence, and this one afternoon, when his wife is out and there is plenty of money in the gas-meter, he will do.

A is free. Are B and C? I assume that A will reply that B and C are not free. If A asserts that B and C do enjoy real liberty, most of us, without further definition, will know what to think of A's idea of liberty. But a Wells, a Forster, or a Russell would doubtless agree, as vehemently as us, that this is not liberty, but a degrading slavery to environment. He will say that to free B and C we must raise them to A's level, the level, let us say, of the Oxford don. Like the Oxford don, B and C must have leisure and a modest income with which to enjoy the good things and the good ideas of the world.

But how is this to be brought about? Bourgeois social relations are what we have now. No one denies that the dynamic motive of such relations is private profit. Here bourgeois economists and Marxists are agreed. Moreover, if causality has any meaning, and unless we are to throw all scientific method overboard, current economic relations and the unfreedom of B and C must be causally inter-related.

We have, then, bourgeois social relations on the one hand, and these varying degrees of unfreedom—A, B, and C—on the

STUDIES IN A DYING CULTURE

other hand, interconnected as cause and effect. So far, either might be cause, for we have not yet decided whether mental states arise from social relations, or *vice versa*. But as soon as we ask how action is to solve the problem, we see which is primary. It is useless to give B, by means of lectures and picture galleries, opportunity for understanding philosophy or viewing masterpieces of art. He has no time to acquire, before starting work, the taste for them or after starting work the time to gratify it. Nor is C free to enjoy the riches of bourgeois culture as long as his whole existence is clouded by his economic postion. It is circumstances that are imprisoning consciousness, not *vice versa*. It is not because B and C are unenlightened that they are members of the working class, but because they are members of the working class, they are unenlightened. And Russell, who writes *In Praise of Idleness,* praises rightly, for he is clever because he is idle and bourgeois, not idle and bourgeois because he is clever.

We now see the cause and effect of the situation. We see that it is not this freedom and unfreedom which produce bourgeois social relations, but that bourgeois social relations alike give rise to these two extremes, the freedom of the idle bourgeois, and the unfreedom of the proletarian worker. It is plain that this effect, if undesirable, can only be changed by changing the cause.

Thus the intellectual is faced with another problem, like that when he had to define more precisely who enjoyed the liberty he regarded as contemporary. Does he wish that there should exist for ever these two states of captivity and freedom, of misery and happiness? Can he enjoy a freedom which is sustained by the same cause as the workers' unfreedom? For if not, he must advance further, and say, 'bourgeois social relations must be changed'. Change they will, precisely because of this unfreedom they increasingly generate; but to-day the intellectual must decide whether his will be part of the social forces making for change, or vainly pitted against them.

But how are bourgeois social relations to be changed? Not by a mere effort of the will, for we saw that the mind was made by social relations, not *vice versa*. It is matter, the quantitative foundation of qualitative ideology, that must be changed. It is not enough to argue and convince. Work must be done. The environment must be altered.

Science shows us how. We achieve our wants always, not by the will alone, not by merely wishing them into being, but with action aided by cognition, by utilising the physical laws of reality. We move mountains, not by the mere movement of desire, but because we understand the rigidly determined laws of kinetics, hydraulics, and electrical engineering and can guide our actions by them. We attain freedom—that is, the fulfilment of our will—by obedience to the laws of reality. Observance of these laws is simple; it is the discovery of them that is the difficulty, and this is the task of science.

Thus, the task of defining liberty becomes still harder. It is not so easy after all to establish even a contemporary definition of liberty. Not only has the intellectual already had to decide to change bourgeois social relations, but he must now find out the laws of motion of society, and fit social relations into a causal scheme. It is not enough to want to be free; it is also necessary to know.

Only one scientific analysis of the law of motion of social relations exists, that of Marxism. For the understanding of how, physically, at the material level of social being, quantitative movements of capital, of matter, of *stuff*, provide the causal predictive basis of society, and pass via social relations into the qualitative changes of mind, will, and ideology, it is necessary to refer the bourgeois intellectual to Marx, Engels, Plekhanov, Lenin and Bukharin. Let us suppose that he has now done this and returns again to the difficult pursuit of liberty.

His causal conception of society will now enable him to realise that the task of making social relations produce liberty is as rigidly conditioned by reality as the task of making matter fulfil his desire in the form of machines. All matter—machinery, capital, men— and the relations which they exhibit in society—can only move in accordance with causal laws. This involves first that the old relations must be broken down, just as a house must be pulled down if we would entirely rebuild it, and the transition, putting up and pulling down, must follow certain laws. We cannot pull the foundation first, or build the roof before the walls.

This transitional stage involves the alteration of all the adherences between humans and the capital, machinery and materials, which mediate social relations. These must no longer adhere to individual persons—the bourgeois class—but to all members of society. This change is not a mere change of ownership, for it also involves that no individuals can derive profit from ownership without working. The goods are not destined to go the round of the market—the profit movement—but directly into use—the use movement. Moreover, this involves that all the visible institutions depending on private profit relations—laws, church, bureaucrary, judiciary, army, police, education—must be pulled down and rebuilt. The *bourgeoisie* cannot do this, for it is by means of these very institutions—private property (the modest income), law, university, civil service, privileged position, etc.—that they attain their freedom. To expect them to destroy these relations on which, as we saw, their freedom, and the workers' unfreedom, depend, is to ask them to go in quest of captivity, which, since liberty is what all men seek, they will not do. But the opposite is the case with the unfree, with the proletariat. The day they go in search of liberty, they revolt. The bourgeois, fighting for his liberty, must necessarily find himself in antagonism to the non-bourgeois, also fighting for liberty. The eventual issue of this struggle is due to the fact that capitalist economy, as it develops, makes ever narrower the class which really owns liberty, until the day comes when the intellectual, the doctor, the petty bourgeois, the clerk, and the peasant, realise that they too are not after all free. And they see that the fight of the proletariat is their fight.

What, to the proletarian, is liberty—the extermination of those bourgeois institutions and relations which hold them in captivity—is necessarily compulsion and restraint to the bourgeois, just as the old bourgeois liberty generated non-liberty for the worker. The two notions of liberty are irreconcilable. Once the proletariat is in power, all attempts to re-establish bourgeois social relations will be attacks on proletatian liberty, and will therefore be repulsed as fiercely as men repulse all attacks on their liberty. This is the meaning of the dictatorship of the proletariat, and why with it there is censorship, ideological acerbity, and all the other devices developed by the bourgeois in the evolution of the coercive State which secures his freedom.

There is, however, one vital difference. Bourgeois social relations, generating the liberty of the bourgeois and the non-liberty of the proletarian, depend on the existence of both freedom and unfreedom for their continuance. The bourgeois could not enjoy his idleness without the labour of the worker, nor the worker remain in a bourgeois relationship without the coercive guidance and leadership of the bourgeois. Thus the liberty of the few is, in bourgeois social relations, built on the unfreedom of the many. The two notions dwell in perpetual antagonism. But after the dispossession of the bourgeoisie, the antagonism between the expropriated and therefore unfree bourgeois, and the inheriting and therefore free proletariat, is only temporary. For the owners of the means of production, being also the workers of that means, do not need the existence of an expropriated class. When, therefore, the transition is complete, and the bourgeois class is either absorbed or has died out, there is no longer an unfree compelled class. That is what is meant by the 'withering away' of the State into a classless society, after the transitional period such as is now taking place in Russia.

This, stated in its simplest terms, is the causal process whereby bourgeois social relations can change into new social relations not generating a mass of unfreedom as the opposite pole to a little freedom. We have purposely made it simple. A fuller discussion, such as Marx gives, would make clearer the fluid interpenetrating nature of the process; how it is brought about causally by capitalist economy itself, which cannot stand still, but clumps continually into greater centralisation, giving rise to imperialistic wars, which man will not forever tolerate, and to viler and viler cash relations, filling men with hate, which will one day become hate for the system. And as capitalism perpetrates these enormities, the cause of revolt, it gives the proletariat the means of revolt, by making them unite, become more conscious and organised, so that, when the time of revolt comes, they have both the solidarity and executive ability needed to take over the administration of the bourgeois property. At the same time bourgeois social relations reveal that even their freedom is not real freedom, that bourgeois freedom is almost as imprisoning to its enjoyers as the worker's unfreedom. And thus the *bourgeoisie* does not find itself as a solid class, arrayed against the proletariat, but there are divisions in its own ranks, a few at first, and then more and more. The revolution takes place as soon as the proletariat are sufficiently organised by their fight against bourgeois social relations to co-operate, sufficiently harried by their growing unfreedom to demand a new world at all costs; and when, on the other side, as a result of the developing contradictions of capitalism, the bourgeois themselves have lost their grip.

Let us, therefore, go deeper, and examine more closely the true nature of bourgeois freedom. Are H. G. Wells, Bertrand Russell, E. M. Forster, you, reader and I, really free? Do we enjoy even mental freedom? For if we do not enjoy that, we certainly do not enjoy physical freedom.

Bertrand Russell is a philosopher and a mathematician. He takes the method of science seriously, and applies it to various fields of thought. He believes that thoughts are simply special arrangements of matter, even though he calls matter mind-stuff. He agrees that to every psychism corresponds a neurism, that life is a special chemical phenomenon, just as thought is a special biological phenomenon. He is not taken in by the nonsense of entelechies and pure memory.

Why then does he refrain from applying these categories, used everywhere else, to the concept of liberty? In what sense can he believe man to be ever completely free? What meaning can he attach to the word freedom? He rightly detects the idealistic hocus-pocus of smuggling God into science as the Life-Force, entelechy, or the first cause, for the sleight of hand it is. But his liberty is a kind of God; something which he accepts on faith, somehow intervening in the affairs of the universe, and unconnected with causality, Russell's liberty and his philosophy live in different worlds. He has made theology meet science, and seen that theology is a barbarous relic. But he has not performed the last act of integration; he has not asked science's opinion of this belief that the graduate of one of the better universities, with a moderate income, considerable intelligence, and some leisure, is really free.

It is not a question of whether man has in some mysterious fashion free will. For if that were the problem, all men either would or would not have free will, and therefore all men would or would not have liberty. If freedom consists in having free will, and men have free will, we can will as freely under a Fascist, or proletarian, as under a bourgeois government. But everyone admits that there are degrees of liberty. In what therefore does this difference in liberty consist?

Although liberty does not then depend on free will, it will help us to understand liberty if we consider what is the freedom of the will. Free will consists in this, that man is conscious of the motive that dictates his action. Without this consciousness of antecedent motive, there is no free will. I raise my hand to ward off a blow. The blow dictated my action; none the less, I was conscious that I wanted to ward off the blow; I willed to do so. My will was free; it was an act of my will. There was a cause; but I was conscious of a free volition. And I was conscious of the cause, of the blow.

In sleep a tickling of the soles of the feet actuates the plantar reflex. Such an action we call involuntary. Just as the warding movement was elicited by an outside stimulus, so was the bending of the leg. None the less, we regard the second as unfree, *in*voluntary. It was not preceded by a conscious motive. Nor were we conscious of the cause of our action. We thus see that free will exists in so far as we are conscious of an antecedent motive in our mind, regarded as the immediate cause of action. If this motive, or act of will, is itself free, and not forced, we must also be in turn conscious of the antecedent motive that produced it. Free will is not therefore the opposite of causality; it is on the contrary a special and late aspect of causality, it is the *consciousness* of causality. That is why man naturally fits all happenings outside him in a causal frame; because he is conscious of causality in himself. Otherwise it would be a mystery if man, experiencing only uncausality in free will, should assume, as he does, that all other things are linked by causality. If, however, he is only assuming that other objects obey the same laws as he does, both the genesis and success of causality as a cognitive framework for reality are explicable.

Causality and freedom thus are aspects of each other. Freedom is the consciousness of necessity. The universe as a whole is completely free, because that which is not free is determined by something else outside it. But all things are, by definition, contained in the universe, therefore the universe is determined by nothing but itself. But every individual thing in the universe is determined by other things, because the universe is material. This materiality is not 'given' in the definition of the universe, but is exactly what science establishes when it explains the world actively and positively.

Thus the only absolute freedom, like the only absolute truth, is the universe itself. But parts of the universe have varying degrees of freedom, according to their degrees of self-determination. In self-determination, the causes are within the thing itself; thus, in the sensation of free will, the antecedent cause of an action is the conscious thought of an individual, and since the action is also that of the individual, we talk of freedom, because there is self-determination.

The freedom of free will can only be relative. It is characteristic of the more recently evolved categories that they contain more freedom. The matter of which man is composed is in spatio-temporal relation with all other matter in the universe, and its position in space and time is only to a small degree self-determined. Man's perception, however, is to a less degree in relation with the rest of the universe; it is a more exclusive kind of perception that sees little not in the immediate vicinity of man, or in which it is not interested, and it is largely moulded by memory, that is, by internal causes. Hence it is freer, more self-determined, than the spatio-temporal relations of dead matter. Man's consciousness is still more self-determined, particularly in its later developments, such as conscious volition.

Man constantly supposes that he is freer than he is. Freudian research has recently shown that events at the level of being— i.e. unconscious physiological events—may give rise to disturbances which usurp conscious functions. In such circumstances a man may not be conscious of the motives of his actions, although he believes he is. He is therefore unfree, for his will's determination arises from events outside consciousness. An example is the neurotic. The neurotic is unfree. He attains freedom by attaining self-determination, that is, by making conscious motives which before were unconscious. Thus he becomes captain of his soul. I am not now discussing the validity of the various methods by which this knowledge is obtained, or what neurological meaning we are to give to the Freudian symbolism. I agree with this basic assumption of Freudian thereapy, that man always obtains more freedom, more self-determination, by a widening of consciousness or, in other words, by an increase of knowledge. In the case of his own mind, man, by obtaining a knowledge of its causality, and the necessity of its functioning, obtains more freedom. Here too freedom is seen to be a special form of determinism, namely, the consciousness of it.

But man cannot simply sit and contemplate his own mind in order to grasp its causality. His body, and likewise his mind, is in constant metabolic relation with the rest of the universe. As a result, when we want to trace any causal mental sequence, in order to be conscious of it, we find it inextricably commingled with events in the outer world. At an early stage we find we must seek freedom in the outer as well as the inner world. We must be conscious not only of our own laws, but of those of outer reality. Man has always realised that whatever free will may mean it is not will alone, but action also which is involved in liberty. For example, I am immersed in a plaster cast so that I cannot blink an eyelid. None the less, my will is completely free. Am I therefore completely free? Only extremely idealistic philosophers would suggest that I am. A free will is therefore not enough to secure liberty, but our actions also must be unconstrained. Now everyone realises that the outer environment continually constrains our freedom, and that free will is no freedom unless it can act what it wills. It follows that to be really free we must also be able to do what we freely will to do.

But this freedom, too, leads us back to determinism. For we find, and here no philosopher has ever disputed it, that the environment is completely deterministic. That is to say, whatever motion or phenomenon we see, there is always a cause for it, which is itself caused, and so on. And the same causes, in the same circumstances, always secure the same effects. Now an understanding of this iron determinism brings freedom. For the more we understand the causality of the universe, the more we are able to do what we freely will. Our knowledge of the causality of water enables us to build ships and cross the seas; our knowledge of the laws of air enables us to fly; our knowledge of the necessary movements of the planets enables us to construct calendars so that we sow, embark on voyages, and set out to meet each other at the times most conducive to achieving what we will to do. Thus, in the outer world too, determinism is seen to produce freedom, freedom is understood to be a special form of necessity, the *consciousness* of necessity. We see that we attain freedom by our consciousness of the causality of subjective mental phenomena together with our consciousness of the causality of external phenomena. And we are not surprised that the characteristic of the behaviour of objects—causality—is also a characteristic of consciousness, for consciousness itself is only an aspect of an object—the body. The more we gain of this double understanding, the more free we become, possessing both free will and free action. These are not two mutually exclusive things, free will versus determinism—but on the contrary they play into each other's hands.

From this it follows that the animals are less free than men. Creatures of impulse, acting they know not why, subject to all the chances of nature, of other animals, of geographical accidents and climatic change, they are at the mercy of necessity, precisely because they are unconscious of it.

That is not to say they have no freedom, for they possess a degree of freedom. They have some knowledge of the causality of their environment, as is shown by their manipulations of time and space and material—the bird's flight, the hare's leap, the ant's nest. They have some inner self-determination, as is shown by their behaviour. But compared to man, they are unfree.

Implicit in the conception of thinkers like Russell and Forster, that all social relations are restraints on spontaneous liberty, is the assumption that the animal is the only completely free creature. No one constrains the solitary carnivore to do anything. This is of course an ancient fallacy. Rousseau is the famous exponent. Man is born free but is everywhere in chains. Always in the bourgeois mind is this legend of a golden age, of a perfectly good man corrupted by institutions. Unfortunately not only is man not good without institutions, he is not evil either. He is no man at all; he is neither good nor evil; he is an unconscious brute.

Russell's idea of liberty is the unphilosophical idea of bestiality. Narkover School is not such a bad illustration of Russell's liberty after all. The man alone, unconstrained, answerable only to his instincts, is Russell's free man. Thus all man's painful progress from the beasts is held to be useless. All men's work and sweat and revolutions have been away from freedom. If this is true, and if a man believes, as most of us do, as Russell does, that freedom is the essential goal of human effort, then civilisation should be abandoned and we should return to the woods. I am a Communist because I believe in freedom. I criticise Russell, and Wells, and Forster, because I believe they are the champions of unfreedom.

But this is going too far, it will be said. How can these men, who have defended freedom of thought, action, and morality, be champions of unfreedom? Let us proceed with our analysis and we shall see why.

Society is a creation by which man attains a fuller measure of freedom than the beasts. It is society and society alone, that differentiates man qualitatively from the beasts. The essential feature of society is economic production. Man, the individual, cannot do what he wants alone. He is unfree alone. Therefore he attains freedom by co-operation with his fellows. Science, by which he becomes conscious of outer reality, is social. Art, by which he becomes conscious of his feelings, is social. Economic production, by which he makes outer reality conform to his feeling, is social, and generates in its interstices science and art. It is economic production then that gives man freedom. It is because of economic production that man is free, and beasts are not. This is clear from the fact that economic production is the manipulation, by means of agriculture, horse-taming, road-building, car-construction, light, heating, and other engineering, of the environment, conformably to man's will. It enables man to do what he wills; and he can only do what he wills with the help of others. Without roads, food supplies, machines, houses, and clothes, he would be like the man in a plaster cast, who can will what he likes, and yet is not a free man but a captive. But even his free will depends on it. For consciousness develops by the evolution of language, science, and art, and these are all born of economic production. Thus the freedom of man's actions depends on his material level, on his economic production. The more advanced the economic production, the freer the civilisation.

But, it will be argued, economic production is just what entails all the 'constraints' of society. Daily work, division of labour under superintendents, all the laws of contract and capital, all the regulations of society, arise out of this work of economic production. Precisely, for, as we saw, freedom is the consciousness of causality. And by economic production, which makes it possible for man to achieve in action his will, man becomes conscious of the means *necessary* to achieve it. That a lever *must* be of a certain lenghth to move the stone man *wills* to move is one consequence; the other is that a certain number of men *must* co-operate in a certain way to wield the lever. From this it is only a matter of development to the complicated machinery of modern life, with all its elaborate social relations.

Thus all the 'constraints', 'obligations', 'inhibitions', and 'duties' of society are the very means by which freedom is obtained by men. Liberty is thus the social consciousness of necessity. Liberty is not just necessity, for all reality is united by necessity. Liberty is the consciousness of necessity—in outer reality, in myself, and in the social relations which mediate between outer reality and human selves. The beast is a victim of mere necessity, man is in society conscious and self-determined. Not of course absolutely so, but more so than the beast.

Thus freedom of action, freedom to do what we will, the vital part of liberty, is seen to be secured by the social consciousness of necessity, and to be generated in the process of economic production. The price of liberty is not eternal vigilance, but eternal work.

But what is the relation of society to the other part of liberty, freedom to will? Economic production makes man free to do what he wills, but is he free to will what he will?

We saw that he was only free to do what he willed by attaining the consciousness of outer necessity. It is equally true that he is only free to will what he will by attaining the consciousness of inner necessity. Moreover, these two are not antagonistic, but, as we shall now find, they are one. Consciousness is the result of a specific and highly important form of economic production.

Suppose someone had performed the regrettable experiment of turning Bertrand Russell, at the age of nine months, over to a goat foster-mother, and leaving him to her care, in some remote spot, unvisited by human beings, to grow to manhood. When, say forty years later, men first visited Bertrand Russell, would they find him with the manuscripts of the *Analysis of Mind* and the *Analysis of Matter* in his hands? Would they even find him in possession of his definition of number, as the class of all classes? No. In contradiction to his present state, his behaviour woud be both illogical and impolite.

It looks, therefore, as if Russell, as we know and value him, is primarily a social product. Russell is a philosopher and not an animal because he was taught not only manners, but language, and so given access to the social wisdom of ages of effort. Language filled his head with ideas, showed him what to observe, taught him logic, put all other men's wisdom at his disposal, and awoke in him affectively the elementary decencies of society—morality, justice, and liberty. Russell's consciousness, like that of all useful social objects, was a creation. It is Russell's consciousness that is distinctively him, that is what we value in him, as compared to an anthropoid ape. Society made him, just as it makes a hat.

It goes without saying that Russell's 'natural gifts' (or, as we say more strictly, his genotype) were of importance to the outcome. But that is only to say that the material conditions the finished product. Society is well aware that it cannot make a silk purse out of a sow's ear or, except in special circumstances, a don out of a cretin. But it is also aware that out of iron ore you can make rocks, bridges, ships, or micrometers, and, out of that plastic material, man's genotype, you can make Aztecs, ancient Egyptians, Athenians, Prussians, proletarians, parsons, or public schoolboys.

It also goes almost without saying that a man is not a hat. He is a unique social product, the original of Butler's fantasy of machines that gave birth to machines. He himself is one of those machines. The essential truth about man, as compared with hats, is that he is not a hat, but the man who wears it. And the essential truth about this fashioning process of man by society, is that the fashioning is primarily of his consciousness, a process that does not take place with anything else. Now it is precisely because society elaborates his consciousness, that man, although a social product like a hat, is capable of free will, whereas a hat, being unconscious, is not capable of free will. The coming-to-be of a man, his 'growing up', is society fashioning *itself*, a group of consciousnesses, themselves made by previous consciousnesses, making another. So the torch of liberty is handed on, and burns still brighter. But it is in living that man's consciousness takes its distinctive stamp, and living is simply entering into social relations.

But, it will be urged, man—the individual— sees the world for himself alone—mountains, sky, and sea. Alone in his study he reflects on fate and death. True. But mountains and sea have a meaning to him, precisely because he is articulate-speaking, because he has a socially-moulded consciousness. Death, fate, and sea are highly-evolved social concepts. Each individual contributes a little to altering and elaborating them, but how small a contribution compared to the immense pressure of the past! Language, science, and art are all simply the results of man's uniting with his fellows socially to learn about himself and outer reality, in order to impose his desires upon it. Both knowledge and effort are only possible in co-operation, and both are made necessary by man's struggles to be freer.

Thus man's inner freedom, the conscious will, acting towards conscious ends, is a product of society; it is an economic product. It is the most refined of the products society achieves in its search for freedom. Social consciousness flowers out of social effort. We give vent in effort to our instinctive desires. Learning how to accomplish them, we learn something about the nature of reality and how to master it. This wisdom modifies the nature of our desires, which become more conscious, more full of accurate images of reality. So enriched, the desires become subtler, and, in working to achieve profounder goals, in more elaborate economic production, gain still deeper insight into reality, and, as consequence, themselves become yet more enriched. Thus, in dialectic process, social being generates social mind, and this interplay between deepening inner and outer reality is conserved and passed on by culture. Man, as society advances, has a consciousness composed less and less of unmodified instinct, more and more of socially-fashioned knowledge and emotion. Man understands more and more clearly the necessities of his own being and of outer reality. He becomes increasingly more free.

The illusion that our minds are free to the extent that, like the beasts, we are unconscious of the causality of our mental states, is just what secures our unfreedom. Bourgeois society to-day clearly exhibits in practice this truth, which we have established by analysis in theory. The bourgeois believes that liberty consists in absence of social organisation; that liberty is a negative quality, a deprivation of existing obstacles to it; and not a positive quality, the reward of endeavour and wisdom. This belief is itself the outcome of bourgeois social relations. As a result of it, the bourgeois intellectual is unconscious of the causality that makes his consciousness what it is. Like the neurotic who refuses to believe that his compulsion is the result of a certain unconscious complex, the bourgeois refuses to believe that his conception of liberty as a mere deprivation of social restraints arises from bourgeois social relations themselves, and that it is just this illusion which is constraining him on every side. He refuses to see that his own limited liberty, the captivity of the worker, and all the contradictions of developing bourgeois relations—pacifism, Fascism, war, hate, cruelty, disease—are bound in one net of causality, that each is influenced by each, and that therefore it is fallacious to suppose a simple effort of the will of the free man, without knowledge of the causes will banish Fascism, war, and slumps. Because of his basic fallacy, this type of intellectual always tries to cure positive social evils, such as wars, by negative individual actions, such as non-co-operation, passive resistance or conscientious objection. This is because he cannot rid himself of the assumption that the individual is free. But we have shown that the individual is never free. He can only attain freedom by social co-operation. He can only do what he wants by using social forces. If, therefore, he wishes to stop poverty, war, and misery, he must do it, not by passive resistance, but by using social relations. But in order to use social relations he must understand them. He must become conscious of the laws of society, just as, if he wants to lever up a stone, he must know the laws of levers.

Once the bourgeois intellectual can see that society is the only instrument of freedom, he has advanced a step farther along the road to freedom. But until then he is unfree. True he is a logician, he understands the causality of nature, Einstein's theories, all the splendid apparatus of social discovery, but he still believes in a magic world of social relations divorced from these theories, in which only the god of bourgeois liberty rules. This is proved, not only in his theory, in the way his doctrine of liberty is accepted like a theological dogma, and never made to square with all his philosophic and scientific knowledge; but it is also proved in action, when the bourgeois intellectual is powerless to stop the development of increasing unfreedom in bourgeois society. All the compulsions of militancy, Fascism, and economic distress harry contemporary society, and all he can oppose to them is individualistic action, conscientious objection and passive resistance. This is bound to be the case if he is unfree. Like a man who believes he can walk upon the water and drowns in it, the bourgeois intellectual asserts a measure of freedom that does not in fact exist, and is therefore unfree mentally and physically. Who cannot see iron compulsion stalking through the bourgeois world today? We are free when we can do what we will. Society is an instrument of freedom in so far as it secures what men want. The members of bourgeois society, all of them, worker, capitalist, and capitalist-intellectual, want an increase in material wealth, happiness, freedom from strife, from danger of death, security. But bourgeois society to-day produces a decrease in material wealth and also creates unemployment, unhappiness, strife, insecurity, constant war. Therefore all who live in bourgeois society—democratic, Fascist or Rooseveltian—are unfree, for bourgeois society is not giving them what they desire. The fact that they have, or have not, votes or 'freedom of speech' does not alter, in any way, their unfreedom.

Why does not bourgeois society fulfil the wants of its members? Because it does not understand the laws of economic production—it is unorganised and unplanned. It is unconscious of the necessities of economic production, and, because of that, cannot make economic production fulfil its desires. Why is it unconscious of the necessities of economic production? Because, for historical reasons, it believes that economic production is best when each man is left free to produce for himself what seems to him most profitable to produce. In other words, it believes that freedom is secured by the lack of social organisation of the individual in the function of society, economic production. As we saw, this individual freedom through unconsciousness is a delusion. Unconscious, deluded bourgeois society is therefore unfree. Even Russell is unfree; and in the next war, as in the last, will be put in gaol.

This very unfreedom—expressed as individualism—in the basic function of society, ultimately generates every form of external constraint. The bourgeois revolutionary asserted a fallacious liberty—that man was born good and was everywhere in chains, that institutions made him bad. It turned out that this liberty he claimed was individualism in private production. This revealed its fallacious nature as a freedom by appearing at once as a restraint. For it could only be secured, it was only a name, for unrestricted right to own the means of production, which is in itself a restriction on those who are thus alienated from their livelihood. Obviously, what I own absolutely my neighbour is restricted from touching.

All social relations based on duty and privilege were changed by the bourgeois revolution into exclusive and forcible rights to ownership of cash. I produce for my individual self, for profit. Necessarily, therefore, I produce for the market, not for use. I work for cash, not from duty to my lord or retainer. My duties to the State could all now be compounded for cash. All my obligations of contract, whether of marriage or social organisation, could be compounded for cash. Cash appeared as the only obligation between men and men, who were otherwise apparently completely free—free master, free labourer, free producer, free consumer, free markets, free trade, free entrepreneur, the free flow of capital from hand to hand and land to land. And even man's obligations to cash appeared an obligation of cash to him, to be absolutely owned by him.

This dissolution of social obligations could be justified if man was free in himself, and if, doing what seemed best for him, for his own good and profit, he would in fact get what he desired, and so secure freedom. It was a return to the apparent liberty of the jungle, where each beast struggles only for himself, and owes no obligations to anyone. But this liberty, as we saw, is an illusion. The beast is less free than man. The desires of the jungle cancel each other, and no one gets exactly what he wants. No beast is free.

This fallacy at once revealed itself a fallacy in the following way. Complete freedom to own property meant that society found itself divided into haves and have-nots, like the beasts in the jungle. The have-nots, each trying to do what was best for him in the given circumstances, according to the bourgeois doctrine of liberty, would have forcibly seized the property from the haves. But this would have been complete anarchy, and though anarchy, according to bourgeois theory, is complete liberty, in practice the bourgeois speedily sees that to live in the jungle is not to be free. Property is the basis of his mode of living. In such circumstances social production could not be carried on, and society would dissolve, man return to savagery, and freedom altogether perish. Thus the bourgeois contradicted his theory in practice from the start. The State took its distinctive modern form as the enforcement of bourgeois rights by coercion. Police, standing army and laws were all brought into being to protect the haves from the 'free' desires of the have-nots. Bourgeois liberty at once gives rise to bourgeois coercion, to prisons, armies, contracts, to all the sticky and restraining apparatus of the law, to all the ideology and education centred round the sanctity of private property, to all the bourgeois commandments. Thus bourgeois liberty was built on a lie, bound to reveal in time its contradictions.

Among the have-nots, bourgeois freedom gave rise to fresh coercions. The free labourer, owning nothing, was free to sell his labour in any market. But this became a form of slavery worse, in its unrestricted form, than chattel slavery, a horror that Government Blue Books describing pre-Factory Act conditions make vivid for all their arid phraseology. They show how unrestricted factory industrialisation made beasts of men, women, and children, how they died of old age in their thirties, how they rose early in the morning exhausted to work and knocked off late at night only to sink exhausted to sleep, how the children were aged by work before they had ceased to be infants. Made worse than a slave—for he was still free to be unemployed—the labourer fought for freedom by enforcing social restraints on his employers. Banding with others in trade unions, he began the long fight that gave rise to the various Factory Acts, wage agreements, and all the elaborate social legislation which to-day coerces the bourgeois employer.

And, after all this, even the bourgeois himself is not free. The unrestricted following of his illusion of liberty enslaves him. His creed demands unrestricted competition, and this, because it is unrestricted, works as wildly and blindly as the weather. It makes him as unfree, as much at the mercy of a not understood chance, as a cork bobbing on the waves. So he too seeks freedom in restraint—industry is increasingly sheltered by amalgamations, rings, tariffs, price agreements, 'unfair competition' clauses, subsidies, and Government protection for the exploitation of colonial areas. Bourgeois liberty makes overt its self-contradictions by becoming monopoly.

Here is the secret paradox of bourgeois development and decline. The bourgeois abandoned feudal relations in the name of a liberty which he visualised as freedom from social restraints. Such a liberty would have led to savagery. But in fact the liberty he claimed—'unrestricted' private property—really involved restraint, that is, it gave rise to complex forms of social organisation, which were more manysided, more incessant, and more all-pervading, than feudal restraints. Thus the cash relation, which he conceived as putting an end to all social restraints, and thus giving him liberty, did give him a larger measure of liberty than in feudalism, but in the opposite way

71

to his expectations, by imposing far more complex organisations than those of feudal civilisation. All the elaborate forms of bourgeois contracts, market organisation, industrial structure, national States, trade unions, tariffs, imperialism and bureaucratic democratic government, the iron pressure of the consumer and the labour market, the dole, subsidy, bounties—all these multifarious forms of social organisation—were brought into being by a class that demanded the dissolution of social organisation. And the fact that bourgeois civilisation obtained a greater measure of control over its environment than feudal—and was that much freer—is precisely because all these complex social organisations were brought into being—but brought blindly.

Blindly brought into being; that is the source of the ultimate unfreedom of bourgeois civilisation. Because it is not conscious of the fact that private ownership of the means of production, unrestricted competition, and the cash nexus, of their natures involve various forms of restraint—alienation from property, captivity to slump and war, unemployment and misery—bourgeois society is unable to control itself. The various forms of social organisation it has blindly erected, as an animal tunnelling for gold might throw up great mounds of earth, are all haphazard and not understood. It believes that to become conscious of them fully, to manipulate them consciously for the ends of the will, is to be an advocate of determinism, to kill liberty, to bring into birth the bee-hive state. For still, in spite of all the havoc the bourgeois sees around him, he believes that only the beast is free, and that to be subject to all the winds of chance, at the mercy of wars and slumps and social strife, is to be free.

Any definition of liberty is humbug that does not mean this: liberty to do what one wants. A people is free whose members have liberty to do what they want—to get the goods they desire and avoid the ills they hate. What do men want? They want to be happy, and not to be starved or despised or deprived of the decencies of life. They want to be secure, and friendly with their fellows, and not conscripted to slaughter and be slaughtered. They want to marry, and beget children, and help, not oppress each other. Who is free who cannot do these things, even if he has a vote, and free speech? Who then is free in bourgeois society, for not a few men but millions are forced by circumstances to be unemployed, and miserable, and despised, and unable to enjoy the decencies of life? Millions are forced to go out and be slaughtered, or to kill, and to oppress each other. Millions are forced to strive with their fellows for a few glittering prizes, and to be deprived of marriage, and a home, and children, because society cannot afford them these things. Millions and millions of men are not free. These are the elements of liberty, and it is insane—until these are achieved—for a limited class to believe it can secure the subtleties of liberty. Only when these necessities are achieved, can man rise higher and, by the practice of art and science, learn more clearly what he wants, and what he can get; having only then passed from the sphere of necessity to that of freedom.

Each step to higher consciousness is made actively with struggle and difficulty. It is man's natural but fatal error to suppose that the path of liberty is easy, that liberty is a mere negative, a relaxation, the elimination of an obstacle in his path. But it is more than that. True freedom must be created as strenuously as we make the instruments of freedom, tools and machines. It must be wrested out of the heart of reality, including the inner reality of man's minds.

That is why all lovers of liberty, who have understood the nature of freedom, and escaped from the ignorant categories of bourgeois thought, turn to Communism. For that is simply what Communism is, the attainment of more liberty than bourgeois society can reach. Communism has as its basis the understanding of the causality of society, so that all the unfreedom involved in bourgeois society, the enslavement of the have-nots by the haves, and the slavery of both haves and have-nots to wars, slumps, depression and superstition, may be ended. To be conscious of the laws of dead matter: that is something; but it is not enough. Communism seizes hold of a higher degree of self-determination, to rescue man from war, starvation, hate, and coercion, by becoming conscious of the causality of society. It is Communism that makes free will real to man, by making society conscious of itself. To change reality we must understand its laws. If we *wish* to move a stone, we *must* apply the leverage in the proper place. If we *wish* to change bourgeois

STUDIES IN A DYING CULTURE

social relations into communist, we *must* follow a certain path. The have-nots, the proletariat, must take over the means of production from the haves, the bourgeoisie, and since, as we saw, these two freedoms are incompatible, restraint, in the form of the coercive State, must remain in being as long as the bourgeoisie try to get back their former property. But unlike the former situation, this stage is only temporary. This stage is what is known as the dictatorship of the proletariat, the necessary step from the dictatorship of the bourgeoisie—which is what the bourgeois State is—to the classless State, which is what Communism is. And as Russia shows, even in the dictatorship of the proletariat, before the classless State has come into being, man is already freer. He can avoid unemployment, and competition with his fellows, and poverty. He can marry and beget children, and achieve the decencies of life. He is not asked to oppress his fellows.

To the worker, subject to unemployment, starved in the midst of plenty, this path eventually becomes plain. Despite the assurances of the bourgeoisie that in a democratic or national State he is completely free, he revolts. And who, in those days, will stand by his side? Will the bourgeoisie, themselves pinched and disfranchised by the growing concentration of capital, discouraged, pessimistic, harried into war and oppression by 'forces beyond control', and yet still demanding liberty? On the answer to that question, which each individual bourgeois must make, sooner or later, will depend whether he strives in those days to make men free or to keep them in chains. And this too depends on whether he has understood the nature of liberty. The class to whom capitalism means liberty steadily contracts, but those once of that class who are now enslaved to war, and imperialism and poverty, still cling to that bourgeois interpretation of liberty that has abundantly proved its falsehood. They can only escape and become free by understanding the active nature of liberty, and by becoming conscious of the path they must follow to attain it. Their will is not free as long as they will liberty but produce unfreedom. It is only free when they will Communism and produce liberty.

This good, liberty, contains all good. Not only at the simple level of current material wants, but where all men's aspirations bud, freedom is the same goal, pursued in the same way. Science is the means by which man learns what he can do, and therefore it explores the necessity of outer reality. Art is the means by which man learns what he wants to do, and therefore it explores the essence of the human heart. And bourgeoisdom, shutting its eyes to beauty, turning its back on science, only follows its stupidity to the end. It crucifies liberty upon a cross of gold, and if you ask in whose name it does this, it replies, 'In the name of personal freedom'.

IV

BEAUTY

A STUDY IN BOURGEOIS AESTHETICS

What is beauty? Is it a subject for discussion at all? Can it be defined in such a way as to provide a foundation for aesthetics? Is it a product of art? Or of nature?

To define: to limit the boundaries, to give an outline to the defined thing. Beauty, then, is defined by all that is not-beauty. This not-beauty circumscribes, limits, and defines beauty. But beauty is not opposed by not-beauty; it is opposed by ugliness. Yet the recognition of ugliness itself involves an aesthetic 'faculty', and sensibilities responding both to beauty and ugliness; and it is not possible to say where one begins and the other ends. Ugliness itself is an aesthetic value: the villain, the gargoyle, the grotesque, the Caliban, the snake-headed Furies, the triumph of Time's decaying hand, all these qualities interpenetrate with beauty, and help to generate and feed it. All live in the same world. Nowhere can we draw a distinct line and say, on this side lives the beautiful, and on that the ugly. All man's experience, all the rich complexity of his sculpted, painted, written art forms, all the elaborate multiform crowd of living animals and varied scenery, deny such a simple dichotomy. All form one world even if it contains opposites, and therefore the generating forces must lie at a lower level. Beauty and ugliness, the noble and the petty, the sublime and the ridiculous, all these opposite terms, *when used in an aesthetic way*, involve each other, and must be determined by other, different qualities, from which they spring.

We do not respond to all beautiful things in precisely the same way. The peculiar qualities of each thing colour the emotion we feel with an individual unique shade. If it were not so, the one beautiful thing would suffice; the one vase, painting, mountain would always be sufficient stimulus to our emotion. This is not so. Yet of course there must be a likeness in all our responses for us to group them as one, as *aesthetic*.

Still more striking is the change in the responses to the beautiful from age to age. No age is satisfied wholly with the beautiful things of its forefathers, but produces other things, to the measure of its desires, quite clearly different from those beautiful traditions it inherits. This new vision does not exclude the old, however. The old still seems beautiful, but now its qualities are seen through a kind of mist or aerial perspective of intervening time, changing and toning its hues. The old beauty has been gathered up in the new. And that age which is least able to rest content with the beautiful things of the past, that creates things beautiful to its eyes most different, most revolutionary and most insurgent, is precisely that age which seems to us most in possession of beauty. We value the revolutionary, dissatisfied art works of the Renaissance, and see nothing in those of the Hellenising classicists or tired formalists who mechanically repeat the beautiful things of times gone by.

Man remains throughout this period much the same, but the changing pageant of his art, his poetry, and his buildings proclaims that at no stage does his idea of beauty remain constant, but continually demands expansion and rejection. All contents of the habitable world, of the known cosmos even, come to share in this strange irradiation. The rich Americas, the glassy depths of the 'deep abyss', the spiral nebulae, new birds and insects, jungles and swamps, the silent Poles and the breathless Equator, acquire for man's eyes with each generation a novel aesthetic quality and become things of a nature undreamt of before this time.

Remembering this, we start to define Beauty. The man looks at an object and calls it beautiful. This is a relationship repeatable by this one man with perhaps thousands of objects. What does it involve—what, in this subject-object relation, is the Beauty?

It must be, not in one relation but in all relations of man to object where man says: 'This is Beautiful'. It must be, therefore, something common to all beautiful objects and to all men finding an object beautiful.

The simplest answer is to say that the man is common to

all objects, and therefore beauty is 'in' the man. Beauty is a state of the man. To the bourgeois aesthete this very simple solution of the problem seems so obvious that he has no patience with anyone who can think anything else. This is the solution advanced by I. A. Richards and C. K. Ogden:

'Beauty is attributed to objects which produce coenaesthesia.'*

The common term linking these relations wherein the man says 'This is beautiful' is therefore his 'coenaesthesia'. Here is a common term of the kind we sought for when we sought for something similar in all relations of men finding objects beautiful. Here then is a definition for beauty. Beauty is coenaesthesia.

Coenaesthesia is a wide term, and really includes the totality of proprioceptive impressions as far as they give rise to affects. Most neurologists picture the process as one in which interoceptive stimuli—particularly visceral stimuli—give rise, *via* thalamic activity, to colorations of the conscious field known as feelings. Now it is quite plain that although the aesthetic emotions are coenaesthetic in this sense simply because they are affective, all coenaesthetic sensations are not sensations of the beautiful. That would be to say that all feelings of pleasure or unpleasure are feelings of the beautiful. Consequently the definition of Richards and Ogden is inadequate. A pork chop, well done, may arouse strong feelings of coenaesthesia, but it is not beautiful—or hideous. As an aesthetic object, it is neutral.

Why do the authors then arrive at this definition? It is in fact a typical bourgeois definition; beauty is a state of the bourgeois. This is not very different from many other bourgeois propositions springing out of the decay of bourgeois philosophy after Hegel, shown by the rise of positivism. In the same way Truth becomes an *economical* method for the bourgeois of describing phenomena. Causality becomes the way it *suits* the bourgeois to think of phenomena. And so on. It is the product of a 'tired' philosophy.

The definition of beauty as coenaesthesia is the ultimate product of mechanical materialism, of a philosophy that defines

* *The Meaning of Meaning*, by I. A. Richards and C. K. Ogden.

the environment as 'all that is not the bourgeois', while the bourgeois stands outside it free and separate. The world thus becomes divested of all values arising from the relation of bourgeois to environment, for all such values, since they contain the bourgeois, are abstrated from the environment, for otherwise they would tie him to it. Such a non-valued environment ultimately contains nothing knowable and contains therefore nothing at all, but by the time this is discovered bourgeois culture is in such an advanced stage of disintegration that it seems immaterial whether the world is a real, coloured, qualified world or a ghostly ballet of equations.

(i) If on the one hand the environment is robbed of all values in which it shares, the bourgeois is presented with all such values. They are his. Beauty is *in him*. But it is soon found that this by no means aggrandises such values.

For what is the bourgeois, according to the mechanical materialist? A body, a group of electrons, a collection of blood, bones, and neurones, subject to physiological laws, conditioned reflexes, and 'instincts'. Beauty and all similar values thus become physiological activity. Having dissolved the environment into moving molecules, atoms, ultimately into tensors and moved all values into the bourgeois, this type of bourgeois philosopher now starts to operate on the bourgeois himself. He also is the environment to other bourgeois; he also is matter. Therefore all the accumulation of values stripped from the environment and concentrated in him can now themselves quickly be shown to be nothing but physiological functions, biochemical and electronic phenomena—mere tensors.

This is the bourgeois nightmare of a predetermined Universe which includes the bourgeois, from which he shuddered away into absolute idealism.

(ii) If we start from the other end, with the mind as primary, all qualities which partake of the environment are stripped from mind. Applied to relations of the beautiful, this involves that the singularities of the beautiful objects, due to the way in which they differ among themselves, are to be abstracted from these relations in order to discover the essentially beautiful. The liquid eyes of the deer, the massive solidity of the mountain, the fatness of Falstaff, the coldness of an iceberg, are qualities not common to mind but peculiar to the objects on which mind rests. They must all be stripped away and finally, by removing all environmental individualities from beauty as it inheres in beautiful relations, we are left with absolute Beauty, the Idea or concept of Beauty, which is homogeneous and bare of individualities, and is therefore completely mental.

But the objects of beauty vary from generation to generation of men, and appear to have existed before men existed. There is therefore a Beauty which is independent of the brain. Thus we get the absolute Idea of Beauty existing apart from the brains of men. This is that 'Beauty' of which aestheticians talk; meaning nothing but an Idea, something colourless, a kind of vague white-robed bare-footed personification going about the world. Such an idea is parasitic, because it sucks an emotive colouring from all beautiful objects, and yet has denuded those objects of just that in them which was the source of our delight—their self-hood and individuality. It is death to Art, because in the artist's flair for the difference, for the newness, for the intrinsic and peerless individuality of the beautiful object, lies his power to make new beauty. It is equally deadening to the lover of beauty, for he loves beautiful *objects*—the daffodil, the Cézanne—*for themselves*, not because in them is a manifestation of an Idea of the Beautiful. Thus, when the extremes of bourgeois idealism and bourgeois mechanical materialism in the realm of Value are reached, there is not so much difference after all—to both Beauty dissolves and becomes something homogeneous, empty, dead—coenaesthesia or the Absolute Idea.

★

It is true of course that coenaesthesia enters into the beautiful relation, just as a neuronic wave of potential difference enters into the perceptual relation. How much is there to this side of the story?

Let us pick out at random a few generalised qualities and values:

Heat,	Cold,	Glory,	Happiness,
Pleasure,	Beauty,	Fear,	Pain.

All these may be regarded as affective: Man feels happy, pleased, afraid, feels pain, fear, that a thing is hot, that a thing is beautiful. But of course, in the way these feelings arise, each expresses a relation of the man to his environmental relation. *Something* makes man happy, he finds *something* to be pleasant. Yet there is plainly a difference in man's use of these concepts. Happiness, fear, pain and heat are all the accompaniment of nervous disturbances, are all in possession of a common physiological term. We locate happiness *in ourselves,* and this we do also with fear and pain, and yet we locate heat and beauty *out there,* in the object.

We locate it as the outcome of our experience. Take the concept of happiness. Experience shows us that certain objects in certain cases are associated with happiness, in the other cases with not-happiness. We find that movement away from those objects to others does not necessarily mean the removal of unhappiness. We find that happiness has a persistent quality through a large number of different 'I' environmental situations. Happiness is common to these situations. So is the 'I'. The environment is not common, but changes in these situations; so we locate happiness in the 'I'. A happy person is therefore to us a person who has *in him* happiness.

But fear, or joy, while showing a certain congruity in changing environmental situations, also show a certain incongruity. We may indeed find fear and joy persisting in certain changes, but we may find a given situation, particularly with fear, forcibly and abruptly changing the stability of the ego, from happiness or boredom to fear. Therefore we conceive fear and joy, as *a* fear and *a* joy, separate and impersonal, situated neither in the environment nor ourselves, but abruptly breaking in on both.

A pain we locate in ourselves but yet as something alien to us which has gained a seat in us. This concept is necessitated by our experience (*a*) that we act immediately by withdrawing our bodies from the environment (therefore pain is alien, imposed on us by the environment), (*b*) that often pain cannot be so diminished but is still, after such actions, present in our bodies, as for example a toothache, or the pain of a wound after the blow. (Therefore pain is inside us.)

Heat and cold we locate entirely in objects because experience has shown us that movements of our body always remove us from the source of heat or cold. It is therefore not in ourselves, but the environment. In the sum of ego-environment relations, *happiness* vanished while the environment *changed*. Hence, just as happiness is located in the ego, heat is located in the environment.

Finally beauty, like heat, and unlike pain, fear, joy, pleasure or happiness is located entirely in the environment.

The object is beautiful; we ourselves do not feel beautiful when we see a beautiful object.

In other words, it is man's experience that beauty is un objective quality—not wholly objective, because it is a relation between subject and object—but objective in the way that heat is. Like heat, beauty appears or disappears in man's conscious field according as he moves towards or from the beautiful object in his environment, the object itself remaining unchanged during this process. That is what men have felt when they called Beauty timeless, eternal, Divine. But we have already seen that to accept this, to separate the lover of beauty from beautiful objects, is to make Beauty either a colourless Idea or a physiological disturbance.

We find men agree about what is hot and what is cold in all ages. Moreover we can correlate differences of heat with differences of molecular movement and with the temperature of man's blood, above which temperature all seems 'hot' and below which all seems 'cold'. By inference, we hold that these molecular movements with which heat is identified were the same in character long before man existed. This gives heat, in all its degrees, an objective existence independent of man. It is now described or compared with other qualities (motion), more or less independently of the sensory nerves.

But we do not find men agreeing about what is beautiful in all ages. We find on the contrary that in each age:

(*a*) Men pick out different objects as beautiful, or pick out different aspects or details of objects already recogniced as beautiful, for praise.

(*b*) Men not only pick out different objects as beautiful (beauty in nature) but make different beautiful objects (beauty in art) from age to age.

(c) Usually, however, the objects that earlier generations found or made beautiful, are accepted by later generations as beautiful, and the rôle of the later generation is that of either adding to them by enriching our perception of them, or subtly modifying our appreciation of their qualities.

We cannot find any non-aesthetic qualities in terms of which beauty can be exactly described independently of man, although we can find non-thermal qualities in terms of which heat can be exactly described. Thus we cannot infer back to describe the beauty of the world before man came into existence; we can only suppose that, 'if man could see such a world, he would find it beautiful'. But, to do so, we must imagine the observer already there; ourselves looking at such a world; we cannot imagine the world as a ballet of impersonal equations with the beauty expressed by these equations, as they express the heat of molecular movement.

How are we to reconcile the fact that we regard beauty, unlike happiness, as a property of the environment, with our failure to produce comparative environmental qualities, as we can in the case of heat, which would suffice to determine it independently of man? We could only reconcile it if there were a triadity in the subject-object relation of man to beautiful object; if in addition to naked subject and naked environment, we had a third mediating term, something which remained unchanged while the subject changed and so could stand to it as environment and account for our projection of Beauty outside ourselves, and yet which changed while the bare environment remained unchanged, which would account for the historic change in what particular objects are found to be lovely or made beautiful.

We have actually such a third term; we have already referred to it; it is men as opposed to man—society. The *man* as born, as innate, uneducated and 'wild', changes little in the course of history, but of course he does not span all human history; only *men*-in-society does that. So in commenting on the change in man's estimation of beauty from age to age, we have already in fact admitted society as the cause of change in beauty, of the coming into being of new beauty. In conmenting on the constancy of the environment thoughout, we have in fact admitted that the objective environment in which beauty is situated is social rather than natural. If it were the unchanging environment in which beauty was situated, how could it change? If man, substantially unchanging in his innate make-up, faced the unchanging earth and stars without material mediation, how could an ever-changing beauty be generated? But man sees nature through social spectacles. 'Spectacles' is a partly incorrect analogy, for man is a part of society, and nature is a part of society. Society is a genuine middle term. To an individual man society stands as environment, and is included with the sun, earth and air. To nature, however, society stands as an active human force. The antimonies of beauty as a value can therefore only be resolved by regarding it as a social product, something secreted in the process of society. In the process of society, all nature enters. Man measures himself against infinite space, and takes his time from the sun. He feels the hot breath of the desert in his cities, and he goes out alone or in bands to establish himself in the jungles. He moves on the face of the lonely sea in man-made ships. The threads of social process penetrate, under the hands of Einstein and Amundsen, Freud and Rutherford, Kepler and Magellan, into remoter and remoter cracks of reality. The labouring masses of society root deep in the face of the earth. The farmer sowing the fruitful prairies, the lone hunter in untamed woods, and the sailor on the 'wine-dark' sea are all parts of the social process. As such, the social process generates everywhere beauty, not as a universal but as a specific social product, just as it generates science, politics, or religion.

We referred to the possibility of expressing heat in terms of other, non-sensory, qualities, so that heat had an objective metrical scale, correlated to but independent of man's experience. If it were possible completely so to describe heat, we should be discovering a self-contained, self-determined world. The complete goal is impossible. The completely non-human self-determined world of physics does not exist. There is something in heat as felt which can only be expressed in terms of the observer. But none the less such feeling, in its degree and appearance, can be completely *determined* by other qualities.

Bourgeois philosophy attempts to close one world or the other, to make heat objective or mental. Dialectical materialists refuse to do this. Heat is determined by objective qualities but its appearance contains a newness, something peculiar to it as an event.

This is equally true of beauty. Beauty is determined by other non-aesthetic qualities, which account for its appearance and disappearance, its change and development. These qualities are not, as in the case of heat, kinetic, but sociological, they arise from the interaction of systems of men with the environment, in the course of labour processes. Such sociological qualities are not aesthetic: there is a distinct realm of aesthetics. Beauty can only be known, felt or described in the experience, and the experience is real, it is not a chance iridescence on the surface of atomic clouds, but a real intense property of the Universe. A man who had never felt heat would never be able to imagine it from a study of the kinetic theory of heat, however familiar he was with motion. A man who had never seen beautiful things would never know beauty, however complete his sociological data. Beauty is social. It is objective because it lives apart from me, in society. The smile of a Polycletan Hermes has qualities, not only in me, but in the Hellas which produced it, and all that has happened since and before to man. It is not, however, merely resident in society considered as a group of men. It stretches into all parts of the Universe because society, as active subject, is related to all other reality as object.

Happiness is not a social product, any more than a man is a social product. It is true that happiness arises out of the relation of me to my environment; my experience generates it. But it is like my flesh, instinctive and unsophisticated. It is like sorrow, anger and love, a quality which is as yet untransformed by society and is born the same in each man. It is genotypical. I, as individual subject, generate it in relation to the environment, as object. It is not independent of the environment, any more than my body is in its health. But happiness is not a social product any more than illness, which is produced by the environment, is a social product. We need not suppose it will always be so. A day may come when man, become increasingly conscious of himself, may be able to make happy things, a happy environment, as he makes a beautiful thing. Happiness will then seem to him like beauty, not in himself but in his environment. He will be the creator, not the slave of happiness and sorrow, as he is now the creator of beauty and ugliness. Then perhaps happiness will seem higher than beauty, or perhaps it will seem as if beauty, by a simple expansion, has taken up happiness within itself, and it is still beauty, but a larger, more universal beauty which we serve, a happiness which we now consciously create and actually see.

Beauty is not alone in playing a dual rôle as object to the individual and subject to the environment. Morality and goodness are the same; they are conceived of as greater than man and outside him, and yet change with society and are not expressible except in sociological terms. God as he appears in all myths, religions and metaphysics, is such a value. Just as Beauty, imagined as a real indwelling goddess, ceased to exist at a certain stage in social development, and yet beauty the objective value persisted, so God, conceived as a person, to-day ceases to exist, and yet morality and goodness, as objective values outside the individual, persist. Both are social products. Truth is another such value. We cannot conceive truth apart from a true statement—something human, and yet we know that truth is not just what I, the individual, think to be true. Truth is a social product; it is a particular relation of the individual, *via* society, to the rest of the Universe.

But truth, goodness, and beauty are not 'just' social products. Their specific social rôles, in which man as individual, men as society, nature as environment and reality as including individual and society and environment, all figure, differ among themselves and generate their peculiar quality. What is this peculiar quality in the case of beauty? Beauty tells us something not as a statement tells us something, but as a glance tells us something. It is the apprehension of a genuine quality. A beautiful thing has a significant content, just as a true statement has. But it is not the same significance. What is this difference between true statements and beautiful things?

In the course of the contact of the individual with reality, he experiences various emotions. These emotions, or affects, are new qualities. Instinct is what we call a simple repetition of hereditary habits, the mechanical reappearance of the old. Such simple responses to external or internal stimuli change from age to age, but, in relation to the rapid tempo of social life, there is a consistency about them which leads us to separate them as hypothetical entities, the instincts. Situations which, while evoking instinctual responses, do not permit their emergence unchanged, but cause a suspension or interruption of the pattern, produce affects or emotions. The result of such a situation is the transforming, or conditioning (Pavlov), repression or sublimation (Freud) of the response. Thus the affects or emotions are the sign at once of an instinctive response and of its change in a certain *sitation* or subject-object pattern.

The instincts as mechanical responses are unconscious. It is consciousness itself—a particular group of innervations and their relation to reality—which calls them 'unconscious'. What it means by this term is: 'not included with us'. But all innervations, being innervations of one nervous system, are related. Thus even the unconscious group, those innervations 'not included with us', are in indirect connexion with the conscious group. In so far as they leave mnemenic traces, unconscious innervations can be known by consciousness. The nature of this 'unconscious' excluded group is such that they leave crude mnemenic traces but, once left, these traces are enduring. Unconscious 'memories' are simple, poor, and permanent; conscious memories are subtle, rich, and fluid.

Affects are conscious. A feeling is felt. But the affects, the emotions, emerge as a specific relation between a situation and an innate response. The relation between situation and response generates these emotions. Consciousness is a relation of two unconscious terms, body and environment.

The organism encounters situations through its exteroceptive neurones, through sight, hearing, touch, and smell, of which in man sight and ·hearing are dominant. The organism has responses because of innate potentialities buried in it, in its chromosomes, in its sympathetic and parasympathetic systems, in its visceral innervations. Of course there is no gulf between situation receptors and response-effectors. The eye itself has innate responses; and stimuli arise inside the organism. A stomach-ache is a situation. But the *situation* is sencory, is *external;* the *response* is somatic, is *interior.*

An emotion which expresses a particular new relation between a situation and a response therefore has both a sensory component and a somatic component. It is not a mixture, it is a quality—a relation of two terms. The situation appears as the form: the present situation as a percept, sound heard, odour smelt or tactile sensation; the past situation as a memory. The response appears as the feeling content, as the fear, desire, or boredom associated with the presentation. Both are intimately mingled. In thought the situation appears as the memory-image, thought, dream and so forth, and the response as the feeling tone, or affective colouring of the thought. In reflection, affective tone and percept are more closely entwined, for whereas the organism is the same, there is no real situation 'outside-now'. The affect has almost sucked up into itself the sensory presentation; hence the possibility of imageless thought.

Thus all consciousness may be regarded as groups of entities which may be divided into feelings, the *content;* and situations being met or remembered, the *form.* Feelings are common to all contents, but the form is different for present and for past situations. The form of the one is a percept; of the second, a memory or thought. But the affect differs subtly according to whether the form is a memory or a percept.

A thing may be unconsciously perceived if it evokes no new response. It is habitual, always there; we do not notice it.

The field of consciousness therefore represents the ingression of the new into the organism-situation relation. The affective basis is the organismal basis and the thought or perceptual form is the situation form. But they completely interpenetrate; they are not separable. They determine each other. Each change in consciousness involves a change in the environment. Of course, for each component of consciousness, the change may be chiefly organismal or chiefly environmental. This difference of degree, which never proceeds so far as to enable us to call any component *absolutely* one or the other, is important. Too 'pure' a percept, or too 'deep' a feeling is in either case unconscious. It is not the purity or vividness of either that consciousness expresses, but a change in their relation, an impact of the two. Consciousness is therefore change, it is the ingression of the new. It is the seat or aggregation of the novelties in a man's relations with reality. Such new qualities clump to form a conscious field, as bacteria clump in serum. The field is not static; it grows, changes and expands. It is not self-determined; on the contrary the field is the expression of the determining relation between the organism and the rest of reality.

In examining these contents we may sort them so as to pay special attention to the *forms*, to the percepts and memories of situations encountered in reality, to the bits of reality apparently embedded in consciousness.

The study of consciousness then becomes a study of the bits of reality embedded in consciousness, or the portions of outer reality in the conscious field. There is a tendency to call the outer reality quite simply 'Reality', so that this sorting becomes the study of reality.

The objective of such a study is truth. It is the goal of science. In so far as the 'situation' portions of the conscious field separate themselves out, a greater and greater grip of reality is presumed to be obtained. Such a programme is of course the programme above all of 'physics'.

But just because all contents of the conscious field, in so far as they represent the ingression of the new into the subject-object relation, contain both emotion and percept, feeling and memory, it is never possible in fact to find a conscious quality which is all situation and bare of feeling. The following-out of the programme of physics therefore gradually strips the world of reality of all qualities in consciousness in which a feeling tone or 'subjective factor' is concerned. This means stripping the real world, the object of science, of all reality. It becomes simply a group of equations.

But equations are mental. They represent the laws of the comparison of qualities between themselves. Thus the real world becomes virtually nothing—unappetising and bare of interest. It becomes, finally, meaningless. Thus, although science, alone of activities, has as its goal objective truth and the extracting from consciousness of the 'pure' situation elements, this will, if carried to its utmost extent, rob truth of truth. For truth implies some affective attitude, some relation of organism to environment, by which it is generated. Truth can never be a criterion of a complete system of metrics, considered as self-sufficient in themselves, for the circle of metrics is closed. They constitute a world in themselves. The only criterion here is consistency. The question we ask of metrics is: 'Is the world fully closed? Do we arrive back finally at our initial axioms?' Now this consistency is quite different from what we mean by truth, the goal of the scientist, which spurs him on in his arduous labour.

What then is this Truth? For what do we in fact search the field of consciousness in its name? The field of consciousness is not static, it is generated by change. Conciousness is the product or affective heat of a clash between the response of the organism and a situation to which the response is not exactly geared. The impact, changing both, is preserved in the organism's behaviour as a modification and in its consciousness as a feeling and a thought. This conscious field changes; it has its laws of flow and recombination. Man thinks, plans, wills, introspects. Consciousness is the continual ingression of the new. Consciousness is the sign of a behaviour modification. Man 'learns' by experience, by the ingression into his organism of the new. Consciousness is the result of interaction, and is a guide to action.

But action implies the organism. The organism acts. If consciousness is simply the individual's sum of behaviour modifications, available as a guide to fresh situations, if each impact changes organism and environment, truth is a criterion of action. A component of consciousness is only generated by a tension between response and situation which do not fit like hand in glove, and because there is a discrepancy there is energy, heat, perception, feeling, as the hand is forced into the glove and as a result hand and glove are both altered in shape. Truth then is given man in his attempt to change the world. In changing it, of course, he changes himself.

That is why science is never hypothesis alone. It is always hypothesis plus experiment. In the experiment there is a tension or contradiction between man's beliefs—the sum of his responses as a result of previous experience—and a given situation—the crucial experiment or discovery of a piece of reality which does not fit the response. As a result the hypothesis is changed. Man's consciousness is changed.

Hence science's history is a continual modification of hypothesis by experiment. As the result of each modification, man's relation to objective reality is changed—he alters from a being at the centre of the Universe to one on the limits of it and then to a man in no absolute place. Truth always appears as a result of man's successful interaction with his environment. Always he can only find truth by changes and reality. By analysing, by setting up a mock world in the laboratory, by moving his position somewhere to view an eclipse, by making experiments in artificial lightning—in all such ways he changes reality, and all these are precursors to far vaster changes—bridges, ships, roads, tilled land. Each time, in altering reality, he generates new truth, and finds it only thus.

Hence, except in action, truth is meaningless. To attempt to find it in a mere scrutiny of the conscious field, by 'pure' thought, results not in truth but in mere consistency. The contents of the mind are measured against themselves without the incursion of a disturbance from outside, which disturbances in fact, in the past history of the field, are what have created it. Since innumerable consistent worlds are possible, there would be as many criteria of reality as there were people with different conscious experiences.

But action upon nature demands co-operation if it is to be fully effective. The organism which will be most in possession of truth, which will most deeply penetrate and widely change the environment, will be an organism able to co-operate with other organisms in that change. The very combination, by division of labour, produces a qualitative change. What millions of organisms do separately is nothing compared to what they can do in co-operation to a common goal. Truth appears as an outcome of the labour process, for it is the labour process that demands and at the same time dictates the co-operation of organisms.

Thus a mediating term now appears in truth, which we first

analysed as an outcome of the bare organism faced by bare environment. But now the bare organism faces society and its culture, and the bare environment faces, not the lone organism, but the tremendous apparatus of co-operating men.

In fact this occurred from the very beginning. The labour process itself generates the co-operation which changes and expands the responses of the organism, and gives rise to sufficiently many new situations to make it possible to talk of 'truth'. From the very start the labour process, by the society it generates, acts as a mediating term in the production of truth.

From the very start the labour process gives rise to material capital. Simple enough at first, taking the form of mere tools, customs, magico-scientific objects, seeds, huts, these were yet all-important as the beginnings of culture. To our argument they bear this important relation, that all such enduring products represent social truths. The plough is as much a statement about the nature of reality as the instructions how to use it. Each is useless without the other; each makes possible the development of the other. All these social products are generated by the nature of reality, but their form is given by the organism in its interaction with reality. The nature of fields and plants imposes on the organisms specific types of co-operation in sowing and reaping and determines the shape of the plough. It imposes on them language, whereby they signify to each other their duties and urge each other on in carrying them out. Once established the labour process, extending as remotely as observation of the stars, as widely as organisation of all human relations, and as abstractedly as the invention of numbers, gathers and accumulates truth. Faster and faster it proliferates and moves. The bare organism is to-day from birth faced with an enormous accumulation of social truth in the form of buildings, laws, books, machines, political forms, tools, engineering works, complete sciences. All these arise from co-operation; all are social and common. Generated by this capital, truth is the past relation of society to the environment accumulated in ages of experience. It is actually created by the conflict of social organisms with new situations in the course of the labour process.

But the very richness and complexity of this 'frozen' truth, the very elaborateness of an advanced culture and a functioning society, ensure that the naked organism will be confronted with the greatest possible variety of 'situations'. This will ensure the greatest possible activity of a man's consciousness, and the maximum of mutual transformation of his responses, his instincts, and the material environment. There will be a rapid ingression of newness. This itself will generate new truth. Man, as experiencing individual, will find himself constantly negating the truths given in his social environment.

Thus we see the cause of the apparent antinomies in truth. Truth appears to be in the environment, to be objective and independent of me. Yet the attempt to extract a completely non-subjective truth from experience produces only metrics. Moreover the environment changes only slowly, but the truth of science or reality as known to man has changed rapidly.

Truth, then, is in my environment, that is, in my culture, in the enduring products of the labour process. Thus truths, although similar in their lack of newness and fixation to my inherited responses, are yet different in that responses emerge from the unconscious, *inside* me, whereas the inheritances of culture come to me as 'situations', as things learned, taught, or told me, as experience, as *environment,*. But I do not regard myself as bound to the social criteria of truth; on the contrary it is my task to change their formulations, where my experience contradicts them.

★

But, it will be urged, we were to discuss beauty, and now it is only truth we have obtained. Writing when bourgeois English poetry was at its height at the same time as bourgeois German philosophy was reaching its climax, Keats said:

> 'Beauty is truth, truth beauty'—that is all
> Ye know on earth, and all ye need to know.'

A modern bourgeois poet, T. S. Eliot, has announced himself unable to understand these lines of Keats, just as modern bourgeois philosophers show themselves unable to understand

Hegel's dialectics. But we saw that the pursuit of truth was the study of the objective elements in the conscious field. We saw further that completely objective elements could never be obtained. A world built up in such a way dissolved into mere metrics, and truth became consistency. To every percept and thought, an affect or subjective tinge inevitably attached itself. We never had a mere situation but always response to a situation.

Thus truth never stands by itself as 'pure'. It is always generated in action, in instinctive organismal response going out into the situation and modifying both itself and the situation, begetting emotion as a result. Absolute, static, eternal truth is thus impossible.

But every such action involves a desire, a volition, aim, fear, disgust, or hope. Thus truth is always tinged with the subject and with emotion. This is not a discoloration. As we saw, any thoroughgoing attempt to wash truth clean of such affective discoloration simply washed the world away, for it becomes bare geometry. We do not feel ourselves passively responding to a situation, we feel active and subjective and seats of innovation. Necessarily so, because each transaction with a situation changes us, and therefore makes us a new centre of force. This is expressed directly in consciousness.

If we sort out of consciousness all the subjective elements we now orientate the same field *in an entirely different way*. The connexion between conscious contexts is no longer outer reality, but the responses. We now group all the conscious contexts into like responses (love, fear, self-preservation). The laws of thought now become the laws of affective association. The affective association of ideas discovered by Freud, which threw a flood of light upon dreams, is not so much the discovery of a secret connexion as a law arising from our mode of analysis of conscious contents. If we sort them according to the responses or somatic components, we discover ideas to be affectively associated. If we sort them according to the situation or environmental components, we find them to be associated by contiguity and other laws taken from the environment. Both methods are equally correct. Both affect and thought, both response and situation, are given in the one conscious glow.

When we are concerned with dream and day-dream, attention is introverted; the body ceases to be closely concerned with the situation. The response or instinctive element in consciousness then becomes dominant. Hence the value of the Freudian or affective analysis of consciousness in such states. The 'deeper', and more somatic, the innervations, the more dominating becomes the response. The more external and sensory the innervations, the more dominating becomes the situation. The environment rather than the intinct gives the main clue to the structure of the perceptual field; the response lays bare the secret structure of the phantastic field.

A development may take place. The body may be introverted, and unconcerned with its immediate environment, and yet it will not be dreaming, it will be thinking. It will be striving to mould its dream according to the ntaure of all past situations, according to its experience of outer reality. It will be attempting to realise the laws of outer reality, and penetrate its nature. This is science. It is a scientist thinking, however crudely, for there has been genuine synthesis between almost unconscious dream full of somatic drives and conscious perception, full of environmental shape. These have been fused in thought. Dream draws vividness and restraint from perception; perception gets a flexibility of recombination, an onward drive to a goal, from dream. The result is thought, as rational scientific thought.

But the same development leads to another. Behaviour is not only intra-somatic and conscious; it is also overt and visible in action. The organism is conscious, and is acted on by the environment, but it also behaves and acts on the environment. In its behaviour it is guided by perception, but perception cannot present it with a goal. Perception guides it but it is impelled by 'instinct'. The somatic element in consciousness now figures as a programme for change—what we 'want to do'. In trying to bring about our wishes, they too are transformed.

But perception is not 'pure' perception—perception *only* of the present situation. By introversion, by stiffening dream with the memories of past perceptions, perception has become 'rational' thought. Perception is widened into a general scheme of reality as experienced over a time. Reason, or congealed cognition, now guides instinct. In helping to change the environment, cognition too is modified and becomes truer and subtler.

But how can I by myself effect more than the slightest change in my environment? I need the co-operation of other men. But this involves perceptions held in common: we must all have similar views of reality. Reason and perception therefore become social, become crystallised in languages, tools, techniques. This has the advantage that I can now draw not only on my brief experience of percepts, but on the combined and sifted experiences of thousands of generations, preserved in language, tool, or technique. This has become dominating. Even from the start it was so; man found himself, by the necessities of the labour process, sharing a common view of reality, and inheriting the seeds, experience, and advice of a preceding generation. Even before language, the labour process, if it involved only common hunting tactics not inherited but taught, would involve a common world-view however crude, and would generate a Truth resident not wholly in oneself but also in one's environment. Thus long before science has a name or a distinct existence, it is generated as a social product. Truth is created and extended before the concept could exist, as part of the labour process.

But the labour process, involving a social view of the necessities of the environment, a general consciousness in man of laws existing outside him in reality, involves also a social unity of response to these necessities and this environment. The interaction produces a change, and as the change becomes more willed, it generates increasing consciousness not only of the structure of reality but also of one's own needs. The goal is a blend of what is possible and what is desirable, just as consciousness is a blend of what is response and what is situation. Or, to be more precise, just as consciousness is the product of a tension between response and situation which do not precisely fit each other, so the goal is a product of a tension between what is possible and what is desirable. They are forced to meet; they are synthesised; and as a result both are changed, are fused into an attainable goal. Of all possibles and all desirables, the laws of reality enforce only one wedding, and the child is a new generation.

But if the desirable is to be held clearly in mind, if all action is somatically motivated, or *willed*, and therefore has an affective as well as a perceptual element—then there must be a community of desire as well as a community of perception. There must be a community of instinct, as well as a community of cognition. The heart, as well as the reason, must be social. The community must share a body in common, as well as an environment in common. Its hopes, as well as its beliefs, must be one. This hope, which is the opposite to science, we may call art. Just as Truth is the aim of science, Beauty is the end of art.

But both deflate abjectly if we attempt to isolate them. If we try to get them 'pure' we get nothing. Both are products of the living organism in the real world, and this means that every element is determined both by organism and environment.

We saw that the pursuit of Truth, and the separation of all environmental elements in the conscious field, produced not Truth but consistency. It produced an unreal dematerialised world, devoid of quality; in fact a mere series of equations. The pursuit of Beauty, and the separation of all affective elements in the conscious field, produces not Beauty but physiology. We get merely the body with its reactions.

But both Truth and Beauty are in fact generated, already blended in action, in the social labour process visualised throughout human history. In this they are indivisible. Both continually play into each other's hands. Science makes the percepts, the possibilities, the world with which the body's desire concerns itself, continually richer and more subtle. Art makes the body's incursions into reality always more audacious, more curious, and more indefatigable.

Of course to the bourgeois with his ideal closed worlds, Truth and Beauty, art and science, appear not as creative opposites but as eternal antagonists. Even Keats, who saw their kinship, could yet complain that science had robbed the rainbow of its beauty. This is because science and art, as long as they seem something distinct, situated in the environment entirely on the one hand (science) and in the heart entirely on the other (art), must seem exclusive and inimical. They seem to raise up two different worlds, of which we can choose one only. One is bare of quality, and the other is destitute of reality, so that we cannot rest easily on either horn of the dilemma. Only when we see that the separation is artifical and that response and situation are involved throughout consciousness and are part and parcel of the social process which generates both truth and beauty—only then can we see that there is no such deadly rivalry as we supposed, but that on the contrary these opposites each create the other. The 'secret' connexion between the two is the world of concrete society.

In all social products, therefore, affect and percept, response and situation, inevitably mingle. They do not merely mingle, they activate each other. In language every word has an affective as well as a cognitive value. The weight of each value varies in each case. Some words, such as interjections, are almost entirely affective. Others, such as scientific names, are almost entirely cognitive. But an entirely affective language— that is, sounds having only affective associations—ceases to be language. It becomes music. An entirely cognitive language— that is, sounds having only cognitive associations—also ceases to be a language; it becomes mathematics. In doing so, both seem to exchange rôles. Music no longer refers to outer reality; but it does not disappear into the body; it becomes for the body outer reality. For the body, listening to the music, the sounds are now environment; nothing is referred to. Mathematics, though it has no affective reference, does not disappear into the environment. On the contrary it becomes pure thought; it becomes the body operating on the environment. Cognition and affection can never be separated. The attempt to do so simply begets a new thing, in which they are united again.

Not only language but all social products have an affective rôle. Each society evolves its own gestures, deportment, and manners. These include a reference to reality, a pointing to something, the necessary opening of doors to get through them, or lifting of food to feed oneself, or moving of legs to get from one place to another. But these actions also include an affective element: all can be done 'beautifully' or artistically. One can point with an air, open a door politely, feed oneself quietly and 'off silver', walk slowly and with dignity. All this is beauty; all this is desirable; all this is a social product. Different societies have quite different notions of what is desirable in these things.

All objects, from a house to a hat, share these cognitive and affective elements. A hat has a real cognitive environmental function, so has a house. The hat must keep rain and sun off our heads; the house must keep out wind and weather, resist perhaps the robber and marauder. But both are modified by the affective element. The hat must add honour, dignity and grace to the head. The house must express respectability or power; and must contain rooms of a certain shape and size, because of the manners and social customs of the age.

Action designed only to express an affective purpose becomes, like music, an environment; dancing is a *spectacle*. Action designed only to express a cognitive purpose, and to achieve a goal which is not in itself really desired, becomes action in itself desirable, as in the mock-fights and trivial goals of sport, in which all energies are bent on securing something not really to be desired. Between sport and dancing stretch all the forms of action designed to secure an affective but real goal, that is, all forms of work, from sowing and reaping to factory production.

All forms of representation have the same duality. The faithful congruence of representation to reality, robbed of all affective elements, becomes not really a representation at all, but a symbol—the diagram. The attempt to make representation purely affective, without reference to environment, produces what is in itself an environment—the town and the building. Between lies the richness of pictorial illustration—the painting, the sculpture, the film, and the play.

In primitive civilisation this intimate generation of truth and beauty in the course of the labour process and their mutual effect on each other are so clear that it needs no elaboration. The harvest is work, but it is also dance; it deals with reality, but it is also pleasure. All social forms, gestures, and manners have to primitives a purpose, and are both affective and cognitive. Law is not merely the elucidation of a truth in dispute, but the satisfaction of the gods, of the innate sense of rightness in man's desires. Myths express man's primitive instincts and his view of reality. The simplest garment or household utensil has a settled beauty. Work is performed in time to singing, and has its own fixed ceremony. All tasks have their lucky days. Truth and beauty, science and art are primitive, but at least they are vitally intermingled, each giving life to the other.

It is the special achievement of later bourgeois civilisation to have robbed science of desirability and art of reality. The true is no longer beautiful, because to be true in bourgeois civilisation is to be non-human. The beautiful is no longer real, because to be beautiful in bourgeois civilisation is to be imaginary.

This itself is simply a product of the fundamental bourgeois position. Our own proposition about beauty is this: whenever the affective elements in socially known things show social ordering, there we have beauty, there alone we have beauty. The business of such ordering is art, and this applies to all socially known things, to houses, gestures, narratives, descriptions, lessons, songs and labour.

But to the bourgeois this proposition seems monstrous, for he has been reared on the anarchy of the social process. He refuses to recognise it. He recognises only social process—commodity-manufacture, and one social tie—the market. The bourgeois produces for and buys from the market, governed as an individual by social relations masquerading as laws of supply and demand.

Thus any attempt at social consciousness which necessarily involves the manipulation of desires, i.e. of 'the laws' of supply and demand, seems to him outrageous. But this is just what art is—the manipulation or social ordering of desires, and therefore of the laws of supply and demand. Art gives values which are not those of the market but are use-values. Art makes 'cheap' things precious and a few splashes of paint a social treasure. Hence the market is the fierce enemy of the artist. The blind working of the market murders beauty. All social products, hats, cars, houses, household utensils and clothes, be-

come in the main unbeautiful and 'commercialised', precisely
because the maker in producing them does not consider social
process, does not scheme how to order socially their affective
values in accordance with their use, but merely how to satisfy
a demand for them with the maximum profit to himself. This
extends finally to those products which have no other purpose
than affective ordering—paintings, films, novels, poetry, music. Because here too their affective ordering is socially unconscious, because it is not realised that beauty is a social product, there is a degradation even of these 'purest' forms of art
products. We have commercialised art, which is simply affective massage. It awakens and satisfies the instincts without expressing and synthesising a tension between instinct and environment. Hence wish-fulfilment novels and films; hence jazz.
The bourgeois floods the world with art products of a baseness
hitherto unimaginable. Then, reacting against such an evident
degradation of the artist's task, art withdraws from the market
and becomes non-social, that is *personal*. It becomes 'highbrow'
art, culminating in personal fantasy. The art work ends as a
fetish because it was a commodity. Both are equally signs of
the decay of bourgeois civilisation due to the contradictions in
its foundation.

The ravages of bourgeois unconsciousness destroy not only
the social product but the producer. Labour now becomes, not
labour to achieve a goal and to attain the desirable, but labour
for the market and for cash. Labour becomes blind and unconscious. What is made, or why it is made, is no longer understood, for the labour is merely for cash, which now alone
supports life. Thus all affective elements are withdrawn from
labour, and must therefore reappear elsewhere. They now reappear attached to the mythical commodity which represents
the unconscious market—cash. Cash is the music of labour in
bourgeois society. Cash achieves objective beauty. Labour in
itself becomes increasingly distasteful and irksome, and cash
increasingly beautiful and desirable. Money becomes the god
of society. Thus the complete disintegration of a culture on
the affective side is achieved, and has resulted from the same
causes as its disintegration on the cognitive side.

Beauty, then, arises from the social ordering of the affective elements in socially known things. It arises from the labour process, because there must not only be agreement about the nature of outer reality, but also agreement about the nature of desire. This agreement is not static. In the social process, outer reality becomes increasingly explored, and this makes the social process more far-reaching and deeply entrenched in the environment, while each fresh sortie into reality alters the nature of desire, so that here, too, fresh integrations are necessary. This pressure, both in science and art, appears as an individual experience. A scientist inherits the hypotheses, and an artist inherits the traditions, of the past. In the scientist's case an experiment, and in the artist's case a vital experience indicates a discrepancy, a tension, whose synthesis results in a new hypothesis or a new art work. Of course the scientist feels the tension as an error, as something in the environment; the artist as an urge, as something in his heart.

★

Science and art, as we use them in current language, are more partial and restricted than in my use. Science, as generally used, involves not all the cognitive elements in the labour process but only the *new* elements. The scientist is on the borderline where new hypotheses are generated to modify technique. In factory, in building, in housework, and all daily occupation, the cognitive elements are familiar and traditional. They are technique rather than science. The world-view is not expanding here; reality is as our fathers knew it; but the scientist is situated on the very expanding edge of the world-view. Here new regions are continually coming into sight; discrepancies in experience continually arise to make him modify yesterday's formulations. The same applies to the artist. In daily life, in manners, desires, morals, hopes and patriotisms we tread the daily round; we feel as our fathers do; but the artist is continually besieged by new feelings as yet unformulated, he continually attempts to grasp beauties and emotions not yet known; a tension between tradition and experience is constantly felt in his heart. Just as the scientist is the explorer of new realms of outer reality, the artist continually discovers new kingdoms of the heart.

Both therefore are explorers, and necessarily therefore share a certain loneliness. But if they are individualists, it is not because they are non-social, but precisely because they are performing a social task. They are non-social only in this sense, that they are engaged in dragging into the social world realms at present non-social and must therefore have a foot in both worlds. They have a specially exciting task, but a task also with disadvantages comparable to its advantages. The scientist pays for his new realms by travelling without affective companionship, with a certain deadness and silence in his heart. The artist explores new seas of feeling; there is no firm ground of cognitive reality beneath his feet; he becomes dizzy and tormented. Those not on the fringes of the social process get their life less new but more solid, less varied but more stable. Their values are more earthy, more sensuous, more mature. They are rooted, certain, and full. It is time for the antagonism between scientist and artist to cease; both should recognise a kinship, as between Arctic and tropical explorers, or between bedouins of the lonely deserts and sailors on the featureless sea.

But they must not suppose that a line can ever be drawn between science and other social cognition, and art and other social affection. The social process is far too closely woven for that. The ingression of new values takes place at all parts; only we call certain operations scientific or artistic because there we see the ingression most clearly. In education cognitive and emotional tradition is chiefly at work, but on the one hand even here there is an ingression of the new, and, on the other hand, the artist and the scientist are being educated as well as learning new things all their lives.

If they remember this, they will not make the mistake of supposing they are opposite poles, between which the whole social process is generated. This is to suppose profit produces capital. In fact profit is produced by capital, and yet continually augments it. Science and art represent the profit on social capital. They are pushed out into the deserts of the unknown by the very workings of society. They lead, but they were instructed; they find new worlds of life, but they were supported by the old. Always we find only terms drawn from the labour process to be adequate to describe their function, and only this can explain the nature of Beauty and Truth, how man can never rest on the truth his eyes tell him or the beauty his heart declares, but must go about finding new truth, and cannot rest until he has created with his hands a new beauty.

The artist takes bits of reality, socially known, to which affective associations adhere, and creates a mock world, which calls into being a new affective attitude, a new emotional experience. New beauty is thus born as the results of his social labour.

But if art works were artificial, and beauty is a social product, how do we find beauty in the natural thing, in seas, skies, a mountain, and daffodils?

To separate in this way natural things from artificial is to make as dangerous a distinction as that between environmental and affective elements in the conscious field, or between mental and material qualities. Society itself is a part of nature, and hence all artificial products are natural. But nature itself, as seen, is a product of society. The primitive does not see seas, but the river Oceanus; he does not see mammals, but edible beasts. He does not see, in the night sky, blazing worlds in the limitless void, but a roof inlaid with patinas of bright gold. Hence all natural things are artificial. Does that mean that we can make no distinction between nature and art? On the contrary, we can clearly distinguish two opposites, although we must recognise their interpenetration. In all phenomena, from hats to stars, seasons to economic crises, tides to social revolutions, we can distinguish varying portions of change, varying portions of the ingression of the unlike. The most rapid evolution is that of human society, of its customs, towns and hand-made products. The next that of animals and plants. The next that of the solar system. The next that of our galaxy. The whole universe in fact changes but it changes at different rates. The region of most change, human society, as it were, separates itself out from a background of least change, which we call 'nature'—stars, mountains and daffodils. The line can nowhere be precisely drawn; and in all cases it is man, a social product, confronting nature, and finding beauty in it. Nature finds no beauty in nature; animals do not look at flowers or stars. Man does, and therefore it is the social process which has generated in him the ability to see beauty in flowers and stars. This ability changes in character. The sea is beautiful to a European, to an ancient Athenian, to a Polynesian islander, but it is not the same beauty; it is always a beauty rooted in their cultures. The frozen sea is to the Eskimo a different beauty from the warm sea of the Gulf; and the blazing sun of the Equator a different beauty from the faint six-months-dead sun of the Arctic.

Those elements in nature which are most universal and have changed least in the history of man, may be expected to produce, in interaction with him, the most constant quality. Hence we feel rightly that there is something simple, primitive, and instinctive in the beauty we see in certain primitive, simple things. This must never be pushed too far. The richest and most complex appreciation of natural beauty belongs to the civilised man, not to the primitive. We may oppose the art-work just made to the enduring mountain as an artificial to a natural beauty, but the difference is one of degree. In both cases beauty emerges as a quality due to a man, in the course of social process, gazing at a piece of his environment. The ancient town, with weathered walls, full of history and character, is a part of nature, and is yet a completely artificial product; the sun lights it and the wind weathers it. There is no dichotomy between nature and art, only the difference between pioneers and settled inhabitants.

Art, then, conditions the instincts to the environment, and in doing so changes the intincts. Beauty is the knowledge of oneself as a part of other selves in a real world, and reflects the growth in richness and complexity of their relations. Science conditions the environment to the instincts and in doing so changes the environment. Truth is the knowledge of the environment as a container for, and yet known by and partly composed of, one's own self and other selves.

Both are products of the labour process—that is to say, both are realised in action. Truth and Beauty are not the goals of society, for directly they become goals in themselves, they cease to exist. They are generated as aspects of the rich and complex flow of reality. The scientist or the artist is only a special kind of man of action: he produces truth or beauty, not as an end but as the colour of an act. Consciousness, society, the whole world of social experience, the universe of reality, is generated by action, and by action is meant the tension between organism and environment, as a result of which both are changed and a new movement begins. This dynamic subject-object relation generates all social products—cities, ships, nations, religions, the cosmos, human values.

Bourgeois culture is incapable of producing an aesthetics for the same reason that most of its social products are unbeautiful. It is disintegrating, because it refuses to recognise the social process which is the generator of consciousness, emotion, thought, and of all products into which emotion and thought enter. Because ideology is rooted in the labour process, the decay of an economy must reappear as a similar disintegration in the art or science which is rooted in it. Bourgeois economic contradictions are bourgeois ideological contradictions. The scientist and artist are forced on by the tension between past and present, tradition and experience. But tradition is the accumulated product of the past labour process as preserved; and experience is an experience in contemporary society.

Such a disintegration can only be revitalised by a transformation of the relations which, at the very roots, are destroying the creative forces of society. Change is dialectic; one quality gives birth to another by the revelation of the contradictions it contains, whose very tension begets the synthesis. The contradiction at the heart of bourgeois culture is becoming naked, and more and more clearly there is revaled the inextinguishable antagonism between the two classes of bourgeois economy, the bourgeoisie and the proletariat. The ruling class, the bourgeoisie, which exploits the labour power of the proletariat for profit, in doing so generates an illusion which sets the pattern for all the structure and ideology of bourgeois civilisation. Man is held to be free in proportion to his ignorance of the social process, as a part of which he functions. Instead of bourgeois activity being governed by knowledge of the social process, it is governed by the market, by the 'laws of supply and demand', by the free circulation of cash, in short, by mere 'accident', for accident is man's name for his ignorance of determinism. Man is held to be free by virtue of unrestricted rights over property: but this merely conceals the domination of a few, who own the means of production and can traffick in labour-power, over the many who have nothing but labour-power to sell. The few believe that this dominating power they exercise makes them free, that in the act of domination their actions are not determined; but the event—the internal collapse of their economy in war and crisis and of their ideology in anarchy—reveals that not even they the lords are free, but their desires have disrupted their culture.

And who can transform it? Only those who are conscious of the cause of its collapse, who realise that to be without conscious social organisation is not to be free, and that power over men by men is not freedom, even though concealed, but all the more if concealed, is mere ignorance of the necessities of society. It is precisely the proletarians who know all this by the pressure of the economy whose cruel weight they support. In their struggles against exploitation they learn that only conscious organisation, Trade Unions and Factory Acts, can give them freedom from oppression. When they see their masters, the bourgeoisie, powerless to prevent war, unemployment, and the decay of the economy they have built up, the proletariat learns that this power of men over men, exercised by a simple act of the will and congealed in a property right, is not freedom for either class. It is only a delusive short cut in which humanity was for a time lost. Freedom appears, socially, when men take no short cuts of 'will' but learn the necessities of their own nature and of external reality and thus share a goal in common. Then the common goal and the nature of reality uniquely determine the only possible action without compulsion, as when two men combine, without 'orders', to lift a stone that lies in their path. In such an understanding, a new science, a new art, and a new society are already explicit, and to build it involves a proletariat which has already overthrown the bourgeoisie, and in revolution and reconstruction has transformed civilisation. In a society which is based on co-operation, not on compulsion, and which is conscious, not ignorant, of necessity, desires as well as cognitions can be socially manipulated as part of the social process. Beauty will then return again, to enter consciously into every part of the social process. It is not a dream that labour will no longer be ugly, and the products of labour once again beautiful.

VI

FREUD

A STUDY IN BOURGEOIS PSYCHOLOGY

Freud is certain to be remembered and honoured as one of the pioneers of scientific psychology. But it is probable that like Kepler he will be regarded as a scientist who discovered important empirical facts but was unable to synthesise these discoveries except in a primitive semi-magical framework. Kepler with his divine Sun God, lived in the religious age of physics. Freud for all his honesty lives in the mythical era of psychology:

'It may now be expected that the other of the "two heavenly forces", eternal Eros, will put forth his strength so as to maintain himself alongside of his equally immortal adversary.'

This is Freud's prognosis of the future of our civilisation. It is no bad symbolisation of the psychological trend of the present, but it will be seen that it is mythological symbolisation. Examination of the remainder of his psychology shows that it is generally religious in its presentation. It is a psychology of forces and personifications. Freud is no exceptional psychologist here. Psychology still awaits its Newton. At least Freud has refused to accept the outworn shams of Christianity or of idealistic metaphysics. In *The Future of an Illusion* he maintains the fruitful materialistic traditions of bourgeois science, which bourgeois science itself to-day as it loses its grip is deserting. The metaphysical psychology with its memory, reason, conation, perception, thought and feeling which Freud helped to destroy is more mythological than Freudism. This psychology, of which Freudism is an enemy, belongs to an even earlier age of science. It reduces mentation to verbiage, and then the organisation of this verbiage is called thought. It is, however, real mentation with which Freud deals always, only he symbolises the inner structure of this neurological behaviour in terms of real entities as glamorous and personal as the Olympian gods of old. The Censor, the Ego, the Super-ego, the Id, the Oedipus complex, and the Inhibition are mind deities, like the weather deities who inhabited Greek Olympus. Freud's picture of a struggle between eternal Eros and eternal Thanatos, between the life and death instincts, between the reality principle and the pleasure principle, is only the eternal dualism of reflective barbarians, carried over by Christianity from Zoroastrianism, and now introjected by Freud into the human mind. It represents a real struggle but in terms of a Western bourgeois myth.

As confirmation of his fable about Zeus, the Greek could point to the thunder and lightning. As confirmation of the endless war between Ormuzd and Ahriman, the Parsee could remind the sceptic of the endless warfare that tears life in twain. Freudians point to the psychic phenomena of dreams, hysteric and neurotic symptoms, obsessions and slips of the pen and tongue as confirmation of their intricate mythology. The early scientists could claim the fall of every stone as the evidence of the mysterious force of gravity and all phenomena of heat and cold as testimony to the passage of a mysterious 'caloric'. In Freudism 'libido' plays the part of the mythical 'caloric' of eighteenth-century heat mechanics, or of the 'gravity' of Newtonian physics.

It may be urged with some reason that psychology is an appropriate sphere for fables and emotive symbolisation, but this claim withdraws it from the circle of science to that of art. It is better to demand that mythical psychology should exist only in the novel and that psychology should be a science. If so, the obligation falls upon psychoanalysts either to leave any empirical facts they have discovered in thin air for some abler mind to fit into a causal scheme, as Newton correlated Kepler's separate and arbitrary laws of planetary motion, or else they must clearly exhibit the causality of their discoveries without recourse to mythological entities. This Freud and his followers have failed to do. Thus instead of being causal and materialistic, their psychology is religious and idealistic. Yet Freud is a materialist and is clearly aware of the illusory content of religion. But he is also a bourgeois. This class outlook

110

affects his psychology through certain implicit assumptions from which he starts, assumptions that appear in all bourgeois culture as a disturbing yet invisible force, just as Uranus until discovered was for us only a mysterious perturbation in the orbits of the known planets. These implicit assumptions are firstly that the consciousness of men is *sui generis*, unfolding like a flower from the seed instead of being a primarily social creation, and secondly that there is a source of free action in the individual, the 'free will', the 'wish', or the 'instincts', which is only free in proportion to the extent to which it is unrestrained by social influences. These two assumptions are of vital significance for psychology, and just because they are implicit, they act like buried magnets, distorting all Freud's psychology and making it an unreal kind of a science tainted with wish-fulfilment.

Freud has been exceptionally unfortunate in that his school of psychology has been rent repeatedly by schisms. Jung and Adler are the most notable schismatics, but almost every psychoanalyst is a heretic in embryo. Now this must necessarily have been a matter for sorrow to Freud although he has borne it as calmly as he has borne the numerous attacks from all with vested interests in contemporary morality whom his discoveries seemed to menace. The Freudian schisms are not paralleled in other sciences. The disciples of a discoverer of new empirical principles, such as the disciples of Darwin, Newton and Einstein, do not as a rule turn and rend him. They work within the general limits of his formulations, merely enriching and modifying them, without feeling called upon to attack the very foundations on which the structure is based.

Freud is himself indirectly to blame. Schism is the hallmark of religion, and a man who treats scientific facts as does Freud, in a religious way, must necessarily expect the trials and tribulations, as well as the intense personal relationship, of a religious leader. In approaching science in a religious spirit, I do not mean in a 'reverent' spirit. The scientist necessarily approaches reality, with all its richness and complexity, with a feeling of reverence and insignificance which is the more intense the more materialistic he is, and, the less he feels that this reality is a mere offshoot or emanation of a Divine friend of his. I mean by a 'religious' approach, the belief that scientific phenomena are adequately explained by any symbolisation which includes and accounts for the phenomena. Thus 'caloric' accounts for temperature phenomena. None the less, no such mysterious stuff exists. In the same way Freud supposes that any fable which includes a connected statement of genuine psychical phenomena is a scientific hypothesis, whether or no it exhibits in a causal manner the inner relations of the phenomena. Of course such explanations break down because they do not fit into the causal scheme of science as a whole.

Now this is precisely the way religion sets about explaining that the world, thunder and lightning are caused by deities. The world exists because it was created by a God. Disaster is the will of an omnipotent deity, or the triumph of an evil deity over an omnipotent deity. We die because we sinned long ago. Moreover, religion naïvely supposes that the fact that there are thunder and lightning, that the world exists, that disaster occurs in it, and that we die, is a proof that deities exist, that God created the world, and that we sinned long ago. This is what theologians mean by the Cosmological and Teleological proofs of God's existence. But this kind of 'proof' was long ago banished from science, and it is strange to see a man of Freud s intellectual gifts impressed by it. It is a sign of the crisis reached in bourgeois culture when psychology cannot escape from this kind of thing.

It follows from presuming that an adequate explanation of certain facts will be furnished by any fable connecting these facts, that for any group of facts an indefinite number of myths can be advanced as an explanation. Thus an indefinite number of religions exist which explain with different myths the same facts of man's unhappiness, his cruelty, his aspirations, his sufferings, his inequality and his death. Religion by its method of approach spawns schisms. The only reason that Churches can exist without disintegration is because of their material foundations in the social relations of their time.

Science can recognise only explanations which with as little symbolisation as possible exhibit the mutual determination of the phenomena concerned, and their relation with the rest of reality. Thus one scientific hypothesis is intolerant. It drives out another.

Scientific explanations, because of their austere structure, are not equally good, as different religions are equally good. One or other must go to the wall. And the test is simple. If, of two hypotheses one exhibits more comprehensively and less symbolically the structure of the determinism of the phenomena it explains and their relation to the already established structure of reality, that hypothesis will be more powerful as an instrument for predicting the recurrence of such phenomena in real life. Hence arises the crucial test, which decides between one hypothesis and another. For example, the crucial tests of the Einstein theory, as compared with the Newtonian, were the bending of light, the perturbation of planetary orbits, the increase of mass of alpha particles, and the shifts of the spectra of receding stars. But it is never possible to demonstrate by a crucial test the rival truths of the Protestant and Catholic theories, simply because they deal with entities assumed to be outside the structure of determined reality. The crucial test of the two theories is presumed to occur at the Last Judgment, that is, never in this life. The theories are expressly so formulated that it is not, for example, possible to test the Eucharist by chemical analysis. The Catholic theory states that in being turned into Christ's body the bread retains all the chemical and physical properties of ordinary bread. In the same way the Protestant theory makes it pointless to test for the salvation of a soul, precisely because the soul is asserted to be completely non-material and therefore inaccessible to determinism.

No hypothesis, religious or scientific, can have any meaning unless it can give rise to a crucial test, which will enable it to be socially compared with other hypotheses. Thought must interact with external reality to be of value or significance. Capitalist and socialist economists dispute as meaninglessly as theologians as long as they base their defences of the rival systems on justice, liberty, man's natural equality, or any other 'rights'. No one has yet devised an instrument to measure or determine justice, equality, or liberty. The Marxian can be concerned only with the structure of concrete society and he will on this basis advance socialism as a superior form of organisation at a certain period of history because it permits a more efficient use of the means of material production. This makes possible the crucial test of practice—is communism more productive than capitalism? Thus economics remains scientific because it remains in the sphere of reality and does not deal with entities that cannot be determined quantitively. For this reason, historical materialism has not given rise to as many brands of socialism as there are theorists. It can only be opposed by an hypothesis more penetrative of reality. The 'cast-iron inflexible dogmatism' of the communist corresponds to the scientists' 'rigid' and universal adherence to a methodological principle, such as the conservation of energy, until a fresh hypothesis, capable of a crucial test, has shown the need for its expansion or modification.

When we see a scientific 'school' rent by schism, or engaged in vigorous persecution, we may assume that a certain amount of the religious spirit has entered its science. Science has never been wholly free of it, but it has rent psychoanalysis into fragments.

Adler, Freud and Jung deal with the same mental phenomena. They are as follows: psychic phenomena consist of innervations of some of which we, as subjects, have a privileged (subjective) view. Some of these innervations, the smallest and most recent group phylogenetically, form a group often called the consciousness, the ego, or the subject. This group appears to be more self-determined than the other groups but all affect each other and form a kind of hierarchic process. Those which do not form part of the consciousness are called unconscious. At the moment of birth the neurones capable of innervation exhibit certain specific patterns of innervation, involving certain specific somatic behaviour, as a result of internal and external stimuli. These patterns are known as 'the instincts'. But the experience resulting from the awakening of these patterns modifies, by means of a phenomenon which may be called *memory* but is not peculiar to consciousness, the patterns themselves. At any moment of time, therefore, the system as a whole has a slightly different resonance or totality of patterns as a result of previous behaviour due to the then totality of patterns. The result will be to increase with lapse of time the range and complexity of the behaviour response to reality, and the hierarchy of groups of possible innervation combinations. We say, therefore, in ordinary language, that in the course of life a man learns by experience, or, a little more technically, that his instincts are modified or conditioned by situations. Such expressions contain a certain amount of mythology, perhaps at present unavoidable. In particular the more autonomous group called the 'consciousness', in whose language all explanations of other less autonomous groups must be phrased, will necessarily tend to write everything from its angle, and give a peculiar twist to the description. Science itself is a product of consciousness.

Experiment leads us to believe that the innervations concerned in consciousness are phylogenetically the most recent in evolution, and that the older the neurone groups, the less modifiable they are in their behaviour, i.e. the less they are able to 'learn' by 'experience'. Hence they may be described as more infantile, primitive, bestial, archaic or automatic, according to the mythological language one is adopting at the time.

In every innervation, however simple, the whole system of neurones is really concerned. If we play a chord on the piano, the strings we do not strike are as much concerned as those we do, because the chord is what it is being part of the well-tempered scale, and to the chord contribute also the wood, the air of the room, and our ears. Though consciousness deals with psychic phenomena in its own terms, yet in all conscious phenomena the innervations of the rest of the system are concerned and their innate responses, modified or unmodified, give all behaviour, including conscious phenomena, the 'ground' of their specific pattern. Hence we may say that the Unconscious modifies all behaviour, including consciousness; that is, that unconscious innervation and experience are a part of consciousness.

The study of this modification of the consciousness by the unconscious is naturally of great interest to our consciousness. To understand it we must know accurately the innate responses of all parts of the nervous system, and the laws of their harmony. Sometimes as a result of the temporary instability of the conscious innervation pattern (e.g. in situations of emergency or difficulty or in sleep), the tune of behaviour is called chiefly by the phylogenetically older neurones, and these, as we saw, are less teachable than the newer groups. We then have behaviour in which there is a return to the earlier and less experienced state, the so-called infantile regression. In it some of life's experience is thrown away. We may also call this behaviour instinctive.

Now these disturbances have been studied by Freud, and he has made some interesting empirical discoveries about them. He has shown how much more common they are than we suspect and has elaborated a technique for detecting them. All his discoveries have been embodied in an elaborate and ingenious myth, or series of myths. This is due partly to the fact that he has not taken his own doctrine seriously. He has not realised that, since it is consciousness which is formulating psychoanalysis, all unconscious phenomena are likely to appear as seen by consciousness, not as causal phenomena with the same physiological basis as consciousness and ultimately homogeneous with it, but as wicked demons which burst into the neat ordered world of consciousness. Just as causal phenomena, such as thunder and lightning, which burst into the accustomed world of the primitive, were attributed to the arbitrary acts of deities, so unconscious 'influences', causing perturbations in the conscious world, are by Freud called by such rude names as distortion, inhibition, regression, obsession, the id, the censor, the pleasure-principle, Eros, libido, the death instinct, the reality principle, a complex, a compulsion. Freud does not perceive the implications of the physiological content of his theory. All innervation patterns consist of an innate response (instinct) modified by experience (inhibition), and thus all innervation patterns contain varying proportions of conscious and unconscious elements, connected in various ways, but all forming the one circuit, overtly visible in behaviour. Freud has accepted for this part of his theory the prejudiced view of consciousness. He treats all unconscious components of behaviour as perturbations, distortions, or interferences, just as the treble part in music might regard the bass as distortion by some primitive unconsciousness. Just as mythological and consistent a psychology as Freud's might be written from the point of view of the 'unconscious' in which, instead of the 'instincts', the 'experiences' would now play the part of energetic imprisoned demons distorting or inhibiting the stability and simple life of the innate responses. And, in fact, when Freud comes to treat civilisation and man as a whole, he does swing over to this point of view. It is now experience or consciousness (culture) which is thwarting or distorting instinct(the unconscious). Naturally, therefore, Freud's doctrine contains a dualism which *cannot* be resolved.

But of course both consciousness and unconsciousness, as sharply distinct entities, are abstractions. In all the innervations which are part of behaviour, a varying proportion make up the group which at any time we call the consciousness or the ego. And they are not separate; consciousness is made vivid and given its content by the unconscious innervations, whose contribution we know consciously only as affect. A thought without affect is unconscious; it is simply one of the cortical neurones mnemonically modified, but not at that moment affectively glowing, and therefore not part of the live circuit of consciousness. It is only an unconscious memory. Equally an unconscious innervation or affect without memory is not an affect at all, but simply an instinctive reflex, a tendency unmodified by experience. Consciousness and unconsciousness are not exclusive opposites, but in any hierarchy of innervations forming the behaviour of the moment we have a certain amount with high mnemonic modifiability and others with high innate predisposition, and the proportion of these may be varying. But they are in mutual relation, like the positive and negative poles of a battery activating a circuit, and it is only by abstraction that we separate out the complex called consciousness, as we might separate out the threads forming the pattern on a tapestry. The same threads pass through to the other side and form the reverse pattern there, the unconscious, and each pattern determines the other.

Freud gave to these discoveries of his, which were founded on the previous work of Charcot, Janet, Morton Prince, and Bleuler, formulations drawn from his consciousness, without the rigorous causality demanded in physical or chemical hypotheses. As a result Freud's terminology consists of little but the abusive names coined by the consciousness for its distortion by the unconscious, or of the pitiful complaints by the unconscious of its modification by the experience embodied in conscious innervations. On the whole our sympathies will be with the consciousness, for the consciousness represents recent experience, and recent experience is the richest; but reality reminds us that we cannot simply live in the new experience of the present. If we do, we shall be unable to advance beyond it; we shall be trapped in the limitations of the present. We must accept the present more thoroughly than that, we must accept the past *included* in the present. That does not mean that we must accept the past as the past, for, in being included in the present, it is changed. That indeed is what each present *is* in relation to the precedent past, it is that precedent past modified by the impression of an additional experience; and that present itself becomes the past when it is synthesised in a new present. This may sound metaphysical, and yet in the human body we see it given a 'crude' and material physiological basis. Everything below the optic thalamus represents the inherited experience of the ancestral past. The cerebrum is the organ for storing each present as it becomes the past, and sensory perception is the process by which the past, acquiring new experience, becomes the present. This ingression gives rise to the will, to the future.

Thus though we accept consciousness as latest and richest, we must not reject the Unconscious, as the worship of the consciousness may too easily lead us to do. Those who accept consciousness only are entrapped in immediate experience, and can never progress to a richer consciousness; just as those who ignore the past in the present in the form of history are unable to grasp the richer future, which they write only in terms of the barren present. This is the lesson of historical materialism, that the future is not contained in the present, but in the present *plus* the past.

Still less can we accept *only* the past. That is worse than the other, it is a return to outworn things, it is infantile regression. It is the path that perpetually appeals to man when, as to-day, his consciousness seems to fail him at the tasks with which he is faced, but it is the way of defeat. The Unconscious has its wisdom, certainly, for it contains the condensed experience of ages of evolution, stamped in by natural selection. Our life is built on the foundations of the somatic wisdom of unconscious innervations. None the less, the spearpoints of life's insertion into the reality is the present, it is new experience and this new experience is unseizable by unconsciousness. It *is* consciousness.

Freudism does not accept the story of one party to the exclusion of the other's. It accepts *both* uncritically, and so involves itself in an irreconcilable dualism. After showing how the wicked complex-devils of the Unconscious distort and obsess the consciousness, Freud goes over to the other side and paints the Unconscious as it would like to paint itself. He shows us the Instincts tortured by the inhibitions of culture, martyrs to the present and to consciousness. Yet the scientist ought in these matters to be impartial, otherwise he will never synthesise these two opposites, past and present, new and old. Freud raises only the barren trichotomy of metaphysics: (i) infantile regression (or worship of the past); (ii) conservatism (or blind acceptance of the present); (iii) dualism (the conception of present and past as eternal antagonists). Only the man who sees how the past is included in the present, can proceed to the future, child of a 'Marriage of Heaven and Hell'. They are included in the primary process of becoming, exhibited in the organism as active behaviour, in which unconscious and conscious innervations are the bass and treble of the innervation harmony in whose theme we distinguish instinct, thought, feeling and conation.

Directly Freud clothed the elements of this harmony in the fabulous and emotional symbols of psycho-analysis, Freud invited schism. Jung and Adler have invented symbols which are at least as good explanations of the same phenomena, and yet they are totally opposed to each other and to Freud's in their significance. In Adler's fable the sexual 'instinct' makes hardly any appearance, yet his 'instinct of self-preservation' explains everything as satisfactorily as Freud's 'libido'. Since separate entities—such as an instinct of self-preservation or a Censor—are fabulous descriptions of certain innate physiological responses, it is not possible to find a crucial experiment to judge between Adler and Freud. They are disputing about myths, though the myths refer to real phenomena. In the same way Grecians might have disputed about inconsistencies in rival accounts of the birth of Athene from Zeus's head. What was actually being discussed by them was the modification of behaviour by experience or—more picturesquely—the Birth of Wisdom. Since both Athene and Zeus were mere symbolic fictions, such disputes about them were wasted time. Adler, Jung and Freud have wasted much of their time in precisely the same way.

Of them all, Jung is perhaps the most scientific theoretically, even if he has made the fewer empirical discoveries, because he does realise the dualism inherent in Freud's approach. But he never escapes from that daulism. On the contrary, he makes it the foundation of his theories.

★

So far we have been concerned with psychology as shown by the organism's behaviour, and have neglected the environment except as simple stimulus. Restricting our study to the organism, we regard all psychic phenomena as simply certain patterns of innervations. Some of these innervations in ourselves are consciousness. As a whole they are part of a body's behaviour and we see part of this behaviour overtly as action, in ourselves or others. In the act of behaviour, the basic innervation patterns become modified. Thus the tune of a man's life begins with a simple hereditary phrase, on which experience plays endless variations, continually increasing in richness and subtlety. This is part of the fact that a man's life is lived in Reality, whose nature it is that each new present includes the previous past, so growing increasingly in complexity.

But all behaviour is interaction between body and stimuli from outside, or between one part of the body and another. The organism never behaves alone; there is always an 'other', the environment, which is a party to its behaviour. Moreover the environment too has its history, for it is subject to time. Thus it is never the same environment, and each transaction the organism has with it is subtly different because since the previous transaction it has become more full of history. Hence the behaviour of the organism is a counter-point, in which the organism furnishes one part and the environment the other part. We may for purposes of analysis consider the melody of each separately, but actually behaviour is not a melody but a harmony. Thus the harmony of the psyche is itself a reflection of the harmony of the body's being in reality. The treble of the consciousness is a reflection of the melody of the environment; the bass of the unconsciousness is a reflection of the melody of the organism. The fundamental principle of physics is that each action has an equal and opposite reaction. Thus, after each act of behaviour, in which organism and environment interact, environment has affected organism and organism environment, and the resulting positions of each are different. Indeed that is why there is history, for the environment itself is simply a collection of mutually-interacting bodies. In between the act of an organism one moment and its act the next, the environment has changed, simply because the elements of which the environment is composed have interacted and changed each other.

Now of all known organisms, the human organism is the most elaborate in its melody and the most sensitive in its reaction to intercourse with reality. It is the organism which learns most from behaviour, from experience. Nothing changes so quickly as the human organism. In the same way the social environment, because the organisms of which it consists are chiefly human beings, also changes most quickly in between the acts of a human being. The study of this dialectic change is psychology from the point of view of the individual; but from the point of view of the sum of human beings it is sociology or history, and in its causal statement in must include all portions of the environment with which human beings interact, even the fixed stars. But since in the short periods usually studied, cosmical conditions do not change importantly, they may be neglected. They might become important in a study of humanity which included the Ice Ages. Of primary interest to history are however the material elements in the environment that do change rapidly in the periods generally studied, i.e. machines, transport, cities, and, in brief, all the social relations arising from social production, for the change in the organism will necessarily be related to these changing features in its environment. The organism does not enter consciously or of its own will into these relations. They are prior and determine its consciousness and will. It is in fact impossible to study psychology without a background of sociology. If one does do so, either it is impossible to find the causal connexion in the change of the human psyche, or else one accepts the human psyche as unchanging and all laws discovered from a study of contemporary psyches seem true for all time.

As it happens, no modern school of psychology has ever studied social relations as primary, as conditioning the consciousness which is generated by them. None study concrete society and its non-psychical basis. No modern school of psychology has ever yet got so far as to formulate its basic approach to the environment of the psyche it studies, continuous interaction with which is the law of psychic life.

Freud approaches his psychological problems with the assumptions of a bourgeois idealist, to whom nothing exists of reality save an unchanging backcloth before which the ideas play their parts. It is true that these ideas are now rather like the 'ruling passions' of older philosophers, and have been given the name of 'the instincts' or 'libido', but the story is still the same fabulous drama, in which are performed the 'miracles' of inhibitions, sublimation, cathexis, narcissism, transformation and displacement, by those good and bad fairies, the censor, the ego, the super-ego and the id. There are even cannibal instincts and incest instincts, though it staggers the imagination of the biologist to infer how these variations evolved and became hereditary. These is no causality.

Freud imagines a pleasure-principle attempting to gain freedom for its pleasures within the bounds of the prision house of reality. Beyond those bounds of causality we must not stray, Freud admits, but inside their ever-contracting boundaries there appears to be true freedom. It is a fine fable. The instincts, like bourgeois revolutionaries, desperately attempt to gratify themselves, oppressed by the tyrant Reality's laws. Has such a conception any place in science?

Freud, like all bourgeois intellectuals, like Eddington, Russell and Wells, cannot lose his faith that there is a separate cell called liberty, mysteriously existing in the granite of scientific causality. Scientific thought is continually (it is supposed) contracting the dimensions of this chamber of little ease, but still it exists.

In particular, these thinkers suppose that man is more free, more at liberty, the more he is free from the pressure of culture, consciousness, and social organisation. Russell, Eddington, Freud, and Wells are alike in this supposition, which, carried (as they do not carry it) to the logical conclusion, means that the only beings with real liberty are the unconscious brutes.

But the truth is, the world is not a prison house of reality in which man has been allotted by some miracle a honey cell of pleasure. Man is a part of reality, in constant relation with it, and the progress of consciousness, in so far as it increases his knowledge of causality, increases his freedom. In the same way, civilisation increases his freedom, in so far as it increases his causal control over reality, including himself. In this last, in the self-control of men as compared with their environmental control by machines, we are least advanced, and this is precisely because psychology, which would show us how to control ourselves, is always trying to evade causality. Science does not seem to be telling man about freedom. On the contrary, it seems only to be dicovering cast-iron laws, of whose existence and rigidity he did not guess. But is an animal in a cage free because it does not realise it is a cage? Will it not only become free when it realise that a locked cage completely restricts its movements and that to be free it must *necessarily* unlock the door?

Bourgeois civilisation is built on this rock, that complete freedom consists in complete personal anarchy, and that man is *naturally* completely free. This Rousseauism is found distorting all bourgeois thought. Freud cannot help visualising civilisation as the enslavement of the completely free instincts by culture.

Hence the honest bourgeois is always either pessimistic or religious. Man must have some conscious social organisation to exist socially (police, judges, factories, education), and all these seem to him so many limits to his freedom, not because of the *imperfection* of the organisation, which is the communist criticism, but because there is organisation at all. Thus to the bourgeois, civilisation seems damned by its premises and there is no hope in this life of attaining freedom. All organisation, all consciousness, all thought eventually seem to the bourgeois intellectual the corruption or inhibition or repression of the completely free natural man; but this natural man is an anthropoid ape, for man without society is a brute.

Can we talk of the inhibition or repression of that which is not free? And are the instincts free or are they, as we see so clearly in the insect, blind mechanical enslavements, deaf to individual learning, heeding only the slow ancestral experience of the species? Then society, creating by its 'inhibitions' and 'repressions' *consciousness*, is leading the instincts on the path not of slavery but of freedom. To call, as Freud does, that which frees the enslaved instincts 'inhibitions' or 'repression' is prejudiced.

Freud sees in the evolution of each individual psyche nothing but the drama of the instincts fighting among themselves, and so giving rise to the repressions of culture. He sees in culture nothing but the projection of this drama into the environment, on a collective scale: 'And now,' he says, 'it seems to me, the meaning of the evolution of culture is no longer a riddle to us. It must present to us the struggle between Eros and Death, between the instincts of life and the instincts of destruction, as it works itself out in the human species.' Thus to him culture is autonomously psychic, and without internal causality, just because it has no external connection. The material environment is ignored.

In another passage he attributes the organisations of society to the identifications of all individuals with each other through the father, thus explaining both social cohesion and leadership. And he adds (explaining our present discontents): 'This danger (i.e. social discontent) is most menacing where the social forces of cohesion consist predominantly of identifications of the individuals of the group with one another, whilst leading personalities fail to acquire the significance that should fall to them in the process of group-formation.' Here bourgeois idealism, long before the advent of Hitler, unwittingly writes the charter of barbarous Fascism, Führership, and the Corporate State. Withdrawing from the future, Fascism appeals to a savage past for salvation. By a strange irony, Freud becomes the apologist of the Fascist philosophy which rejects him, which burns his books, and seems repugnant to him. Yet this is the irony of all bourgeois culture, that because it is based on a contradiction, it gives rise to the opposite of what it desires. It desires freedom and individual expression, but, because it believes freedom is to be found in abolition of social organisation, it gives rise to all the tyrannies and blind crippling necessities of the modern world. Freudism, attempting to cure civilisation of its instinctive distortions, points the way to Nazism.

Is Freud, then, an ally of Fascism, whose psychological mechanism in the individual his theory explains and condemns? In one sense, yes! All bourgeois consciousness breaks down before new reality, it is aware of its failure and this sense of failure is itself a disintegrating force. It is part of the rôle of Freud to make overt the rottenness in bourgeois social relations, but there are no 'absolutely hopeless' situations, and bourgeois culture defends itself from these humiliating awarenesses by the mechanism of barbaric pseudo-religious constructs, such as that of Fascist ideology. When consciousness reveals its inadequacy to a situation, one can either advance to a wider consciousness which will include the new situation that brought about the crisis, or one can regress to a former solution of a similar problem in the childhood of the individual of the nation. This is the mechanism of neuroses. But this is no solution, for the old situation is not the same situation, and the mind that faces it too has changed. So one gets only a false and pathological infantilism, full of illusion and phantasy. Freudism can point this out but, because of its lack of a scientific basis, it cannot show the way to attain the wider consciousness. Thus, after all, it is not a therapy, it is only a diagnosis. The analyst vainly exposes the regressive nature of the neurotic's solution, if he cannot himself provide a better solution. And Freud cannot. We can only cast out error with truth, and

Freud had no new truth to offer, only a fairy-tale recording the breakdown of bourgeois civilisation as seen in its own mythological terms.

In answer to criticism of Freud's mythology, it has often been urged that Freudism is a therapy, not a science. Such defenders admit that emotively-charged concepts such as libido, the censor, the Oedipus complex and inhibition have no place in a scientific hypothesis. But (they argue) the neurosis is an emotional crisis, and the neurotic can only be cured emotionally. It is no use talking to him about conditioned reflexes. His emotions must be stirred, and this justifies the myths of psychoanalysis, by which truths are conveyed to him fabulously but vividly.

But just because Freudism is not a science, it fails as a therapy. Granted that the neurotic must be touched emotionally, are individual psychoanalysts really arrogant enough to believe that the enormous, creative force of emotion, the dynamism of society, can be directed by them, as individuals, and by means of such arid concepts as those of Freudism? Emotion, in all its vivid colouring, is the creation of ages of culture acting on the blind unfeeling instincts. All art, all education, all day-to-day social experience, draw it out of the heart of the human genotype and direct and shape its myriad phenomena. Only society as a whole can really direct this force in the individual. To imagine that one psychoanalyst can shape it is to believe that one can bring down the houses of London with a shout. Could any discipline rooted in scientific causality have made so rash a misjudgment of the powers of the individual, as to believe that the mighty social force of emotion could be harnessed by 'transference of libido' to the earnest, middle-aged and bald physician? At least the Victorian heroine who wished to reform the sinner by a good woman's love had personal charm and unlimited opportunity.

The innate responses of an organism, the so-called instincts, as such are unconscious, mechanical, and unaffected by experience. Psychology therefore is not concerned with them, for they are the material of physiology. Psychology, in its study of consciousness or unconsciousness, can only have for its material all those psychic contents that results from the *modifi-*

cation of responses by experience. It is this material that changes, that develops that is distinctively human, that is of importance, and psychology should and in practice does ignore the *unchanging* instinctual basis as a cause. It concerns itself with the variable, which changes not only from age to age but from individual to individual and in an individual from hour to hour.

Reflexes are conditioned by experience, by action upon the environment. In man the environment consists of society, and action of education, daily work, daily life, what man sees, eats, hears, handles, travels in, co-operates in, loves, reverences, is repelled by—the whole fabric of social relations. These in the developing instinctual organism, produce the psyche, give consciousness its contents and the unconscious its trend, and make man what he is. Consciousness is the organ of social adaptation, but society is not composed of conciousnesses.

It is true that each contact of organism with the environment not only affects the organism but also affects the environment. But in studying any one psyche, which is the task of individual psychology, we see on the one hand a naked genotype, dumb, ignorant and without tradition, whereas, on the other hand, forming its environment, we see not only millions of other individuals but the formulation in bricks and mortar, in social organisations, in religions, sciences, laws and language of the experience of aeons of human activity. Consequently the action of the organism upon this mass of conciousness is minute compared with its reaction upon the organism, except in those cases where, owing to its own instability, the smallest touch is already sufficient to send it over violently into a new position. Such touches are administered by Marx. But in formulating a scientific psychology as in formulating a mechanics, the spectacular side is of no importance compared to the underlying causal laws, good for the ordinary as well as the exceptional event. The fact that in certain conditions of instability a cricket ball could cause the sun to explode, does not justify us in imagining that cricket balls exert forces greater than suns. In psychology, as in mechanics, the reaction of a body on its cosmic environment can be neglected, as compared to the effect of the world on the body.

Thus psychology must be extracted from sociology, not *vice versa*. For sociology, if scientific (and the only school of scientific sociology was founded by Marx), already includes the conscious formulations and the material accretions, arising from the dialectic of social relations, which provide the environment of the developing infant psyche. These are the social relations into which the organism enters irrespective of its will. The single organism is a slave to its environment, just as the particle is a slave to time and space, in spite of the fact that the social environment is composed of the activities of human organisms and time and space are the sum of the relations of particles. We must establish sociology before we can establish psychology, just as we must establish the laws of time and space before we can treat satisfactorily of a single particle. This is not to say that psychology and sociology are the same. Psychology has a province of tremendous importance to the human race, but it can only be studied scientifically on a background of more general laws, just as biology is impossible without the prior laws of physics and chemistry. Sociology is the foundation of psychology.

This Freud has failed to see. To him all mental phenomena are simply the interaction and mutual distortion of the instincts, of which culture and social organisations are a projection, and yet this social environment, produced by the instincts, is just what tortures and inhibits the instincts. Freud is powerless to explain causally the intricate and rich movement of cultural development, because he is in the position of a man trying to lift himself off the ground by his bootlaces. All this rich culture, its art, its science, and its institutions, is to Freud merely a projection of man's instinctive turmoil into unchanging reality, and yet this projection continually changes, although the individual instincts and reality remain the same. Why do social relations change? Why do psyches alter from age to age? Freud, like all modern psychologists who base themselves on the unchanging instincts of the genotype, is powerless to explain the only thing that interests psychology, the thing that *constitutes* psychology, the perpetual variation and development of the mental phenotype. Like Plato's men in the cave, psychoanalysts try to deduce from shadows what is happening outside. Looking into the psyche, they are mystified by the movements caused by currents in outer reality and mistake them for the distortions of the cunning and oppressed instincts, or for the interventions of mysterious 'forces' that are generated by the instincts. Seeing the shadows make a circular detour round one place, they assume this to be an eternal law of the psyche, the Oedipus complex. It does not occur to them that it may be due to an obstacle in the environment, round which the shadows have to move, and that the complex will alter if the obstacle is moved.

Unable to see psychology causally simply because they cannot see it sociologically, Freudism can attain to no psychology beyond bourgeois psychology. They never advance beyond the view-point of the 'individual in civil society'. Whether they study primitive man or lay down general laws of the soul, it is always with ideas formulated from a bourgeois psyche studying other bourgeois psyches, and so the instincts play always the part of splendid and free brutes, crippled by the repressions of a cruel culture. It is true that to-day the system of production relations is crippling man's splendid powers, but Freudian 'libido' in bondage to 'repression' is a very inadequate myth to convey this reality. It is a pale subjective reflection of the vital objective situation. The old bourgeois symbol of 'original sin' is better. The psyche, a creation of its environment, becomes to Freud, who ignores the environment or is ignorant of its mode of change, a creature whom mysterious self-generated entities force to become an unhappy bourgeois psyche. It is as if a man, seeing a row of trees bent in various ways by the prevailing winds, were without studying the relation between growth and environment to deduce that a mysterious complex in trees caused them always to lean as the result of a death instinct attracting them to the ground, while eternal Eros bade them spring up vertically. Freud's error is so much the worse because the psyche, studied by psychology, is far more the result of environmental conditions than the whole tree. The psyche is the organ of adaptation to social relations, therefore for psychology the laws determining social relations are fundamental.

Thus Freudism, like all 'individual' psychologies, breaks

down in the most elementary scientific desideratum, that of causality. Though evolved as a therapy, it turns out to be the creed of undiluted pessimism. If we do not know the laws of our environment, we cannot know ourselves, and if we cannot know ourselves, we can never be free. If we are full of bitterness, and this bitterness is the outcome of an inevitable instinctual strife, our hearts can never be sweetened. If we owe no vital part of our consciousness to our environment, it is of no value to change it. 'New skies,' said Horace, 'the exile finds, but the same heart.'—If we regard the categories of the present as final, and the present is full of despair and neurosis, of slumps and wars, we can never pass beyond them to a successful issue. At the best, like the neurotic, we can only return to a former successful solution at an infantile level—to feudalism, barbarian group-leadership, *unanisme,* Fascism. Indeed Jung invokes as our only salvation this very regression, appealing to the old barbarous mythologies to come to our aid. Freud at least has the courage to spurn this way of escape, and so, like a Roman stoic, in decaying classical civilisation he treads the die-hard path, and drinks the cup of poison to its dregs.

This conception, apparently refined, of the last fatal battle of the gods, is really barbarous, and the first step in the path to Hindoo resignation and vegetable sanctity. Spengler is the prophet of this resignation to one's own limitations:

'Only dreamers believe that there is a way out. We are born in this time and must bravely follow the path to the destined end. There is no other way. Our duty is to hold on to the last position, without hope, without rescue.' Freud, too, in *The Future of an Illusion* and *Group Psychology,* sees little hope for culture. Yet he is, in spite of this, more optimistic than the communist in that he believes that while society rushes downhill, the psychoanalyst, as an individual, can do what all society fails to do, and cure the neurotic produced by modern conditions. This contradictory belief that the individual can do what the sum of individuals, of which he is one, cannot do, is characteristic of all these bourgeois pessimists, and makes it difficult to take their pessimism as completely sincere.

It is generally believed that the relation between environment and individual is correctly expressed in Adler, exponent of Individual Psychology, and Freud's former pupil. Let us therefore hear him:

'In a civilisation where one man is the enemy of the other— for this is what our whole industrial system means—demoralisation is ineradicable, for demoralisation and crime are the by-products of the struggle for existence as known to our industrialised civilisation.'

Surely, it will be said, Adler has escaped from the bourgeois cage. Surely he has realised that it is the environment, bourgeois capitalism, that produces our present discontents, and not the struggle-for-existence of the organism, pushed on by its instincts, that produces bourgeois capitalism. True, he here confuses industrialisation (machine technique) with the competition of capitalism which gave rise to it, but is separable from it. He is confounding productive forces and production relations. Yet, at least (it will be urged), the root of the matter is in him. Let us therefore continue the quotation and see his remedy for this 'ineradicable' demoralisation: 'To limit and do away with this demoralisation, a chair of curative pedagogy should be established.'

This is the logic of Individual Psychology! Man's demoralisation, his neurosis, his discontent, his despair, are correctly seen to be due to his environment—capitalist social relations. To cure it, however, his environment is not to be changed, for the environment is always in all bourgeois economics and sociology and in spite of history presumed to be unchangeable. Rather, man is to lift himself off the ground by his bootlaces; to take pedagogic pills to cure the earthquake of capitalism's collapse. The pill takes various forms: it is a chair of curative pedagogy with Adler. With Freud the sufferers, if rich enough, are to go to an analyst for a course of treatment. This is impracticable, Jung realises, for the poorer classes, so we must reintroduce the old myths, of the archetypal hero swallowed by the giant fish ('Psychology of the Unconscious'.) These are the doctors who stand by the bedside of society in its most gigantic agony! Is it surprising that the criticism of the Marxist sometimes contains a tinge of contempt?

131

The Marxian has been often reproached for his antagonism to psychoanalysis. It is even asserted that the founder has no bourgeois illusions; he is a thoroughgoing materialist. But he is not. Freud is still possessed by the focal bourgeois illusion, that the individual stands opposed to an unchanging society which trammels him, and within whose constraints his instincts attempt freely to develop the rich and varied phenomena of the psyche. Because of that illusion Freud thinks society itself is doomed to frustration, and yet thinks that one individual can cure another. He is never able to see that just as man must have a fulcrum outside him to lift himself, so the individual must act on the environment which created his consciousness in order to change it. We owe much to Freud for his symbolic presentation of the discord between the deep and recent layers of men's minds; but he cannot heal us, for he cannot even teach us that first truth, that we must change the world in order to change ourselves.

The revolt of all the instincts against current social relations, which to Freud is everything and obscures his whole horizon, so that he writes all psychology, art, religion, culture, politics and history in terms of this revolt, is only one of many signals to the Marxian that, behind the decayed façade, a new environment is being realised and in man's troubled soul a wider consciousness, too, awaits delivery.

VI

CONSCIOUSNESS

A STUDY IN BOURGEOIS PSYCHOLOGY

1

It is characteristic of bourgeois psychology that it is confused and inconclusive in its treatment of what would seem, to many people, the most important subject of psychological study, consciousness. Bourgeois psychology has a choice between six doctrines about consciousness, and it will throw light on the difficulties with which that psychology is faced if we detail them: —

(*a*) Consciousness contains the sole data of psychology (philosophical and faculty psychologies).

(*b*) Consciousness is an epiphenomenon accompanying neurological activity (neurological psychology and psychophysiology).

(*c*) Consciousness plays no causal part in behaviour, which can be completely described and determined without its use. Since behaviour is the only thing that can be observed in others, the existence of consciousness should on principles of epistemology be denied (behaviourism).

(*d*) The psyche consists of the products of one or a number of transformed instincts; some of these products are conscious, others are unconscious (Freudism and its derivatives; and 'hormic' psychology).

(*e*) Consciousness consists of the shuffling of forms of thought according to dynamical laws (association psychology and gestalt psychology).

(*f*) In so far as any or all of the above theories produce empirically-proven results, they are right (eclectic or academic psychology).

It sounds a hopeless muddle, and in fact it is a muddle

without hope as long as psychologists move within the circle of bourgeois philosophy. Yet would anyone familiar with contemporary psychology accuse me of overstating the case? It is in fact usual to provide many more classifications: for example a gestalt psychologist would insist on being separated from the old-fashioned associationist and the Freudian from the adherent of McDougall, and the follower of Jung or Adler from both.

It is obvious that all these schools cannot be right. For example (a) and (c) also (d) and (e) are exclusive opposites. It is as near certain as anything can be that none of them is right. There is no more depressing spectacle in bourgeois culture to-day than this of a science so important and vital to human knowledge as psychology unable to secure argeement about the most elementary feature of its domain. But may not this be a necessary feature of psychology itself which perhaps, as some scientists have suggested, can never be a science; and is not this more likely than that the failure of its psychology should be a necessary characteristic of bourgeois culture?

The answer is, that not only is the anarchy of psychology a necessary feature of bourgeois culture, but that the very attitude of mind which supposes that psychology can never be a science, is itself an outcome of the same fundamental position. Bourgeois psychology grew out of biology through the influence of physiology on philosophy; but equally bourgeois physics affects it, for it determines on the one hand bourgeois philosophy and on the other hand bourgeois biology. Medicine, too, throws its contribution into psychology through physiology, and it is chiefly philosophical medicine, medicine formulated in terms of the current bourgeois philosophy.

Does this sound an inextricable tangle, accounting for the confusion of psychology, the latest of the empirically developed sciences? It does so only because the bourgeois sciences, as an outcome of the bourgeois position, cannot be conceived except as either confusing or dominating each other. Either the fundamental categories of 'the sciences' are held to be exclusive, and nothing can result from their combination except a mishmash, or, alternatively, one science excludes and suppresses the categories of the others, as in behaviourism the categories of bourgeois biology are allowed to suppress those proper to psychology, and in mechanical materialism the categories of bourgeois physics are allowed to usurp those of all other spheres of science. *Either* the spheres of the positive sciences are distinct, *or* they are the same, that is the dilemma which bourgeois science has posed for itself, and it can never imagine that they are different and yet mutually determinative.

The bourgeois, by his fundamental position, is free 'in himself'. He is free not because he is conscious of his causality, but because he is ignorant of the social causes that determine his being. He pictures himself therefore as standing in a dominating relation to his environment, just as in society he seems by his dominating relation to capital and ownership of social labour power, to be determining society and not determined by it.

He is in fact deluded, for his ownership of capital does not enable him consciously to determine society even though his actions determine its fate. The sum of bourgeois wills produces history, but it is not the history any one bourgeois willed. His efforts for one thing produce another thing—his attempts at profit produce loss, at plenty poverty, at peace war. As his culture collapses all his efforts to shore it up hasten that collapse. He finds himself unfree after all, although he is 'in control' of social forces.

Why then was he unfree? Where did he err? He erred because he did not see that his dominating relation to society was a determining relation, which determined him as much as he determined it. He was unconscious of this, and therefore unable to achieve freedom. His conception of freedom really arose as a special case of a group of illusions about domination which has been associated with all forms of society based on dominating classes. This group of illusions has for a common factor the belief that domination secures self-determination. But it follows from the material unity of the Universe that this is untrue. All the phenomena that constitute the Universe are mutually determined. If any group were completely self-determined it would constitute a closed world, and would not exist. All relations are determining. The earth appears to primitive man to dominate the cosmos—sun and stars appear to rotate round it. This is a pleasant illusion, it does not make us astronomers, much less does it make us people round whom the cosmos revolves. As soon as we realise there is a determining relation, and become conscious of its nature and how it grips us, we are that much freer of cosmic phenomena, and can predict eclipses, construct sidereal time, navigate, and govern our actions according to the necessity of the Universe.

All previous cultures that were ideologically conscious at all have been based on a ruling class which consciously dominated and directed the utilisation of productive forces. As a result all such cultures were subject to an illusion distorting their ideologies. Slave-owning culture conceived freedom to consist in this, in the domination of the will of one man over the will of another, the other passively obeying this one's will. This gives rise to the *teleological* explanation of the Universe, which reaches its subtlest form in Plato's or Aristotle's philosophies, in which all phenomena are determined by Ideas or Forms. These correspond to the plans formed in the mind of the slave-owner which his slave passively fulfils. This explanation applies equally to social and non-social phenomena, and therefore is consistent. The domination inherent in the slave-owning system is not repressed, as with the bourgeois, but is conscious, and the illusion consists, not in supposing that no domination exists, but that society is in fact really determined solely by the will of the master, and does not in turn determine his will. This will, which therefore appears as the first cause in society just because it is conscious, also appears the first cause in the Universe, as the Law of the Universe, as the doctrine of Ends, Final Causes, Perfect Ideas (willed by one or more supreme causes or Divine Masters) whose plans the Universe fulfils and thus develops.

Society is not in fact determined by the will of a slave-owning master, but by the productive forces at the service of such an economy. The master's will is itself determined by the society in which he finds himself and, just because he is unconscious of these causes, the slave-owner is unfree. His world of ends is inadequate, not only as a basis for sociology, but also for physics, biology and psychology. It cannot exhibit true causal relations: only demons disguised as final causes. The slave-owning world, incapable of being deeply scientific or analytical, inevitably marches on to the Empire, whose fiction it is that the whole Empire's activity is controlled by the will of one master, the Emperor. And this Empire as inevitably marches on to ruin, for the productive forces are not controlled by the will of the Emperor but instead, crippled by slave-owning productive relations, the Imperial economy decays for all his efforts, and it is a world whose income has steadily diminished, whose soil is impoverished and whose people is demoralised, that crumbles at any push from the barbarians so easily repelled at the height of the Empire's power.

No less than the slave-owning, the feudal civilisation is in the grip of the illusion of dominion. The dominion is still conscious, as it is in slave-owning civilisation, and therefore necessarily gives rise to a physics and to a worldview in which all causes are final causes—conscious purposes in the mind of a dominating master. In this respect it simply takes over Aristotelianism, the most consistent expression of slave-owning philosophy. But now this domination is regarded as necessarily exercised according to a hierarchy of privilege; the day of unrestricted property in slaves is over. The dominating relation is exercised 'according to law', and this law itself is only the reflection of the Roman technical apparatus of learning, social organisation, and administrative skill taken over with the Church from the Empire by the barbarian overlords. This technical apparatus becomes symbolised as Christendom, as the monopoly of the Church, as benefit of clergy, as an instrument which must be used to sanction all acts of domination from kingship to knighthood. Aristotelianism must therefore be modified: and while final causes are still the explanatory mechanism these final causes are, in Scholasticism and Thomism, causes which are established by a law of God, which can only work themselves out according to a fiat given forth at the Creation. The world works according to God-sanctioned laws which have a purpose, and have had a purpose from the beginning of time. These laws are not self-driving, but require the continual impetus of deity. They can therefore be suspended at any time by the Divine Will, but such miracles are rare.

Science therefore in feudal civilisation is still in embryo but it is yet a stage nearer birth than in slave-owning society. A dominion which, in addition to the free will of the master, requires also the sanction of the impersonal law, is already well on the way to be determined, even if it is determined from above by another dominating will—God's. A world ruled by law is well on the way to being a world ruled by causality.

In a sense this is an accident. Feudal law is only the Imperial law of slave-owning society preserved through the survival of Roman economy in the monastery-farm, example to the barbarian of agricultural efficiency and therefore the ancestor of the manor. But the fact of this survival changes it. In Roman society, law's sanction is simply this, that it expresses the will of the Divine Emperor, who owns his people like a slave-owner. To medieval society, to the barbarian invader, law comes as something outside the will of the ruler, as an impersonal and pre-existing body of law, as Christendom with which he must comply if the social production from which he draws tribute is to be carried on, for that production functions according to these laws, and otherwise collapses in anarchy. The law therefore appears, not as a fiat of any serf-owner's will but as something determining in some measure the range of will of both serf and serf owner, a something existent from the beginning of time. Hence feudal society provides the necessary transition to the bourgeois position.

This transition is achieved within the limits of its own illusion by bourgeois culture. The scholastic world laws are stripped of their final causes and become self-driving, while the question of the reason for and time of their issue by the Creator is postponed or treated as outside the province of science. Science is thus conceived for the first time as the field of laws which connect phenomena in a mutually determining way, and are sufficiently explained by exhibiting the structure of that determinism. These laws do not require as their sanction a final cause nor a clearly expressed divine *place in the cosmos* and do not therefore explain nature as the vehicle of conscious wills exercising dominion.

This ought to be the death of animism. Animism is nothing but the attribution to nature, as the sufficient cause of all phenomena, of human wills, due to the primitive's illusion that the will is a freely determining cause in itself, and not in the act of willing itself determined. In primitive communism, where there is no domination or division of labour, such wills seem present in every individual freely determining his behaviour as a cause, and therefore by analogy they are held to play the same part in the beneficent or maleficent activities of trees, stones, and stars, which obey their own wills without overlords. But the slave-owner is well aware that though the slave may will as he please, the slave's will is not the cause of the slave's activities, which are caused by his master's will. He therefore subtilises animism to this extent, that trees and stones have not wills of their own, but are passive subjects to a god's will:

> From haunted spring, and dale
> Edg'd with poplar pale,
>   The parting Genius is with sighing sent,
> With flowre-inwov'n tresses torn
> The Nimphs in twilight shade of tangled thickets
>   mourn.

So early Greek animism, with the development of its economy, gives place to the teleology of Aristotle.

The slave-owner is at times visited with a nightmare. He finds that his free will, in spite of its freedom, is thwarted, not by a superior will but by things-in-themselves—by inferior wills, accidents, mistakes, and his own ignorance. Yet he is still unable to conceive his will except as being thwarted like that of his slave's by another will, and since he the master is so thwarted, might not even the world's master and his—God Himself—be thwarted in his volition by some grand overriding will, by Will-in-Itself? This is the slave-owning conception of Moira, or Fate, a comparatively late development reaching its noblest expression in Greek tragedy. This Fate, in spite of its closeness to bourgeois determinism, betrays its slave-owning parentage by the fact that it is always visualised as a consciously foreseeing Will, and always as thwarting, not determining human wills *as well as* events, but *interfering* with human wills *by means of* events.

Animism, slave-owning teleology and Fate, feudal teleology

and Law, these then are the steps by which society in its development explains the world. It was the rôle of the bourgeois to carry a step forward, not only society's productive development but also, and necessarily also, its explanation of the Universe.

★

The bourgeois first finds himself as one of a class whose development is restricted by feudal privilege and the reign of law imposed by Christendom. He therefore revolts against it and, in the circumstances in which he finds himself, he necessarily formulates his case as follows: —

(i) The dominating relations of one man over another are evil, and must be eliminated, for they hold up productive forces (that is, the productive forces of my class).

(ii) Law is not something immutable existing from the beginning of time and imposed on men from without. Any such imposed law is wrong. A man's law is in himself. What seems to him in the given circumstances best or proper to do, is right, and there should be no other law.

This means that the bourgeois turns Catholic dogma into personal Protestantism, and that all feudal laws, monopolies, or privileges which restrict his doing what seems best to himself, are abolished in the course of his revolution. Those restrictive laws are, however, all laws interfering with his right to acquire, alienate and own capital. He does not however regard this right as a 'law', but as something given in the nature of things, and in his own nature.

The bourgeois thus emerges to consciousness as a man whose views of the world are determined by social causes, just like the slave-owner or lord. Freedom consists in this, in each man's doing what seems best to himself, consulting, not some good laid down by law, like the service to his overlord by which the feudal landowner held his land, but his own good. Out of this apparent confusion of personal competition will emerge (according to the bourgeois) a world order that is the best possible, because it is the product of freedom. To this illusion the bourgeois is completely committed by his revolutionary programme.

But this society, in spite of its apparent individual freedom, is still based on a dominating relation.

The bourgeois, as the source of uncontrolled free activity in society, must necessarily be uncontrolled in his ownership of social capital. This apparently innocent dominating relation to a thing also involves, after all, dominion over men, just as in previous societies, but unlike the ruling class in previous societies the bourgeois cannot consciously assert dominion over other wills as a law of society; on the contrary he is committed to repress the knowledge or deny the existence of such a law. Moreover the very dominion thus exercised imposes a conflict in society between the haves and have-nots, which would become overt and suicidal to society if it were not forcibly repressed and kept harmless, not once and for all, but as long as the antagonising domination exists, which is as long as culture remains bourgeois.

Thus after a bourgeois revolution, the resultant strife is suppressed by a 'strong man' who forcibly imposes a coercive law on haves and have-nots alike, making possible unrestricted capitalism. In English history this strong man is, after the bourgeois Reformation, the Tudor monarch, and, after the Revolution, Cromwell. In France he is Napoleon. But this 'strong man', though necessary, is by bourgeois standards himself an anomaly, and as soon as he has called into being laws protecting bourgeois rights, he is eliminated in favour of a rubber stamp monarch (the Glorious Revolution of England) or a President (France) and the bourgeois task then becomes simply the preservation of this body of law in its main principles (the constitution, democracy, etc.) with the incorporation of such minor amendments as social development renders necessary (legislation). These laws are now hypostatised as the essence of liberty and justice (freedom and parliamentary democracy).

How is this change reflected in the world of science, with which we are concerned? The world of science follows the same course. The first attempt at a bourgeois world-view as homogeneous as that of Aristotle or Thomas Aquinas necessarily fails from the outset by reason of this split in the bourgeois position. Either classicism or feudalism can achieve a homogeneous world-view in a far more consistent anticipation of Schopenhauer's philosophy: the 'World as Will and Idea' (or rather, as Will and *Aim*). And, unlike Schopenhauer's, such a world-view expresses in a refined form the viewpoint of all thinking men in that culture. This the bourgeois never achieves.

He is divided between two contradictory points of view. In himself he is exempt from determinism, not because of the dominating relation of his class to society (as with classical society) but through the absence of any conscious relation to other men at all. Other men neither dominate him nor are dominated by him (he thinks), and the ideal society, to which all bourgeois strive, is one in which each unit is insulated, and the world of society and of values drives on in the best possible way as the result of the independent, self-motivated action of every free bourgeois.

At the same time he stands, as owner and master of social capital, in a dominating relation to 'Nature', his environment. Social capital is the crystallisation of men's attempts to control nature through their empirical knowledge of its causality. He is in charge of this manipulation of nature, but this is not a relation of will like that of classical society, for the bourgeois by his position is committed to the belief that a dominating relation to a thing (private property) is not a dominating relation at all. It is therefore a relation in which will does not enter in the sense that to will a thing is to have the slave do it if it is do-able, and if not—well, slaves are not perfect and it is not for the master to do the slave's business for him. It is a new kind of relation in which the bourgeois as it were 'administers' a thing, so as to draw out from its intrinsic qualities the maximum benefit to society, which, in bourgeois language, appears translated as 'the maximum profit to himself'. Of course he is not really administering property, he is exploiting labour power.

Unlike the classic or feudal position, such a position is from the outset self-contradictory, and will never be able to generate a consistent world-view; dualism is implicit in it. For from the bourgeois point of view, in the world of society freedom seems to inhere in the individual will unconscious of any causality or outer necessity; but in the world of nature, freedom seems to inhere in the drawing-out by the will of the necessary qualities in Nature and, therefore, in consciousness of the necessity of Nature. The first view is completely fallacious; but the second is nearer reality than a teleological explanation, and therefore bourgeois culture is culture which gives birth for the first time to a science of the environment of Nature, a thing almost unknown to previous cultures. Nonetheless, the fundamental fallacy of this position means that increasing success in the second, or scientific, world-view will add to the inconsistency and anarchy of the first; and ultimately the second world-view will itself become affected, for both are only abstractions from the one reality.

★

We have in other essays explored different aspects of the disintegration of bourgeois science; here we merely concentrate on the duel between physics and psychology. The bourgeois looked round on his social world and unconsciously projected it into the world of physics, into his environment. He therefore discovered new truths about his environment, for the world of society is a part of reality. But, coming back to society, he could not, because the projection was unconscious, see society as determined in the way the world of physics was determined, for to do so would be to make social necessity conscious. He stood in his own light. As a bourgeois he had been unconscious of any necessity determining his action, for the bourgeois law for social action is 'Do as you will'. It forgets to state whether (a) you *can* do as you will; (b) you can *will* what you will.

Hence the world of physics, in which the 'wills' of the particles are determined at first by God but later by the relations of the particles themselves, would have been the basis of an accurate view of bourgeois society, but the bourgeois was unable to achieve it. He kept on getting near it, but always this fundamental conviction that his will and desires were the source of social motion prevented it. If on the one hand he saw society as a network of determining relations and, on the other hand, his own mind as determined by this, he would have seen that not only did society produce from its interaction 'laws of supply and demand', but that his conceptions of justice and right were also determined by society. But this last step he could never make, for to him his own self was the source of the free energy which, interacting with bourgeois society, gave rise to economic law.

This failure meant that he conceived his desires and notions of justice, morality and so forth, as not in any way determined, but as primary and therefore eternal. Necessarily, the type of society of which these were the outcome was the eternal type of society—any deviation was either discredited or was an accident.

This results in three different worlds which are of major importance in understanding the distortion of bourgeois thought.

(i) *The world of physics.* This world, modelled on bourgeois society unconsciously grasped in experience by the bourgeois, is a world of particles trading freely with each other and giving rise to laws of supply and demand which dictate the behaviour of the world as a whole. Because nature is not a dominated slave, but an administered thing, it is non-living and non-mental; a-teleological therefore and stripped of all quality.

It is a closed world, which does not interact with the bourgeois, who surveys it to learn its laws and sue it like a machine —hence it is in absolute space and time, independent of the observing mind. In order that it should not be in determining relation with mind, it is by definition bare of all qualities found in mind (the so-called sensory or secondary qualities). But these ultimately are found to include *all* material qualities. Consequently the bourgeois closed world of physics, by definition restricted to matter, which matter is defined as 'non-mind', becomes barer and barer of real qualities until 'nothing' is left. But something must be left—there are the concepts that describe the 'structure' of this nothing. Thus mechanical materialism by its very premises is pushed on to become its apparent opposite, mentalism, which it reaches with Mach, Eddington, Jeans, and their followers.

The closed world of matter, restricted to non-mental qualities, is bound to collapse. 'Pure' physics is bound to reveal itself as an illusion. This it does by flying into two contradictory halves. On the one hand absolute space and time, independent of the observer, is saved by fusing them (space-time) and using the elaborate apparatus of the tensor to eliminate the determining effect of the observer and close the world by making it 'invariant for all transformations'. On the other hand this is flatly contradicted by quantum mechanics, which is composed partly of matrices of *observations alone,* partly of waves in absolute time-space which *are not however waves of matter* but waves indicating the *probability* of matter being present. In both cases matter is supposed to lurk behind the numbers as an unknowable Ding-an-sich.

(ii) *The closed world of sociology.* Here, once again, the bourgeois surveys a world from outside, and since his mind is not determined by it, though he lives in it, the social concepts in his mind are eternal (the laws of appetite, supply and demand, justice, free trade, etc.). These concepts therefore function in the world of sociology as laws regulating the free clash of individuals, and not as products of certain stages of that clash. Consequently, as in the famous mercantile examples, if two men meet on a desert island, their transactions strangely enough always and inevitably produce bourgeois economics, and this is taken as a proof of the validity of the bourgeois concepts. It follows from this that although the bourgeois can give a fairly accurate picture of contemporary sociology, it is a static picture, and neglects the vital laws of motion. Pigou can seriously devote a book to 'The Economics of a Stationary State'. Hence—not only is all bourgeois economics false as a science, and therefore as a guide to prediction and action, but it cannot give a deterministic and causal picture of the development of society in all its varieties of culture. Thus the closed world of bourgeois sociology is far less accurate than the closed world of physics. Both are absolute, but whereas in the history of man the environment does not to any degree alter, society itself alters rapidly, and thus bourgeois culture precludes itself from writing a scientific history of any feature of its culture from economics to religion. Yet change manifestly occurs and therefore some force must be invoked from an outside world to produce these changes. On the one hand ludicrously simple causes from spheres anterior to the sociological will be brought in as sufficiently explanatory—climatic changes, racial differences, differential birthrate, dietetic deficiencies (Marett), or, on the other hand, causes from spheres posterior to the sociological will be used in explaining the change—great Ideas, the invention of steam, the concept of liberty (H. A. Fisher), a cycle of flourishing and decay (Spengler). Both forms of explanation are equally unscientific but are preferred by the bourgeois to admitting that he is unconsciously determined by social relations, and that the 'fundamental' categories he has carefully established for sociology, are simply the product of his own particular phase of social relations.

(iii) *The closed world of psychology*. It was inevitable that the bourgeois should excel himself when he came to establish the categories of his own mind. The closed world of psychology is as it were the antithesis of the closed world of physics. Now if we abstract from mind all 'material' qualities we travel the reverse road to borugeois physics and we end up with something that contains no qualities at all. That is to say, consciousness is 'nothing'. But mind exists and the brain exists, therefore mind is simply physical matter in its sensory aspects, *the behaviour of the body*. Thus whilst in physics the bourgeois recipe for matter, 'not mind', was producing a matter so stripped of all material qualities as to evaporate into mind (cp. Eddington, Jeans and Russell), in psychology the bourgeois recipe for mind, 'not-matter', was producing a mind so stripped of all mental qualities that it solidified into matter, and became behaviourism. These two doctrines, so apparently opposed, produce each other, and follow from the one bourgeois position.

Before this, however, the bourgeois standpoint had succeeded in generating all the other distortions of psychology we have listed at the beginning of this essay. The simplest bourgeois position is that, since mind is not determined and is therefore free, the laws of the mind can only be studied in its products. Only the world of consciousness exists for psychology and, by this definition, psychology is the study not merely of non-material but of 'non-unconscious' qualities of the mind.

146

The first attempts at this form of bourgeois psychology are systematic. They are merely the classification of conscious phenomena (faculty psychology). Since the psychological field is undetermined there is no reason why faculties should not be anything, and as a result they are merely subsumed according to the prejudices of the moment and the structure of language at the time.

But it is impossible by reason of the very nature of knowledge that any field can be depicted as indetermined within itself, for every positive statement must necessarily express some kind of determinism. The most the bourgeois position claims is that mental phenomena are, in their own sphere, self-determined. The next step from faculty psychology is therefore the study of the self-determination of psychological products. The bourgeois, freely wandering about the world he dominates, acquires images of it or ideas, and these interact and live their lives, and combine and move by virtue of causal laws, parallel to but different from those that rule the world of particles in the closed world of physics. This closed world of Ideas, foreshadowed in Locke, reaches its final development in the associationists, with whom everything is explained by the 'association of ideas'. It still represents an important influence in all modern psychologies, for it appears to solve the problem of the closed worlds by creating two parallel worlds, quite in the manner of Descartes.

But unfortunately biology, itself a closed world, here erupts to shatter this dream of the parallel worlds, one of physics in which particles move according to physical laws, and the other of conscious ideas in which images of the real world move according to mental 'laws'. Biology, in human physiology, discovers a connecting link breaking into both worlds. On the one hand the body is composed of particles subject to physical laws, on the other hand, as aphasia and cerebral injuries show, disturbance of particles of the body leads to a disturbance of 'ideas'. The two absolute worlds must be joined.

This is the function of neurology. To neurology, however delicately its practisers may veil their position, the nerves (and particularly the cerebral neurones), are subject to electrical disturbances or waves of potential variation as the result of stimuli, and these waves are accompanied by ideas, just as the passage of an electric current across two poles in the atmosphere is accompanied by a spark. Great success is achieved by neurology in its correlation of conscious with physiological phenomena.

In this way mind is forced into the closed world of physics. The particles still move about in absolute time and space (for few, if any, neurologists have advanced to Einstein's absolute time-space) but now their movements are accompanied by a kind of iridescence or glow, which is mind.

The closed world of physics is a world dominated by the bourgeois, viewing it from outside and therefore able to foresee, by a Divine Calculation, the whole course of future movements of particles. This is bourgeois *pre*determinism, in which the whole future can be imagined as consciously known in its necessary future evolution, like the movements of a machine, just as in slave-owning fatalism the whole future can be imagined as consciously planned. In the former case the necessity arises from the causality of things; in the latter from the will of the planner; but in both cases the predestination consists in the conscious pre-knowledge of events.

But if consciousness itself is—as it evidently is—a late development of the Universe, such a conception falls to the ground. And if mind is also part of the network of determinism, each act of knowing involved in consciousness plays a determining as well as a determined rôle, and the mere fact of being all-knowing like Laplace's divine calculator, would involve a new determining force not allowed for in the original act of knowledge.

To the bourgeois the world of physics has its lines laid down irrespective of mind; it exists *absolutely*. When facts force him to include mind in this already complete, self-driving world, it is therefore simply dragged round with the machinery. Mind becomes pointless and redundant. What the bourgeois thought was the 'ennoblement' of mind—its separation as a distinct thing from gross matter—is in fact its degradation, for now it becomes involved in the mindless causality of bourgeois physics, a causality abstracted of mental qualities, though consciously envisaged as a whole by impersonal Mind.

Consciousness is to this abstract Mind an irrelevant phenomenon arising from the predetermined clash of particles.

Nothing could in fact be more repugnant to the bourgeois than this logical outcome of his contradictory position. Therefore bourgeois causality, or predeterminism (the only form of determinism he understands), is the bourgeois nightmare, and it induces him to lead an attack in full force on determinism or causality in physics (Jeans, Eddington, Weyl, Born, *et al*). It leads him at last to picture, by whatever immoral stratagem, the movements of the particles as indetermined; and the particles themselves as unknowable. This he supposes, at last secures his menaced free-will. But in fact free-will does not lie along this road at all.

★

Thus the neurological approach is the most fruitful to-day in scientific results, yet it is also the most destructive to bourgeois psychology and bourgeois self-esteem. Mind is a material quality, and therefore all mental phenomena are necessarily phenomena displayed by material neurones. But by 'matter' the neurologist does not understand real sensuous matter, for he is a bourgeois physicist, and moreover in most cases a Newtonian bourgeois physicist. He only understands matter as it appears in the bourgeois closed world of physics, stripped of mental qualities, a completely self-determined world excluding mind as expressing a determining relation. Therefore neurological data, growing in certainty and precision, seem more and more to dissolve psychology into something non-mental and predetermined, until we are ready to believe consciousness is an unimportant illusion. This is necessarily so, for a method of approach that sees colour, for example, as an hallucination, the *real* thing being a wave length, must even more see consciousness as an illusion, the real thing being a moving wave of potential. Thus bourgeois consciousness, in all seriousness(with maudlin regret even) denies its own existence, or, alternatively, if this 'daring' view seems dangerous, as easily and from the same fundamental position, denies the existence of anything else *but* consciousness.

Neurology, like early faculty and associationist psychologies, at first sees the problem in its simplest terms—consciousness or mind on the one hand, and on the other hand the physico-physiological world or matter. The categories of both are regarded as eternal.

Nonetheless, various considerations operate to make this simple dualism more complex. In the field of faculty or associationist psychology there is the problem of memory. Ideas vanish and then return (recollection) and return perhaps changed. But they must have been somewhere meanwhile. Where were they stowed? The answer is 'In the Unconscious'. Needless to say, this is at present no answer. To answer the question 'Where are Ideas when they are not-conscious?' with 'In the not-consciousness' is childish. However, if new laws of the process governing no-consciousness are learned, the answer is the starting point of research, and in modern psychology the Unconscious does therefore mean something.

Neurology is not perplexed by the problem in this form. Ideas, being a chance glow, can come or go, no explanation is needed. The problem here arises in a somewhat different form.

(*a*) The cortex and (*b*) the thalamus, the cerebellum, and the spinal cord represent phylogenetically different stages of the growth of the nervous sytem, and seem to correspond to different kinds of nervous behaviour—(*a*) voluntary behaviour, or willed response, corresponding to a previously conscious idea; (*b*) reflex behaviour, or innate, automatic, unchanging response to stimuli. These two forms of behaviour are not separate, but all behaviour combines differing proportions of each, and the unit of behaviour seems rather the conditioned reflex, in which an innate pattern has been modified by experience. Voluntary behaviour, in which an 'idea' is at work, is in its purest form still like a conditioned reflex, since preexisting muscular reflexes must be used in behaviour of any kind, and the 'idea' itself is a product of experience.

Thus neurology becomes the study of the integration or mutual interaction of the phylogenetically different systems of neurones, and of the modification of innate responses by experience. The 'problem' of consciousness is solved by supposing that consciousness is associated with cortical innervations, for man is highly conscious and the cortex is phylogenetically the most recent development of the nervous system. The whole problem is in fact visualised as that of the human machine, quite in the manner of Frederick's physician. The stimuli excite nervous activity, behaviour results, and at the end of the behaviour the machine is in a new position of equilibrium. This is an improvement on the closed world of physics in that it is more sensuous and therefore more material. Behaviour, attention, perception and appetite cannot be written in terms of Principles of Least Action or Lagrange's equations. But man is still subject to predeterminism; he is still merely a part of the closed world of physics surveyed from without. However much neurologists may dislike to admit it, the philosophy of neurology is mechanical materialism even where (as for example with MacCurdy), an amateurish attempt is made to escape into a Platonic doctrine of Ideas controlling formless matter ('Patterns').

★

Meanwhile gestalt psychology has been making an attempt to reconcile the associationist position with the devolopment, since Mill's time, of neurology. The gestaltists are not, however, neurologists, they do not regard mind as the iridescence accompanying the movement of particles. Since mechanical materialism is not their method of approach the gestalt psychologists are forced into the only other bourgeois alternative —idealism. Gestalt psychology is Platonic idealism.

Needless to say it is not just Platonic idealism, but bourgeois Platonic idealism altered by all that has been learned since, and moreover applied, not to a world view but to a very limited field, chiefly so far that of perception. It starts out with an apparently materialistic programme—all mental phenomena to be explained on a purely physico-chemical basis. Now we are familiar with such programmes. Physics had one —'all matter non-mental'—whose logical outcome, to the surprise of no one but the bourgeois, is that all matter proves to be—equations. In the same way, since physics and chemistry result in bourgeois science from similar restrictive programmes, a physico-chemical explanation of mental data must necessarily be dangerous. It turns out to be purely Hegelian. Gestalt psychology is objective Idealism of a kind. The psychological phenomena dealt with are the result of the activation of forms or configurations (gestalten) which are pictured as fields patterned three or even four dimensionally by variations in potential. Stimuli serve both for the activation and modification of these potential-patterns. But a form or pattern is a *concept*. Is not a concept a late product of consciousness and, if so, how can we explain mental phenomena as the result of the activation of more recent products of itself? We must therefore assume the existence of these concepts, or forms, *objectively*. Now this is Platonism if carried out half-heartedly, or Hegelianism if carried out thoroughly. It is characteristic of the anarchy of bourgeois science that every scientist, in his little province, feels himself at liberty to use for that field only categories which, if applied to the world at large, would seem to him false. The gestalt psychologist is not really a Hegelian. To bourgeois science the closed worlds of modern culture do not seem even a necessary evil; they seem to him part of the method of science, and he feels himself a scientific benefactor in building yet another of them on a small scale.

★

Meanwhile, apart from neurology and gestalt psychology, another psychology has been growing which, while least scientific in its theory, has the largest empirical content. It is perhaps the most thoroughly bourgeois in spirit and is therefore the most powerful in its influence on contemporary thought. This is the varied field of instinct psychology, of which two schools may be taken as representative: Freud's psycho-analysis and McDougall's 'hormic' psychology. There are about half a dozen others, of which Jung's, Adler's, MacCurdy's and Burrow's are the most important.

Both see life as the theatre of an indwelling force or conation (McDougall) or instinct (Freud) which is the free source of life's actions on the static environment. A sharp line is thus drawn between life and not-life, between agent and patient, in which life is always insurgent, creative and changeful, and dead matter always resigned, moulded and eternal.

The drama of the instincts then becomes a kind of bourgeois novel, in which the heroes are the instincts; and their experiences, mutual struggles and transformations generate not only all psychical but also all cultural phenomena.

Such a view is a fairly accurate description of life as it sees itself in bourgeois consciousness. It is a biological psychology, and therefore makes the same mistake as physical psychology (neurology) and mental psychology (associationism). It dichotomises life and the environment, and defines the environment as all that which possesses no living qualities. The environment is stripped of all qualities common to dead matter and life, and therefore becomes something invariant, ghostly, and unimportant. Everything emerges from within life.

This is the closed world of biology. All change, development, and quality are cooped up within it. Outside is only the Sahara of bourgeois physics, quantitative, changeless, bare. All freedom, all self-determination and all motive force therefore come within the world of life. Change is not a quality of matter but of life. It becomes a special case in the Universe, and therefore inexplicable. The biological dichotomy necessarily leads us, if we expand it, to an uncaused first cause, a Life-Force or vital spirit, which by its ingression in matter makes matter change and develop and therefore living, for change is regarded as a characteristic peculiar to life. Of course instinct psychology does not advance to such a world-view, or press its assumptions to their logical conclusion. It simply takes as a proven thing the closed world of bourgeois biology, and from it extracts the essence of living action, the instincts, which then become the postulates of psychology.

What in fact are these instincts? They are innate patterns of behaviour automatically elicited by stimuli. They are therefore inevitable recurrences amid the sea of change, like the seasons. They are determined in fact (predetermined) by past events. The absoluteness at once reveals them as quantitative abstractions, like energy or space in physics.

But this is not how the bourgeois sees them. He necessarily regards all behaviour that bursts 'spontaneously' forth from the individual ignorant of its causality, as above all free.

Therefore the instincts are conceived as freely striving for unconscious goals, and psychology becomes the adventures of the free instincts in their struggles against the restraints of the *environment* (in Freud, of *society*) which impede and cripple their freedom. Out of this struggle cognitive and emotional consciousness is born.

Now the only objection to this bourgeois psychology is that it inverts the picture. The instincts are not free springs of connation towards a goal. They are, so far as they can be abstractly separated, unconscious necessities, as Kant realised. They are unfree. But in their realisation as behaviour, when these innate things-in-themselves become things-for-themselves and interact with their environment (which also changes, and is not the dead world of physics) they also change. Above all, they are changed in human culture. As a result of this change, these necessities become conscious, become emotion and thought; they exist for themselves and are altered thereby. The change *is* the emotion or thought, and now they are no longer the instincts, for they are conscious and consciousness is not an ethereal but a material determining relationship. The necessity that is conscious is not the necessity that is unconscious. The conscious goal is different from the blind 'instinctive' goal. It is freer.

But how can bourgeois instinct psychology grasp this? The magnificent story of human culture becomes in its view simply the tragedy of the crippling of the free instincts by the social restraints they have freely created. The creation of these social restraints is arbitrary, non-causal and pointless, so that history remains thoroughly bourgeois and indetermined; and each psycho-analyst can give a different explanation of any sociological phenomenon. Experience, art and science are in this psychology the fetters of the instinctive energy; all experiences are the scars of the wounds to this freedom (inhibition and repression). Moreover the unconscious plays a strange rôle. Since experience is in this inversion of life's story the prison house of the free instincts, consciousness (the most recent and least innate products of the psyche) acts the part of gaoler to the unconscious (the most archaic and least conditioned psychic products). Quite a little coercive State reigns in the psyche, complete even to the Censor. Abominable things are done to the instincts; screams (dreams and obsessions) issue from time to time from the dungeons where the noble bourgeois revolutionaries are being tortured by the authorities. It is a picture in the best anarchist style, with the instincts resorting even to terrorism when necessary, and this terrorism is very sympathetically treated by its historians.

And yet this is untrue. It is in the process of living, in experience, that the instincts, those blind patterns, are modified by reality and, becoming conscious of its necessity, change it and themselves, and so become more free. This embrace with reality is in man mediated by the social environment. That the environment does wrongs to man's mind to-day none will deny. These wrongs are not done because consciousness imprisons the instincts with the fetters of necessity; but because bourgeois man is unconscious of the determinism of his culture. Because of this the instincts are losing such freedom as they attained, are becoming crippled, and less free. Unconsciousness and inexperience, not consciousness and experience, are the gaolers of modern bourgeois man.

2

Thus bourgeois culture cannot use even those good things which it produces. In the ideological sphere as well as the economic, it is embarrassed because it cannot consume the empirical discoveries it has made. Freud, Jung, Adler, McDougall, Kohler, Koffka, Watson, Head, Sherrington, Parsons and Mac-Curdy have all made discoveries of vital importance for the understanding of mental phenomena, but their full value is lost in the welter of bourgeois culture.

The closed, unplanned worlds of bourgeois science must be broken down, if science is once again to be coherent and fruitful. That is the task of communist science, of dialectical materialism.

Consciousness is a function of life, and we know it primarily as a function of the nervous system. Yet until we see that its relations are not intrinsically peculiar to the nervous system or even to the body as such, but contain elements common to all real matter, though these elements have been carefully rubbed out of the 'matter' of bourgeois physics, we can never escape from mentalism or mechanical materialism. The very nomenclature of modern psychology is mythological.

What is the organ of consciousness? It would be almost as-reasonable to ask of the earth, what is the organ of liquidity? The answer 'water' would not be very helpful. And yet neurology has an answer of sorts.

The optic thalamus and its outgrowths lie buried in those cerebral hemispheres whose convoluted folds of grey matter, known as the cortex, are hypertrophied in man. The properties of the thalamus have been investigated at a more recent date than those of the cortex. It represents the more primitive portion of man's brain, found well developed even in lower animals. The elaborate cortex is a rich outgrowth of this part of the brain. Naturally therefore the thalamus is regarded as the seat of man's more primitive mental functions, and the cortex of his characteristically human mentation, notably 'reason', 'intelligence,' and 'consciousness'.

The thalamus appears to be the grand shunting station for cerebral messages. All sensory relations between brain and objects, save those for smell, are 'projected' in the thalamus and then sent up to be re-projected in the cortex. Smell, however, passes straight through to the cortex. Motor messages to nerve plates in muscles also pass from the motor area of the cortex, down through the thalamus, to be distributed via the spinal cord to the body.*

The cortex consists of fold upon fold of only slightly-differentiated neurones. Its hypertrophy in man is generally correlated with the plasticity of man's behaviour. He comes into the world a *tabula rasa* for habits. Unlike the fixed instinctive reactions of the insects, his behaviour is mainly acquired. It is assumed therefore that the staggeringly complex nerve mesh of the cortex, with its hundreds of millions of cells, is the blank page on which life writes its message.

---

* Motor impulses do not actually pass through the thalamus as this passage might imply. The main motor tract passes between the thalamus and the basal ganglia. The thalamus however has connexions with other, more primitive, motor nuclei. — *Editorial Note in 1949 edition.*

This has been borne out by the study of cortical lesions. The motor habits of speech, the senses of sight and hearing, the habits of word recognition, writing, and of moving various parts of the body, have all been localised in parts of the cortex.

The primitive nature of the thalamus is suggested by comparision with animals. As one ascends in time the evolutionary tree the cortex grows in bulk, whilst the thalamus and its associations do not. Some claim that those have even diminished. It is a matter of terminology. The thalamus itself has perhaps dwindled slightly, but its associated non-cortical outgrowths, which may be assumed to share thalamic functions, have somewhat increased. There is no dispute about the quite disproportionate increase in cortical volume.

However, the argument from morphology might be faulty. The thalamus might after all be like the cortex in function. The experiments of Head, Rivers, Sherrington, and Parsons, have discovered evidence which supports the morphological argument. Where for any reason connexions between the thalamus and cortex are severed, so that the cortex is out of action, activity seems to become more instinctive. Up to a point nothing happens, and then there is a sudden and violent reaction, accompanied by emotions of disproportionate strength. This kind of action has been taken to be characteristic of instinct—the 'all or none' reaction—and hence this is held to confirm the primitive character of the thalamus.

Head's bold experiment of severing a nerve in his arm and noting the return of sensation as it healed, uncovered still more interesting phenomena. The experiment led him to differentiate between two forms of sensation, *protopathic* (or primitive) and *epicritic* (or advanced). As the nerve healed protopathic sensation first appeared; then epicritic developed, repressing the older form. One does not develop into the other: there is a dialectic 'jump'.

Protopathic sensation was discovered to have a high threshold. It was difficult to locate. When, for example in the case of pressure, the high threshold was passed, quite suddenly there was a sensation of acute discomfort, but with very poor discrimination or localisation. This 'hit and miss' character of protopathic sensation, as of a man in a rage swiping blindly at some unknown danger, had already been found to be characteristic of thalamic function. Hence Head and his followers connect protopathic or primitive sensation with the thalamus, as representing a primitive form of sensation, repressed by the evolution of the epicritic system.

The epicritic system by contrast is more discriminating, has a low threshold and does not suddenly pass into acute discomfort. This is normal sensation as we experience it.

It is therefore assumed that the cortex is part of the epicritic system, and contrasts with the thalamus. It is discriminating; it does not act rashly, in gusts, but according to the situation. In Head's view it is continually repressing the instinctive activities of the thalamus, by cortical 'backstroke', and we may equate this cortical control, it is suggested, with that rational consciousness we feel controlling our actions in actual life.

The epicritic sensations are primarily exteroceptive—as for example sight and hearing. The proprioceptive sensations may however be protopathic. As is well known, the internal organs, bones, etc., are not sensitive; we cannot feel our stomach or intestines move in peristalsis. Nonetheless when a certain threshold is passed internally, we experience a sudden agonising pain and a sensation of 'structural discomfort', dull, heavy, and alarming. This kind of sensation, as Head had already found, is characteristic of the protopathic system before the epicritic sensation has manifested itself. Presumably therefore internal sensation is still largely thalamic. Again, when we are 'thrown off our balance' by sudden gusts of rage, it is to be assumed that cortical control has vanished temporarily and our behaviour is thalamic.

This dualism was not accepted without opposition. It was for instance criticised by neurologists of the standing of Pizron. Nonetheless the general trend of research has if anything confirmed Head's distinction between cortex and thalamus, although the sharpness of many of his definitions has been modified. As a result it is usual to schematise the neurological basis of consciousness as follows: All sensation comes *via* the nerve receptors to the thalamus, where it would provoke instinctive 'all-or-none' reaction were it not for cortical control. It then passes on to the cortex, where it emerges as conscious perception. Discriminative motor habits arising out of this perception are assumed to be lodged in the cortex, while the more instinctive motorisms are located in the thalamus. Thus the general view is that consciousness is primarily, if not solely, the activation of sensation or motor traces in the cortex, and that all delicate affective shades are similarly cortical. Thalamic activity, it is assumed, is associated with unconscious or subliminal perceptions and instinctive motorisms. All violent affective outbursts, particularly severe pains, are assumed to be thalamic. The thalamus is the rebel, the seat of the unconscious, the instinctive proletariat, which that well-educated and refined bureaucracy, the cortex, with its unemotional logical consciousness, keeps (not without difficulty) in order.

At a still lower level is the bulbo-spinal system, concerned with simple reflexes. This may be omitted from our discussion for the moment.

Certain psychologists, such as Marston, have suggested that consciousness is primarily a function of the synapses. This however will not affect the present argument. Since wherever there is a nerve connexion there is a synapse, and since no one suggested all synapses are simultaneously active, the synaptic theory leaves it open as to which parts of the nervous system are in fact concerned in consciousness. In any case there are more synapses in the cortex than elsewhere. Therefore it is fair to say that the view we have outlined represents the trend of opinion, as far as there can be such a thing, amongst modern neurologists. It will be seen that it is still influenced by bourgeois biology. The free instincts are controlled by the cortex. Experience throttles unconscious life. Freedom is the unconsciousness of the necessity of reality, learned in experience.

It would however be just as accurate to picture the thalamus as the organ of conscious instinct and the cortex as the organ of unconscious thought. In either case we are simply playing about with terms. Consciousness is not so simple as that.

Cortical consciousness is equated in current neurological theory with epicritic sensation. The essence of epicritic sensation is fine discrimination. Thalamic sensation—which is *un*conscious or (as Rivers visualises it) repressed by cortical control—is lacking in discrimination. Thus a light touch on the skin, easily detected by the epicritic system, has to be increased to a hard pressure before it is perceived by the protopathic system, which then explodes affectively.

How does this theory square with the facts of consciousness?

Few of the doctrines of psychology receive more general assent than that of subliminal impressions. Impressions have to reach a certain threshold value before they are consciously perceived. That such impressions, although not perceived consciously, have yet left memory traces, *i.e.* have been perceived unconsciously, is evidenced by the fact that they can be recovered in hypnotic trance, when what is loosely called 'the unconscious' is made accessible. The phenomena of hyperaesthesia are explained in this way. Sounds, scents and cutaneous and visual discriminations not normally in the conscious field, are made accessible by the inclusion with the ego in hypnotic trance of a large part of what is normally unconscious sensation. In the same way slight impressions, separately unconscious, appear eventually by repetition to summate until they can rise above the threshold of consciousness, when the ego then becomes 'aware' of the previous repetitions.

Now this at once raises the query, damaging for the usual theory, why consciousness should show all the characteristics of protopathic sensation—restricted field and lack of fine discrimination—while unconsciousness proves itself endowed with epicritic discrimination and range of sensation. Head's view, as we have said, is that epicritic sensation 'repressed' protopathic sensation, or made it unconscious. The facts concerning subliminal impressions, if valid, contradict it. They do not however prove the reverse, for Head's own experiments show that protopathic sensation can also be conscious. The conclusion would appear to be that consciousness has nothing to do with either epicritic or protopathic sensation, nor repression with u. ..sciousness, but that we must think along other lines in order to understand what the relations are.

Let us consider such a simple question as the ordinary visual field, and its connexion with degrees of consciousness. It is well known that we do not regard the visual field as an undifferentiated whole, but that different parts of it have different values. This is expressed in the older theory of a faculty of 'attention' (which, like consciousness, has been located in the cortex) and in the *gestalt* or 'field' theory, which is really an elaborate attention psychology made objective. Thus motion of objects attracts the attention to them. We see *interesting* objects. A woman sees a bat; an artist's attention is caught by features of light and shade unnoticed by others; a detective sees a criminal face. We all tend to see shapes in shadows, figures in clouds, to fill out and round off contrasts, according to the schemes made clear by gestalt experiments. Attention is a name for the actual element in perception.

Now though we may say that all the visual field is 'consciousness', it is plain that different degrees of consciousness range over the visual field. Thus the sportsman, watching rabbits, sees a vague background with a very distinct brown animal moving over it. Perceptually the rabbit is more conscious to him than its surroundings, and more discrimination is made as to size, markings of coat, and movements in this rabbit. A botanist surveying the same scene might however see nothing clearly except a flower in the field.

Here is made plain the nature of the contradiction between epicritic and protopathic sensations and consciousness. Consciousness is at its highest point in the rabbit region of the visual field to the sportsman. Even the beast's whiskers are clear to his eye. Here sensation is epicritic.

At the same time, in the rest of the visual field nothing is consciously noted but a green blur. Here then sensation is protopathic. But in both cases sensation is conscious. The weaker conscious sensation is protopathic, the stronger epicritic. If, however, the sportsman were to be hypnotised, our knowledge of subliminal perception compels us to believe that we could recover, out of that green blur, details of perception which the sportsman had not consciously experienced. Thus here sensation, *unconscious* sensation, is epicritic. experiments with eidetic imagery seem to confirm this view.

This compels us to suppose that consciousness, in its vividness or degree or even actual existence, cannot be correlated with either epicritic or protopathic sensation. It can however be correlated with what has come to be called interest or 'attention'. Interest is an affective phenomenon. Consciousness therefore is affective tone.

To return to another feature of the cortex—the richness and plasticity of its reactions. Man's thought is almost certainly more rich and plastic than that of any animal. His range of memories, the subtlety of his discrimination among them and his faculty of language with all the richness of content it involves, are outcomes of this. Consequently we rightly regard the hypertrophied human cortex as the seat of this peculiarly human richness of association and mental structure.

But when we come to consciousness, we find in it a feature which is peculiarly uncortical—its thinness and *linear* character. Consciousness is a one-track activity. Man can normally only follow one train of thought at a time, and this train consists, even in the richest thinkers, of a succession of single images in the spotlight of consciousness, surrounded by a dim, half-conscious fuzz. None of the richness characteristic of human thought in the universal, is characteristic of consciousness in the particular. Everyone knows we can only concentrate on one thing at a time. Moreover the intimacy of the connexion is shown by the kind of inverse law it follows. The more conscious and vivid the mental product, the more linear and sparse its real content. It does not seem poor to us, because of its vividness. The height of its consciousness seems to atone for its simplicity; but still it is simple. The thing that 'worries' us and demands all our attention, obliterates all other associations. The sight of one we love makes us 'forget everything else'. The approach of a mad bull blots out the rest of the visual field.

But this is very uncortical, for the cortex is by hypothesis the seat of immensely complex motor kinaesthetic and sensory co-ordinations. Consciousness appears unable to use more than a few of these at a time; and the richer it is, the fewer they are. If we regard the human cortex, in a well-educated person, as consisting of n potentialities, consciousness at any moment can only be concerned with a minute fraction of n. The rest are unconscious. Therefore the cortex is primarily an unconscious rather than a conscious organ. It is like a library of knowledge with only one owner. Despite its immense resources, the owner at any one instant can only see one word in one line in one book, though given time and opportunity he can read what he likes and find what he likes in the realm of human knowledge.

Therefore, cortical consciousness is really chiefly cortical unconsciousness. The cortex is the great unopened dictionary, the grand reservoir of the temporarily forgotten. Consciousness in the cortex is the glowing of a few neurones out of hundreds of millions—an exception, a tiny localisation. Unless we think the unconscious of no importance, we would do better to regard the cortex as the seat of unconsciousness. This would give man a larger unconscious than the beasts, but is not this just what we would expect—is not the beast's knowledge more at its instant command, less influenced by memory and association and therefore by the temporarily forgotten but recallable? True, though forgotten is recallable, but no one would restrict the name 'unconscious' to the completely unavailable, for, if it is completely unavailable, by no means can it be proved to exist. We make therefore the suggestion that unconsciousness and not consciousness, is the distinctive feature of man's cortical outgrowth; and that this shows the weakness of current distinctions between consciousness and unconsciousnes.

★

These considerations suggest others. What governs the tiny localisation of conscious light in the vast Arctic night of the cortex? The feature of the cortex, histologically, is its lack of differentiation. Each part is like any other part. The localisations of speech and similar functions seem arbitrary. How much more arbitrary seems the local play of consciousness.

What this suggests can be shown by analogy. In a network of electrified wires we see, constant at one point, a glowing 'hot spot'. We might suppose either that this was due to a blowpipe flame from outside, applied to that spot, or to a kind of local short due to the connexions of the wires.

If, however, we saw that the hot spot moved continually about from wire to wire, we should infer, on the normal principle of induction, that there was some mobile outside cause. Either the blowpipe flame was being moved, or there was some switching apparatus continually changing the direction of the current. In either case, though the hot spot was in the wire system, we should regard it as external.

In the same way, considering the moving spotlight of consciousness in the cortical library, it seems that we must regard its movement as due to some other cause, some external switchboard. We have already correlated consciousness, both in existence and vividness, with affective tone. Assuming that the thalamus is primarily concerned in affective activity, the switching organ, directing consciousness into the local cortical channel, must be thalamic. If therefore anything has the right to be called the organ of consciousness, it would be the thalamus. But this again shows the inadequate conception of consciousness current in psychology. A conscious thought is the affective 'heating' of a cortical trace. The greater the heat, the greater the consciousness. The cortical trace is not the consciousness, because the cortex is, by assumption, an enormous mass of traces, all undifferentiated and all unconscious. The consciousness, if we must make a mere quality substantive, is the affective heat, for that and that alone produces consciousness. But actually to separate affect and idea is Aristotelean; it is like separating form and matter.

Our theory has certain analogies with the kinetic theory of heat. The molecules correspond to the cortex. The vibration of the molecules *is* the consciousness. The perpetually boiling organ, selectively communicating its vibrations, is the thalamus. Its boiling is a reflection of the whole relation between body and environment.

Since the organism is a unity, consciousness must be unitary in nature, and the more intense the vividness, the greater the limitation of consciousness. It is wrong, however, to equate this with a constant supply of conscious energy, which must therefore be either deep and thin or wide and shallow.

The reason for the limitations of content when vividness is present must be sought elsewhere. Attention to externals, *i.e.* to objects in the visual or stimulus field, is characteristic of all animals. It is simply that activity which is regarded as characteristic of life. Sensibility is a readiness to respond to certain stimuli, which in itself mplies activity towards such stimuli. Simple organisms respond to food particles in the tactile field; higher animals to prey or mates, or traces suggestive of them in the visual field. Men notice a wider range of 'things and discriminate more subtly, but always the vivid conscious part of the visual field is something that can awake their instincts, which in turn are defined as the entities which are awakened by those particular stimuli.

Thus consciousness is simply a specific feature of sensibility, a form of behaviour. Sensibility involves on the one hand an innate response to certain things and, on the other hand, certain things in the environment to be interested in. For example, in a unicellular organism, sensibility involves the tendency to be irritated by contact with small round objects (potential food) and also the small round objects at any given moment in contact with the organism.

This stimulus elicits the response, and there is no gulf, only a matter of degree, between this simple manifestation of irritability, and the sportsman with a tendency to be irritated by the rabbit and the presence of the rabbit in his visual field, both making up the consciousness of the rabbit in all its vividness.

True he is also conscious of the green blur which is the rest of the visual field. But if an organism is to be highly irritated by all small round objects that are food, like the amoeba, it must be slightly irritated, as the amoeba is, by all small round objects tactually presented. In the same way, if the animal or the sportsman is to be irritated by the presence of prey in the visual field, if he is to 'notice' them, he must be slightly irritated by the visual field as a whole and always must be slightly conscious of it. In other words, before we can become conscious of a thing, we must first become unconscious of it. We must have awareness over a wide general field.

It might be thought that the visual field, in all its inclusiveness, cannot be compared with an amoeba in tactile contact with a hard object. But in fact, the visual field is an empirical and exclusive construction. It neglects most of the possible wave-lengths of radiation, ignores distant features, and does not observe any molecular or atomic phenomena or real movements above and below a certain speed. It is in fact as much a concentration of interest as a protozon's exclusive concern with small round objects. The protozon's whole world is small round objects. Our visual field is similarly limited to phenomena which, as we evolved, have proved of interest to us, such as the common light octave (in colour).

An instinct is an innate response of a certain nature to external or somatic stimuli, or both. We should not consider an animal as possessing instincts but only potential instincts, just as the cortex as a whole is not conscious but only potentially conscious. We should regard instinct only as it appears in behaviour, as a response to some situation. It is true that we should thus never get a pure instinct, for the situation is always slightly different and therefore even in insects the behaviour is always slightly different. This is all to the good.

This would simplify the theory of mentation. Living response or sensibility, including conscious mentation, consists of potential instincts, which is the whole sum of inborn responses to somatic stimuli or environmental stimuli. This is a purely fictive conception, but methodologically useful, like the 'genotype' in heredity. Actually nothing is ever known, either in behaviour or in consciousness, except potential instinct reacting to its somatic or environmental stimuli and being changed thereby. Where we part company with the behaviourist, who does not recognise consciousness, is that we recognise consciousness and include it as a form of behaviour. Thus we regard the visual field as instinctive behaviour modified by experience. It is the instinctive response of the cortical and thalamic projective areas to stimuli. The stimuli are to us so complex in the normal visual field that we naïvely regard them as 'all reality', instead of just a selection from it. This brings conscious perception within the field of causality. It determines and is determined, and this we already know from quantum physics. Observation is an active process—a return to Cartesian theories of vision on a higher plane.

Instincts are modified in experience. Some, like those of the insects, are only slightly modifiable. Others, like the dog's food response or man's various responses to stimuli, are capable of far more conditioning. This can be regarded as an enriching or complicating of them. Thus the instinctive visual field of the baby is modified, and made richer and more discriminating, in the grown man. Innate behaviour becomes in experience complex behaviour. This is a simple dialectic law of development.

The visual field is a conditioned, instinctive response to stimuli. There is a slight response to a large number of stimuli, which we may call simply vision. This slight sensory response guarantees the visual, aural or tactual field as a whole. Under the influence of some more specialised innate response—to prey, mates or danger—we notice more eagerly, more consciously and more vividly some one object in that visual, aural, or tactile field. We behave towards it in a different way. The greater specificity of the response makes us consider a unit instinct is at work, but this is only a name for a consistent difference in behaviour towards a class of objects. It is thus determined also by the environment.

The linear nature of consciousness, limited in proportion to its vividness, is therefore necessary. Instinct is action. The efficiency of the body and its very survival can only be secured by the fact that it acts integrally. The higher the organism, the more true we find this integration of response, a unity in diversity. Since consciousness is part of the complete response, it must be all of a piece with the rest of the response, including the body's overt action. This means we must only see or think of those things most immediately relevant to the instinctive action as a whole. Thus the tendency of the organism to flee from danger ensures that, when danger appears in the visual field, the organism is not conscious of its tailor's unpaid bill, what it ate for dinner last week, or the infinity of the Universe, but only of the mad bull, and the nearest exit from the field, while at the same time the body's response is limited to visceral vaso-motor constriction, emission of adrenalin into the blood from the suprarenal glands, and rapid running movement with the legs.

Plainty the ego, insofar as we regard it as the stream of consciousness, is our name for this fact. The integrity of the organism creates the ego, not the ego the organism.

The association of affects or emotions with the instincts has always been puzzling. The 'instincts' seem to give rise to affects, and yet instinctive activity can appear without them.

Restricting ourself to the case of conscious perception of a dangerous object in the visual field, we see that there are two elements in the response—intra-somatic behaviour (adrenalic secretion and so forth)—and extra-somatic (running). The first assists the scond. Vision is only involved as a part of action, and is stripped of all but its bare essentials for the purpose. Therefore the simpler the extra-somatic response, the more 'one-to-one' its correspondence with innate reflexes, the less the need for the activation of the cortical traces of experience. Both affect and consciousness are therefore functions of the complexity of the potentially stimulating field, and its relation to the modified reflexes of the organism.

Certain animals, for example the insects, in spite of elaborate instinctive activity, are closely geared to an unvarying chain. The sphex will sting only one species of wasp, and only in a certain way. There is therefore in spite of the complexity of the overt behaviour, a poverty of alternative objects and a poverty of alternative behaviour. The correspondence is virtually one-to-one. We should expect such creatures to experience no affects and no consciousness. Stimuli and reflexes match perfectly and weave an almost unvarying fabric.

Nonetheless we must regard consciousness as a matter of degree. Just as heat and cold are simply varying rates of molecular motion, which we divide subjectively into 'hotter than ours,' and 'colder than ours,' consciousness and unconsciousness simply represent degrees of affective vividness. Many states subliminal for us might well be blinding consciousness for fishes. Even in insects there cannot be anything like perfect one-to-one correspondence of innate instinct to stimulus. There is no absolute degree of consciousness. It is the ego that is conscious but the ego in turn is composed of a series of experiences selected above a certain indistinct threshold. Naturally, to this ego anything below the threshold seems unconscious, but this is merely because it is the ego which is doing the description.

★

The conception of a switchboard is often used for neural operations. It seems less objectionable than most analogies, for the neurone undoubtedly has junctions, and transmits impulses along its length by means of waves of potential difference. But it differs from a switchboard in having no operator, a fact which causes psychologists to invent instincts, consciousness, and egos which operate the switches. Perhaps the automatic telephone may eliminate these mythical deities. The brain is an extremely elaborate automatic telephone system, in which the stimuli are the subscribers dialing, in which the apparatus is modified by experience, and in which the body is part of the system—flesh, blood and all.

In all switchboard schematisations of the neural system, the cortex is pictured as the seat of a highly competent Postmaster-General, directing all the other chains of relays, down to the humble reflexes in the basement. This P.M.G. is usually equated with consciousness. Our hypothesis has no use for this over-worked official.

If we must personify, let us personify the thalamus, and let us imagine it, at a primitive level, faced with the task of making more epicritic its sensations, and its action more discriminating. It will do so by manufacturing an intricate system through which sensations and motor activities can be relayed, sorted out, stored and recombined, and where the increased complexity of the possible combinations will make more epicritic the actions. In other words, the cortex (if we must personify) is the *servant* of the thalamus rather than the master. (But either picture is inaccurate.)

Any engineer faced with the task of increasing the possible combinations of a given circuit—*e.g.* the number of telephone numbers dialable—would at once see that some 'hierarchy' must be called for. A must control B and C; in turn B will control D and E and C will control G and F, and so on. Only in this way can unity of action as well as discrimination, be secured. Yet it is just unity which is the feature of consciousness, represented in the ego and its linear form of thought. Hence for the arbiter or controller of cortical activity, we must look to some concentrated organ holding all the cortical threads in its hands. This would be, for sheer mechanical reasons, the optic thalamus.

Consciousness streams on with different contents, yet we

feel there is an unchanging basis for it, sharing all experiences alike. This unchanging basis, this ego, is something that has access to vast stores of experience, but itself maintains its general pattern. This would correspond to the thalamus, through which all active ingoing and outgoing impulses pass, but which has itself little mnemonic grey matter. The cortex on the other hand is highly mnemonic.

Let it be understood that we do not regard consciousness as exclusively thalamic, or the ego as seated in the thalamus and its outgrowths. This is to make the mistake of the mythologists. The thalamus, because of its strategic position, is the spear-point of consciousness. Consciousness is a behaviour of the whole nervous system. It is one of a number of conditioned responses to stimuli.

Inhibition is a feature of consciousness but is not peculiar to it. The amoeba performs, in response to a given stimulus, one out of several possible actions. The others therefore are inhibited. The organism which runs in response to danger inhibits other possible actions. The organism which thinks is innervating certain neurone groups, corresponding to older motor and sensory groupings, and this constitutes a thought or wish or feeling, one out of many possible, the others being inhibited or unconscious.

Consider a definite situation: *There is a bull in the field of vision.* This stimulus, as a result of thalamic switching, activates adrenal and visceral innervations, and produces a general somatic readiness to make the fear-response. Owing to the nature of the situation, the choice of flight or fighting, and the different paths available for both—there is a good deal of thalamic sparking among different possible muscular reactions, and these thalamic sparkings correspond to fear-consciousness. Some of the energy as a result of more thalamic switching flows into the cortex, where it innervates nerve groups corresponding to thoughts of danger, possible paths, and vague remorse at having taken the wrong shortcut—all glowing with the fear affect. No fear affect, no consciousness of these thoughts.

Thus the conscious field consists of protopathic visceral circuits, a mediating thalamic circuit, and an epicritic cortical circuit. We cannot say that consciousness is located exclusively in any one of these circuits. True, no one is conscious without a cortex, but neither are they conscious without a thalamus. All are concerned; all are integrated in the one response to the stimulus; all combine to produce the one common conscious field.

In this pressing danger, we might examine the bull more closely. We then draw on the traces in the cortical retinal area, to discriminate more closely the features of the bull. Could it be pacified? Is it a large one? Could we side-step its charge? This more discriminating perception, in which memory enters, is the thalamus drawing on the cortex for information, or if we like, it is an affectivity piling up and leaking into other cortical areas.

We may visualise the bulbo-spinal area as the home of innate reflexes which experience will not greatly change. The cortex on the other hand is the place where all motor and sensory experiences leave traces, which because of their elaborate wiring, will be more discriminating, more easily split up and more plastic and learnable than elsewhere. Moreover since their knowledge will be required when instinct has not a one-to-one correlation between stimulus and response, it is precisely the cortical cells which will receive the affective glow of a 'puzzled thalamus sparking and trying various alternative lines. This emotion will therefore be always associated with cortical contents, except in severe pains or thalamic protopathic explosions. Hence our mistaken belief that it is a matter of cortical 'control'.

Rather is it a matter of cortical advice. The thalamus might plead that it is only 'human' and cannot remember everything, and neurologists would admit that its deficiency in grey matter would explain its poor memory. Nevertheless, as a result of aeons of experience, with comparatively little differentiation, it is a magnate of strong will and simple notions. It has the main policy of the firm at its finger tips. Such persons are normally put at the helm of power. At its service, however, it has a staff of experts, and in any ordinary circumstance it consults them (thought). Naturally, in view of their experience, it acts on their advice. The body of experts might therefore claim that they control their chief. Nonetheless the reality of thalamic power is shown in all emergencies calling for instantaneous motor response of a nature so simple that the thalamus has known it for centuries. The cortex is ignored. Again, if a complex situation recurs, even the thalamic memory is sufficient to deal with the situation. This is habit.*

Consciousness might be regarded as an affective light, which plays upon cortical, thalamic, visceral and sensory neurones.** They 'clump' together and separate out. Hence our elaborate classifications of conscious affects, feelings, thoughts, memories and percepts—all purely bogus, if we regard them as describing separate entities. Naturally a cortical neurone, under affective activity, 'feels' different to a visceral or sensory neurone, because it has a different chronaxy, composition, architecture and mnemonic past, but its feeling is pooled in the common structure.

If Marston is right, and consciousness is a synaptic phenomenon, this would account for the variation of affectivity. A simple reflex would not be conscious, because the synapses are firmly 'closed'. When however they are open there is a sparking, which is an affect and goes to compose consciousness. In protopathic systems a heavy stimulus would be needed to open the somewhat 'rusty' synapses, but the spark would be correspondingly intense and explosive. The smooth 'frictionless' synapses of the cortex and epicritic sensory system open and close quietly. The cortex appears to control and modify response as a whole, because it forms a part of most circuits. It corresponds to a capacitance effect in radio. There is no 'seat'

---

* There is no evidence to support the view that an habitual response to a complex situation is dependent on 'thalamic memory'. Rather would the work of Pavlov's school and recent experience of head injuries suggest that an intact cortex is essential for this type of response. By contrast with the emergency situation described above however such a familiar situation will evoke a response with a minimum of affect and consciousness—i.e. be another example of the role of the cortex as the organ of unconsciousness. — *Editorial Note*.

** Cortical, 'thalamic', visceral and sensory neurones. The meaning of the passage is obscured by this classification, since sensory neurones are both thalamic and cortical, and visceral are mainly thalamic. What is clearly intended however is a contrast between the cells of the cortex and those of the evolutionariy older parts of the brain, including the thalamus. — *Editorial Note*.

of integration in an organism. Integration, precisely because it is integration, is the function of the entire organism.

Directed thinking is an affective river in the cortex. All thinking has a strong affective component, otherwise it would not be conscious. Why (to take apparently the least affective intance) do we turn over one of thousands of possible mathematical problems? Because that one interests us. Interest is nothing but affect.

The affective association of conscious ideas, rediscovered by Freud and Janet, is not therefore odd, but the only possible law of conscious thought considered subjectively. Affects are the stuff of ideas. Association by contiguity is meaningless neurologically. It explains association of ideas by another idea, that of contiguity. Needless to say ideas whose original stimuli are spatio-temporally contiguous, are likely to share the same affective tone, and as such are likely to revive together. Given in every experience is a subject and object. Association by contiguity is objective association of experiences.

Whether it is the cat springing precisely on its prey, or the mathematician solving a problem, the behaviour is the same in principle. First there is the tendency called forth by the stimulus—the desire to solve the problem. Then the conformity of the behaviour with reality, that is the flowing of the affective current of interest, by elaborate and tortuous synaptic paths, among just those cortical cells which experience has shown to be necessary. The animal stalking its prey fatigued and stung by the brushwood, and the mathematician, with wrinkled brow, solving the thorny problem, are both exhibiting the same behaviour, except that the animal's is overt, the mathematician's intra-somatic. The exultant pounce of the animal, fatigue forgotten, and the joyful 'Eureka!' of the mathematician, his frown changing to a smile, are evidences of similar terminations to the transaction.

Sleep frees us from attention to present reality. It inhibits by closing the sensory roads (a patient with anaesthesia of the

---

* This is controversial but if incorrect does not vitiate the argument, since the rhinopallium, or part of the cortex which deals with smell, is much more akin to the thalamus than other parts of the cortex. — *Editorial Note.*

skin is liable to fall asleep at any moment). Since the cortex is the great storehouse of memory, *i.e.* of recent reality, it is asleep. We never smell in dreams,* and smell alone of the senses goes to the cortex without thalamic intervention. In sleep, the 'instinct', or 'innate tendency' to conform to reality, which is simply the connexion of the cortex to the nervous circuit, is cut off. Our learning is forgotten. We mould our thoughts like a child. The thalamus reveals that, without his advisers he is in spite of his energy a savage. The strongly visual character of dreams is presumably due to the large retinal projection on the thalamus.*. The fact that most dream contents can be referred to the previous day, might be attributed to the unmnemonic character of the thalamus. There may be some cortical activity in dream, but the primitive proto-pathic character of dream sensations, the indistinct faces, the condensation of images—which would be characteristic of a non-discriminating organ—all seem thalamic. Since we have not equated consciousness with the cortex, the vividness and reality of dreams, present no difficulty. Dreams are the op-posite to '*déja vue*' phenomena, in which real percepts seem memories. In dream, memories seem real percepts. The former some psychiatrists attribute to thalamic inactivity; the latter therefore we attribute to thalamic activity. By active and in-active, we mean active and inactive relatively to the cortex.

Now all this is very well as far as it goes. We have tried to join the two ends of mental and biological psychology. But we reach a certain point with neurology, and then are up against the difficulty that neurology is a branch of biology, that outside stands the closed world of bourgeois physics, and, arbitrarily planted on top of the closed world of neurology, is the closed world of mentalism, or bourgeois faculty psycho-logy. By the very definitions of bourgeois psychology, we are

---

* Thalamus and vision. The thalamus was at one time known as the optic thalamus, a misnomer since the fibres of the optic tract do not relay in the thalamus. There are however other relay stations in the optic appa-ratus which may play a similar rôle in regard to visual stimuli. It is ob-vious that dreams are not wholly explicable on the basis of thalamic acti-vity and that a cortical elementt must be assumed. The general argument, that in the dream state the rôle of the thalamus is dominant, can however be supported. — *Editorial Note.*

forced to regard innervations and thoughts, nerves and consciousness, matter and mind as distinct classes of entities, mutually exclusive. Until dialectical materialism has broken down this exclusiveness, not only in psychology but in physics, biology, philosophy and sociology, how can we begin to formulate a theory of consciousness that will not be dualistic and strained?

But we can perhaps indicate the road, starting from the foundations. We must sweep away the concept of the bourgeois in opposition to and separate from the environment.

In this Newtonian schematisation, the bourgeois and the environment obey entirely different laws; the bourgeois stops at his skin. The consciousness is 'something' that sits inside, while outside 'reality' raps on the nerve-endings in code, which code is 'interpreted' inside the skin. This is precisely how Edington formulates the situation, evidently believing it to be the 'scientific' view.

But in fact the bourgeois is only an organised whirlpool of matter in his environment, constantly changing, constantly being renewed. The consciousness is the organisation of a part of it, but the organisation is not separate from the matter, like a concept or universal. The matter is organised. The organisation is a quality of matter.

The Universe becomes. Not merely man becomes, but change motion and development are the law of the Universe. The Universe does not change and become in Time. Relativity and quantum physics clearly show the time *is* the change, and the becoming. All phenomena A, B, and C, etc. are connected so that A is included in B, B in C, C in D, and so on. This inclusion in difference is Becoming, development, and reality. This involves a substratum of likeness in the Universe, that which changes, that which is the same in all change. This we abstract as space, as the aspects of matter expressed in the conservation laws (mass, energy, interval, action). This we regard as the stuff of the Universe. This is what mathematics, is concerned with, what quantity is, what the basis is of all predictive laws of science.

But equally it involves a superstructure of unlikeness in the Universe—the change as change, the difference in all events.

This we abstract as Time, as the qualities in matter not obeying conservation laws (colour, consciousness, beauty). This we regard as the *aspect* of the Universe, precisely because it is the difference that interests us. This is quality, the basis of all art and sensuous culture.

But any absolute dichotomy into reality and appearance, space and time, matter and motion, primary and secondary qualities, or object and subject, is erroneous and denies the reality either of change or of existence. Both are intimately blended in becoming. It is not separate things that become entirely in themselves, but the Universe is one, there are determining relations between all phenomena. These determining relations are the becoming. If any group were self-determined, it would be unknowable and unknowing in its relations to the rest, and would not therefore exist. The Universe is a material unity.

This is true, not merely of life but of all that is, from consciousness to physics, and this guarantees that these worlds cannot in fact be closed nor their laws remain unchanged. And change, the increase in organisation, is newness; it is what consciousness is. But we can never set something aside, and say: this is entirely new, it has no old in it—for that would be to *separate* something from the Universe, to deny change and dichotomise becoming.

The like, that which remains, is, in the biological sphere, instinct and habit and heredity. The unlike, that which is new, is experience, knowledge and acquired characters. Each generates the other in dialectic movement. In the evolution of consciousness, instinct is experience, gives rise to memory and affect, and is now no longer the old instinct. We may lodge experience in the cortex and instinct in the bulbo-spinal system, but both can only be separated in abstraction. There is only bodily behaviour, that is, material becoming in which body and environment are involved.

Body and environment are in constant determining relations. Perception is not the decoding of tappings on the skin. It is a determining relation between neural and environmental electrons. Every part of the body not only affects the other parts but also determines relations with the rest of reality. It is determined by it and determines it, this interchange producing development—the constantly changing series of interlocking events, A, B, C ... Of this multitude of relations, spatiotemporal, perceptual and mnemonic, we distinguish a certain group, changing as the world changes, not with it or separately from it but in mutually determining interaction with it. This election, rich, highly organised and recent, we call the consciousness, or our ego. We do not select it out. In the process of development it separates out, as life separated out, as suns and planets and the elements separated out from the process of becoming. Separated out, and still changing, it is consciousness, it is *us* in so far as we regard ourselves as conscious egos. But in separating out, it does not completely separate out, any more than any elements did. It remains, like them, in determining relation with the rest of the Universe, and the study of the organisation of this developed structure, of its inner relations and the relations of the system with all other systems in the Universe, is psychology—not bourgeois psychology, but the psychology of dialectical materialism.

We can say that such a psychology will only purge itself of the dualisms and anarchy of present-day psychology by realising that it is the science of the minds of men living in concrete society. These men are material bodies entering into social relations with each other and the rest of the material universe. This means the abandonment of the mythical categories of bourgeois psychology, which has proved itself unable to advance beyond the conception of the abstract individual psyche, the self-consciousness of the individual in civil society —in a society where the individual, because society has not yet found itself, has lost himself.

THE CRISIS IN PHYSICS

I

FROM NEWTON TO EINSTEIN

1. THE NEW SCHOOL IN PHYSICS

The crisis in physics, which a few years ago was the secret of physicists, has now become generally shared with the public. Even the man in the street is aware that all is not well with physics; and that in many cases the cracks which are rapidly developing in the structure have been stopped up by mystical notions new to science. It is proclaimed by distinguished physicists that 'determinism' or 'causality' has been expelled from physics; that the Universe is the creation of a mathematician; and that its real nature is unknowable. Jeans, Schrodinger, Heisenberg, Dirac and Eddington are prominently associated with these ideas; all are distinguished physicists. They are opposed by Planck and Einstein, whose prestige is the chief weapon in their defence of the older positions. For their defence is a kind of stone-walling; they are unable to lead any counter-attack on the enemy positions. Planck's justification of 'causality' is that it is the scientist's faith, his anchor, the unprovable fundamental of science. Einstein's tactics are even simpler; he 'cannot understand' what the younger men mean.

Evidently the new school do not need to trouble about dislodging their antagonists from such ineffective philosophical positions and, with the support of the bishops and the spiritualists, they advance to occupy the new territory they have marked out. Of course it is impossible to ignore the opposition of Planck and Einstein. Einstein is the father of relativity physics and Planck the originator of quantum physics. Both were 'revolutionary' in their day. Even Planck's faith and Einstein's incomprehension therefore have pulling power over the undecided. But the younger men include Heisenberg, Schrödinger and Dirac whose technical achievements are of a similarly 'revolutionary' character. There is no doubt that the new school is winning mass support in its struggle for a more mysterious Universe.

The cause of the crisis in bourgeois physics is sometimes held to be the contradiction between macroscopic or relativity physics on the one hand, and quantum or atomic physics on the other. The concepts with which each domain works are irreconcilable. But it would be wrong to suppose that this contradiction is the real cause of the present crisss in physics. The crisis is too general for that. This particular contradiction is only one of the forms in which the crisis comes to light.

2. NEWTON'S UNIVERSE

There has in fact been a contradiction between two domains of physics ever since the days of Huyghens. Newton's system of Nature, which included the corpuscular theory of light, formed a consistent scheme of the Universe, apparently free from contradictions, built up on an atomistic basis. All particles behaved according to a simple law of motion which uniquely determined the life-line of each particle. The system was of such a character that an 'initial push-off' and an initial fabrication of the atoms out of nothing was necessary. These initial acts were creative acts of God. God thus appears in the Universe as force and substance alienated from Himself. But once created, these two categories are subject to laws of the conservation of matter and energy. Given its initial push-off and creation, the atomistic universe is self-running.

Newton however does not regard it in this light, for his conception of substance is such, as we shall see later, that the maintenance of these laws in fact requires the continual intervention of God.

Thus such a Universe does not exclude the possibility of divine interference with its own laws, but it is always a disruption of very simple laws, and hence is bound increasingly to appear an unaesthetic act.

In the medieval and Aristotelian schemes of the Universe, motion requires the constant expenditure of force, apart altogether from laws governing the action of forces. Hence the

Universe needs the continual inflow of Divinity, as a Prime Mover, to keep it going. Evidently therefore Newton's atomistic scheme gives a basis for deleting God from the Universe as a causal influence once it is treated. The laws of God then become qualities of matter. As compared with Aristotle's, Newton's laws of motion desacralize physics; and they culminate in Laplace's divine calculator, who, knowing the speed and location of every particle in the Universe at a given time, can predict the whole future course of events throughout infinite Time. Nature becomes a machine, but of course one can still ask with Paley: 'Who made the machine?'

Newtonian physics excludes God from Nature, but not from Reality, because it makes Nature only a part of Reality as a result of its particulate conception of Matter.

3. THE WAVE THEORY OF LIGHT

The experimental disproof of the corpuscular theory of light shattered this Universe in the eighteenth century and Laplace's divine calculator had in fact already been proved an impossibility before he emerged from the brain of the French mathematician. It was proved that light rays did not have the character of corpuscles but of waves.

Now everyone had seen waves, and therefore there seemed nothing startling in this conception. But waves as witnessed are waves in something: they are a certain type of movement of water particles. But in the succeeding years, light waves, although they continued to behave like waves in water, proved to be waves of nothing. This raised problems of a critical kind, but the deepness of the contradiction and the gravity of the crisis were only gradually realized.

It is true that this nothing was given a name: the ether. Ether, it was explained, was not matter; its properties were *sui generis*. Unfortunately all these *sui generis* properties proved to be negative. Ether offered no resistance to matter. Ether had no chemical properties. Ether was frictionless, weightless, invisible, and unaffected by the passage of matter through it.

Its final and utter negativity was revealed by the Michelson-

Morley experiments. Since the one certain *sui generis* property of the ether was that light waved in it, then at least a property peculiar to light waves in motion could be recorded of it: the speed of this motion as compared to the earth's. An ingenious apparatus was constructed based on this argument: The earth moves through the ether; light waves are waves in the ether; hence if the movement of light waves relative to the earth across a given distance is measured first across the earth's path and then with the earth's path there will be a discrepancy. This discrepancy will show the earth's real speed through the ether.

In fact the result was null. There was no disrepancy. The logical assumption was that the ether moved at the same speed as the earth. But could the earth possibly drag all the ether of infinite space with it? This was contradicted by observations of the stars; and the phenomenon of 'aberration'. These observations, and also experiments with 'ether-whirling' machines, excluded the only logical deduction from the experiment; that bodies dragged along with them the ether in their vicinity.

4. THE BEGINNING OF THE CRISIS

Hence physicists were faced with the proof that light waves were waves of nothing—evidently an unacceptable statement, for it is meaningless. The only escape from this was a theory that circumstances always mysteriously changed to prevent our observing the earth's motion through the ether. This alternative was adopted under the name of the Fitzgerald contraction. It was assumed that matter moving through the ether contracted along the line of advance so as exactly to conceal the very discrepancy of measurement, which would reveal the speed of the earth.

This conception was not so fantastic as it sounds, for meanwhile matter had revealed electro-magnetic qualities, and electric and magnetic fields had been proved to obey a set of equations, developed by Clerk-Maxwell, which also controlled the emission of light. Light waves were special forms of electromagnetic waves. Analysis of the electro-magnetic equations showed that they might be interpreted to mean that matter would contract to the required extent as a result of its motion through the ether. The Fitzgerald contraction was widely accepted as a fact of Nature, and the solution of the crisis.

Meanwhile the nature of ether remained unknown, its specification included factors that insured its unknowability. Science found on its hands that metaphysically **unmanageable** enntity, the unknowable.

For in fact the unknowable cannot exist; even to say that it is unknowable is to say we know something about it; and when further we say it is unknowable for certain reasons(as we must if unknowable is to be more than a mere word) we specify certain of its qualities, although in an inverted way.

If this position was to be taken seriously, either the ether was completely unknowable and therefore did not exist, being merely the nominative of 'to undulate' or else relative motion through the ether was unknowable, in which case this too did not exist. In either case this unknowability defined certain definite characters of the knowable entities, light and motion. 'Omnia determinatio est negatio.'

5. RELATIVE AND ABSOLUTE MOTION

This revealed a contradiction which was already extant in the Newtonian scheme, whereas the other contradiction had emerged as a result of the discovery empirically of what were held to be undulatory characteristics in light. All the Newtonian particles were in motion, and for example each particle's velocity gave its kinetic energy, if squared and multiplied by its mass. Its energy and mass therefore seemed real self-subsistent entities. But no particle can move in relation to itself, only in relation to something else. Thus a car moving along a road at 30 m.p.h. encounters another at 30 m.p.h. moving in the opposite direction. Relative to each other they are moving at 60 m.p.h. However, we say each is 'really' moving at 30 m.p.h. because that is their speed in relation to the earth of which the road is a part. But the earth is turning on its own axis and circling the sun; and therefore that car which moves with the earth's rotation and orbital motion is, in relation to the sun, travelling some thousands of m.p.h. faster than the other car. Indeed in relation to the sun, a more important body than the earth, the car is not moving forward at all, but hurtling backwards. Yet the sun is not fixed, but itself moves in relation to the stars, and these themselves move in relation to each other. Hence unless some body at absolute rest can be found, it is impossible to find the true speed of any particle, and hence its energy, and hence its inertia and hence its mass. These can only be found relatively, and in any case, even if such a body at absolute rest does exist, the mass, energy and inertia are still relative and not self-subsistent. Only the resting body could be regarded as self-subsistent. Newton realized these difficulties in a general way and only talked of bodies absolutely at rest with the proviso, 'if any such exist'.

Now if the speed of the earth through the ether could have been determined, then the ether could have been assumed to be at absolute rest, and this would provide a cosmic framework for detecting the absolute or 'true' motion of all particles. But we have seen that motion produced the Fitzgerald contraction, exactly concealing the velocity.

However this Fitzgerald contraction itself conceals a contradiction. The length of a body contracts as a result of its motion through the ether. But this in itself implies an 'absolute' length, which is the length of a body at rest in the ether. But since it is impossible to establish the rest or motion, of a body in the ether, absolute length is as unknowable as absolute motion. Since the Fitzgerald contraction is unknowable, it cannot be held really to exist. It is merely another negative determination of moving bodies.

Motion *includes* time: a certain space is traversed in a certain time. But in concrete reality time is not built up into motion is 'broken down' into time. The movement of a body is, in a clock, analysed into movement in space and duration of time. Hence if absolute or time motion and length (or space) are both unknowable, then this is equally so of absolute time, for the motion of bodies will be broken down into different components of space and time by different observers.

The ultimate conclusion of a chain of reasoning which we

have only briefly indicated here was that the absolute dimensions, time, and velocity, energy and mass of any particle were unknowable. They did not exist in themselves, or in relation to a unique framework, but were properties of relative frameworks.

6. THE SPECIAL PRINCIPLE OF RELATIVITY

Einstein recognized that these unknowabilities were in fact important principles of knowledge about nature, and he formulated them as the special Principle of Relativity.

This states that absolute length, mass, energy, space, time, and motion do not exist. But before this Principle could be formulated as a scientific principle and not a metaphysical doctrine, it was necessary to establish the relativity of these qualities in a practical way. Although the Principle of Relativity has an epistemological content, it is not a principle of epistemology, but of science. It describes the limits of our knowledge about reality in such a way that these limits become real descriptions of the nature of matter in relation to us. This was only possible because the previous experiments which had established these limits, had furnished a fund of real knowledge about Nature. This fund could not be used by the existing theory of Nature. On the contrary, these practical results contradicted this theory, which therefore had to be recast in a form fuller of practice.

As long ago as Lucretius philosophers have advanced theories as to the relativity of motion and the secondary and dependent character of abstract Time.* But all such theories were purely metaphysical and could be countered by opposing theories of equal logical worth. It was because the Special Principle of Relativity co-ordinated and gave a meaning to a mass of empirical observations, that it was of importance to physics, and made deeper man's understanding of the Universe.

---

* 'Time also exists, not by itself but simply from the things that happen.' Lucretius.

7. UNITY AND ATOMICITY

Yet this at once brought to light a still older contradiction, which had also been immanent in the Newtonian Scheme. The Newtonian 'bodies' were self-contained units which had each been created with an initial mass and an initial packet of kinetic energy in the form of mass multiplied by the square of the speed which enabled them to lead a wholly independent life in the shape of a right line. Unless they collided physically with another particle, the existence of each was self-contained and unchequered. In such a Universe, unless a collision took place, nothing 'happened' and even such a happening merely meant than the two particles continued on right lines at different angles and speeds. Happenings in such a Universe are therefore completely accidental in this sense, that they represent the intersections of two chains of events (the 'life-lines' of the particles) which are self-contained and self-subsistent. They are also completely predetermined in that, given the relative positions and velocities of the particles at any time in their history, it would have been possible to predict their collision with certainty.

Such a Universe is of course completely pluralistic. It has no organic unity. The history of the other particles has no effect on the history of one. From the point of view of the particles all happenings are complete accidents. From the point of view of observers of the particles, all happenings are completely predetermined necessities.

Such an ideal Universe is however only partly the Universe of Newton, which already contains another unifying principle, as 'mysterious' and 'transcendent' as God, contradicting the atomism of the Universe. This mysterious principle is rendered necessary by observation. In fact none of the particles travel on right lines but all are more or less curved by the effects of the other particles. This curvature is therefore of gravity, an intangible entity whose real nature is unknowable—it can only be expressed in terms of its 'effect' on the paths of the particles, which it causes to curve towards each other in different degrees, the shape of the curve depending on the mass-velocity of the particles concerned.

Since this force affects all particles, it is as resolutely monistic as the other conception is pluralistic. In this sense no particle's path it self-contained, for to specify it with perfect accuracy the mass and location of every other particle in the Universe must be known. Thus no happening—no collision of particles—is entirely accidental, for in the life of every particle the lives of all other particles have been bound up from the start, and no collision is a collision of two absolutely independent chains of events. For the same reason no event is completely predetermined, for to estimate it, all precedent events must be taken into consideration by the calculator whose own consideration therefore becomes an element in the problem, provoking a new situation, making it as insoluble as if a man were to try to climb to a height great enough to look down on himself.*

This principle appears to be something apart from the qualities of matter, which are all self-subsistent in the individual particle. In the Newtonian scheme each particle is a complete individualist, unrolling from its past history its complete future fate, even though that fate may be continually interrupted by accidents (collisions). But the force of gravity is a kind of omnipresent Power, apparently non-material, since it acts across a distance. Indeed, it is evident that to Newton all action of this kind is closely associated with the idea of God. Our subsequent examination of seventeenth century metaphysics will show that this whole atomic Universe was built on the hypothesis of God. Hence the force of gravity already appears as the result of a metaphysic which divides the Universe into matter and non-matter. This had important consequences for the subsequent development of physics. The Newtonian combination of monism and atomicity had this logical defect, that it stated certain laws of motion, which determined uniquely the lifelines of all particles. Then to these laws it added the proviso, in the form of the Law of Gravity, that these Laws could never be obeyed, for another force applying to

---

* This is Planck's argument in favour of free will and I have quoted it as an example of the deepest understanding of necessity to which mechanical materialism can attain.

particles between themselves would always modify these laws relating to particles in-themselves.

In the Newtonian Scheme, the quality which carries on the particle in its independent life-line is 'inertia'. That quality which everywhere alters or distorts this life-line from the path it should follow as an independent unit is 'mass'.

'Inertia' is therefore the quality determined by the laws which govern the independent motion of individual particles; mass is the quality determined by the laws which govern the mutual attraction of particles. These laws are expressed by their effects on each other. The laws of motion produce a distortion of gravitational behaviour, as in centrifugal action. The law of gravity produces a distortion of inertial behaviour, as in gravitational force. And yet, by an apparently amazing coincidence, inertia is always equal to mass.

Although this statement endured for over two centuries, evidently there is something gravely suspicious about its formulation. The very facts that inertia and mass are equal and that one set of laws is expressed in terms of deviation from the other set, and vice versa, points overwhelmingly towards a synthesis of these laws into a common set. Yet one—the set of laws regarding motion—is based on the conception of the Universe as composed of independent particles of matter. The other—the gravitational law—gives us a Universe which is an all-containing force of Unification, where the shudder of a leaf on earth is reflected in a corresponding alteration of gravitational forces on Sirius. Evidently then the required synthesis must

(a) Reduce mass and potential energy and inertia and kinetic energy to a common basis.

(b) Express the laws of motion and of gravity as derivatives from one fundamental law.

(c) Reconcile the atomicity of matter particles* with the monism of gravitational attraction.

* 'Mass-points' in the technical vocabulary of physics.

8. THE GENERAL PRINCIPLE OF RELATIVITY

Such a synthesis remains a mere theory as long as it is based only on logical considerations. But meanwhile a number of physical discoveries had intervened to give the contradiction an observational basis. These facts had already led to the Special Theory of Relativity. The Special Theory denied the existence of absolute distance—yet the Newtonian force of gravity is a product of distance and mass. Hence if a universal force is the product of distance and mass, and distance is relative to the observer, mass must be relative to the observer too. Again, since the force of gravity appears as acceleration, or change of motion in objects, and according to the Special Principle of Relativity all uniform motion is relative, how can change of motion be absolute?

The Special Principle of Relativity, therefore, when once established, made necessary the General Principle. Just as the Special Principle states that absolute uniform motion and length do not exist, so the General Principle of Relativity states that absolute change of motion and mass do not exist. Moreover it satisfies the problems (*a*) (*b*) and (*c*) tabulated above as follows:

(a) Mass, momentum, kinetic and potential energy and inertia, are all different forms of the 'inertial' quality of matter. They can all be expressed in the frame of a common geometry, which is not Euclidean geometry but 'real' geometry. Or, put in another way, Euclidean geometry is only real in certain special circumstances.

(*b*) This 'real' geometry synthesizes the Newtonian law of gravity and the Newtonian laws of motion in one basic law: 'The directed radius is constant in empty space.'

(c) The behaviour of the particle is determined by the geometry of the rest of the Universe. In other words Einstein's world is monistic, and eliminates the pluralism of the Newtonian system.

The geometry of this Universe is the geometry of a *continuum*. It has no absolute Space and absolute Time, but these are welded into one block geometrically and each observer will divide the block differently into space and time; no division will be absolute or unique.

Relativity physics does not make all qualities relative—it sets them in a new absolute framework. Interval—in which both space and time figure—takes the place of distance as an absolute separation between events. The velocity of light is an absolute velocity, whatever the observer. The amount of matter in the Universe is absolutely constant and the conservation of momentum still holds absolutely as a law of Nature. And the absolute framework in which these new qualities are set, is the continuum of space-time, specified by four dimensions.

If this is the real world then it is plain that the logical incompatibilities and distortions of the Newtonian world are due to the fact that the continuum has been split up into an absolute Space-in-itself in which the individual particles move, their movements being accompanied by the uniform flow of an absolutely Universal Time.

However, we have no reason to accept one theory because it is more synthetic than another. The important point about the Principle of Relativity is that if it is correct, objects would observably behave differently in certain circumstances from what they would if the Newtonian theories are correct. These differences have been observed and support the theories of relativity physics, which are therefore accepted by physics, to-day. This is proof that Einstein's theories are truer than Newton's: it is not a proof that Einstein's theories are absolutely true—a belief that would obviate the need for further study in this domain of physics.

Although the dimensions which Newton had supposed to be absolute were shown by Einstein to be relative, this does not therefore mean that Einstein believes all dimensions of the Universe to be relative. On the contrary, his whole life's work has been devoted to eliminating relative qualities from physics in order to reach at last a firm absolute foundation. Each revelation of a relativity in dimensions was regarded as a crisis which could only be solved by 'restoring normality' on a new plane—in other words, by again putting physics upon an absolute basis. Relativity in dimensions or qualities is regarded as a kind of unreality and illusory subjectivity about them, which is opposed to the absolute character of objective reality. Absoluteness and relativity are regarded as mutually exclusive qualities.

Now this is a metaphysical assumption. It is an assumption common to Newton and Einstein. The difference between them is the fund of new information about the observable behaviour of objective reality which forces Einstein to damn far more qualities of matter with the label 'relative,' than was found necessary by Newton. It also forces him to look far more deeply into the structure of the Universe in order to find absolute qualities.

The crisis of physics is not therefore the result of any contradictions in relativity physics, or its supersession of Newtonian physics. Relativity physics is all of a piece with Newtonian physics. At every stage contradictions already latent have become open as a result of extended observation of Nature; and at every emergence they have been resolved by means of a new theory which lifted physics to a higher plane. The contradiction between the Galilean laws of motion and the Keplerian laws of planetary motion, led to the Newtonian equation of mass to inertia and the formulation of the Universal law of gravity.

At a later stage the wave theory of light emerged as a contradiction of the particulate theory of matter, and attempts to resolve it not only gave birth to field physics and the electro-magnetic equations of Clerk-Maxwell; but also pointed the way to the modern developments of atomic physics.

To-day, however, the integrations are becoming increasingly unstable.

The solution of the contradictions within mechanics by the relativity theory, and the solution of the contradictions within 'wave' physics* by the electro-magnetic equations of Clerk-Maxwell, and the solution of the contradictions within atomic physics by the quantum theory, have only led to greater contradictions between these three domains of physics. Conditions call imperatively for a synthesis of the laws governing the three domains, but each new discovery makes this less likely, and the conflict more acute. It is this which has given rise to

* i.e. Field physics, covering electromagnetic phenomena, including light.

the present crisis in physics and made it wholly different from previous crises, which merely paved the way for an immediate synthesis. Here however far more drastic revision is necessary. It is significant that in discussing the consequences of these contradictions, scientists find themselves forced to discuss concepts such as free-will and the nature of knowledge which had hitherto been excluded from science as philosophical questions. The scientist in other words is compelled to overhaul his philosophy, which hitherto had been an uncritical and inevitable way of looking at things rather than a conscious metaphysics. It was none the less metaphysics. Indeed, because of this unconsciousness, it was all the more metaphysical.

This overhauling of their philosophy by scientists has been singularly unsuccessful. The very fact that it has been undertaken, however, is a sign that this crisis is different from the previous crises of physics. It is a revolutionary crisis.

A revolutionary crisis occurs when the contradictions discovered in practice, cannot be met by a rearrangement of content within the categories of the domain of ideology concerned. The categories of this domain are in turn dependent on those of other domains of ideology and a revolutionary crisis is the signal that no real solution is possible, unless the most basic and fundamental of categories, those common to all domains of ideology, are more or less rapidly transformed. Hence the crisis 'overflows' from physics into other fields.

Einstein and Planck are the last physicists who accept the old metaphysics of science uncompromisingly, and who therefore attempt to site their empirical discoveries in an ordered world-view. They are the last physicists sharing the philosophy of Newton and Galileo, although of course it is a philosophy transformed by all that has taken place in the meanwhile, transformed, but not revolutionized. Einstein and Planck are the last of the solid 'Old Guard' of Newtonian physics.

II

THE WORLD AS MACHINE

1. REVOLUTION AND MYSTICISM

The integrations achieved by Einstein and Planck in their respective domains, gave rise to a contradiction between the domains which burst asunder the much-patched fabric of physics. This is realized by the 'younger men'—Jeans, Eddington, Heisenberg, and Schrödinger. But it would be wrong to regard this new school as revolutionary in a real sense—as men who can renew the fabric of physics. For it is the essence of a revolution that such a transformation can only take place as part of the transformation of the fabric in all fields of ideology, and this in turn is part of a still deeper transformation.

The physicists we have mentioned show no realization of the fact that there is a causal connection between the crisis in physics, and that in biology, psychology, economics, morals, politics and life as a whole. Where they see a connection it is only the connection of a general 'disease' or 'questioning'. Thus to adopt a genuine revolutionary standpoint in physical theory involves the adoption of a genuinely revolutionary attitude in real life. This is not what any of the 'new men' are guilty of, although in all branches of science still newer men are emerging who show traces of just this solid revolutionary position.* The older antagonists of Einstein and Planck are aware of the untenability of the metaphysics of current science, but their attitude is purely destructive: 'down with all metaphysics!' They regard this as a progressive step. But of course it is in fact impossible to have a theory without a philosophy: the philosophy is implied in the theory. It is impossible even to have a practice without a theory: one is implied in the other. Hence the slogan, 'Down with metaphysics' which also takes the form 'Down with concepts', or 'images', of 'theories', leads

* For example, in biology, J. B. S. Haldane, J. Needham and L. Hogben.

on the one hand to a narrowing and specialization in the field of physics, so as to keep it apart from life as a whole—a so-called empirical and positivist attitude towards science—and on the other hand the exclusion of science from their own general world-view which thus becomes mystical and idea-listic. In other words there is a cleavage of theory and practice —practice becomes specialized, restricted and empirical, and theory becomes abstract, unco-ordinated and diffuse. Hence in spite of an increase in technical competence in the particular field they have made their own, there is a reactionary trend in their general world-view, which regresses to forms left behind by science.

Once begun this cleavage accelerates. As practice becomes more specialized, and bare of theory, it becomes more difficult to integrate the different specializations in one consistent world-view; and ideology as a whole becomes more anarchic and confused.

Because of this Einstein stands out as a larger figure than his successors, because of his possession of a clear and all-em-bracing philosophy which was able to contain a wide domain of physics. His philosophy, however, was not adequate to con-tain and synthesize the whole complexity of modern physics, whose anarchy it has indeed helped to produce. The pending revolution in physics is therefore the incursion of a wider philosophy able to contain the various specialized and contra-dictory domains, and resolve them into a larger synthesis.

2. THE METAPHYSICS OF SCIENCE

It would be absurd to suppose that this philosophy can come into physics except from outside. The present metaphysics of physics was not generated by physics, but physics was generated by it, not in a self-contained way, but by inter-action with reality.

The present metaphysics of physics—its philosophy—did not descend into physics from the air. Before man could func-tion as a physicist he had to live as a man, and not as an ab-stract man, but as a real man in a certain society. If we take

modern physics, as beginning with Galileo and Bacon, then the
physicist was a man who had to live as a member of bourgeois
society before he could function as a physicist. To do so was
to have a whole superstructure of theory, conscious and unconscious, generated by participating in all the myriad functions of
a real man in real society of that kind. To be a physicist was
to apply this most general theory to a particular domain of
quality in reality, that of physics.

What one would find was determined on the one hand by
the nature of reality, and on the other hand by the theory
brought to bear on reality. The operation would be a selective
one, and the selection would be mutually determined by one's
theory and reality's nature. The impact would be mediated by
instruments, and these in turn would depend on the technical
level of the society in question, and the resources it could spare
for research.

It may be argued that this does not allow for the 'genius'.
But in fact the theory of the physicist is not stamped on him
but is the resultant of a tension between his innate qualities
and his experience of society. None the less his qualities can
only be realized throught the categories of society and thus
emerge with the grain of the epoch, however carved. The
greater the genius, the more profoundly he will be penetrated
with the qualities of his experience. In science this means, the
greater the genius, the more penetrative of Nature the categories of society will become in his hands. The theory of a man
is his world-view, and ultimately informs and guides his every
action—is in fact inseparable from it. It may not however be
realized consciously as a world-view. Any new theory, such
as a scientific hypothesis, because it is an extension of his
world-view, necessarily is arranged within its categories, even
if the arrangement brings about some transformation of them.
Hence the genius does not escape from the categories of his
age, any more than man escapes from time and space, but the
measure of his genius consists in the degree to which he fills
these categories with content—a degree which may even result
in their explosion. This explosion is, however, in turn dependent on a certain ripeness in the categories.

Physics separates itself out from the web of thought and

action, but remains in organic connection with its matrix. Bourgeois physics is completely contained within the categories of a bourgeois world-view and when it escapes from them even Einstein 'cannot understand' it. But it can only so escape in a crisis when the web itself is breaking up.

3. THE ECONOMIC CRISIS

It is no accident therefore that the crisis in physics occurs at the same time as an unprecedent economic crisis, which has become world-wide. The crisis is not peculiar to physics, it penetrates all ideology. In its most general form it is the growth of anarchy by and through integration; it is the explosive struggle of content with form. In the words of Planck:

'We are living in a very singular moment of history. It is a moment of crisis, in the literal sense of that word. In every branch of our spiritual and material civilization we seem to have arrived at a critical turning point. This spirit shows itself not only in the actual state of public affairs but also in the general attitude towards fundamental values in personal and social life.

'. . . Formerly it was only religion, especially in its doctrinal and moral systems, that was the object of sceptical attack. Then the iconoclast began to shatter the ideals and principles that had hitherto been accepted in the province of art. Now he has invaded the temple of science. There is scarcely a scientific axiom that is not nowadays denied by somebody. And at the same time almost any nonsensical theory that may be put forward in the name of science would be almost sure to find believers and disciples somewhere or other.'*

These words reveal a general feeling of collapse of the old order, together with a complete helplessness and lack of understanding as to its cause, which is characteristic of certain elements of society in a revolutionary crisis. Everything is confused, culture is tumbling about his ears: that is all Planck knows.

* M. Planck, *Where is Science Going?* 1933.

The symptoms are precisely the same in all spheres of ideology. There is an increasing specialization and technical efficiency inside the different domains of ideology, but this leads to an increasing anarchy and contradiction between the domains. It is not merely that biology separates from psychology, but psychology itself splits up into mutually exclusive disciplines. Hence it is no longer possible to have a synthetic world-view, a living theory in touch at all fronts with practice. The theory is forcibly torn apart. In such circumstances there are three alternative attitudes open to conservatism: (a) A mystical positivistic attitude to all spheres of ideology outside one's little garden (Eddington); (b) A violent reduction of all other forms of thought to the highly limited categories of one's small domain (Freud); (c) An eclectic mish-mash of all the various specializations with no attempt to resolve their contradictions. This leads to a world-view that negates and frustrates itself (Wells). Obviously any of these alternatives merely intensifies the crisis.

But in fact this ideological anarchy is only a reflection of the economic anarchy which is the cause of the general crisis. When I say 'reflection' I mean that the same general development has taken place in the sphere of social relations as in ideological categories, because the latter are merely subtilizations, qualitatively different, of the former.

It is the characteristic of bourgeois economy that its social relations contain a contradiction which brings about its development and also its decline. This contradiction is the contradiction between socially-organized labour, on the one hand, and individual appropriation of the products of that labour, on the other hand. In its early stages this is the only means by which a raising of the productive forces beyond the stage of handicraft can be accomplished.

A time is reached however when increasing organization of labour within the factory, with its tremendously increased productivity, leads to violent conflict between the individually owned factories. This is the imperialistic stage of capitalism: the era of increasing competition between the trusts and monopolies and the nations which are their organized expression. It becomes plain that the social relations are holding back the productive forces and this is apparent in 'over-production'. mass unemployment, slumps, and wars. Humanity is driven forward to revolutionize the productive relations of capitalism, to set free the crippled productive forces. Capitalism turns into its opposite, communism.

The whole superstructure of ideology, which is in active relation with its base, is thus more or less rapidly transformed, and the new categories generated lead to a synthetic world-view on a higher plane. Of course it is not suggested that physical theory is a mirror-reflex of social relations. It gives information about non-social reality. But it gives such information *to* society. The knowledge is conscious knowledge. It has therefore to be cast into the categories of society.

These categories are not like the Kantian categories, eternal and given in the nature of mind, a set of tools which work up into a cognizable shape the unknowable thing-in-itself. Man interpenetrates actively with Nature. The depth of his interpenetration is due to the fact that he works in association. The laws of association, in the most general sense, are therefore the dynamic field along which individual men actively struggle with the object. This struggle is not merely physical—practical —it is also theoretical, a relation of cognition. Only in abstraction can the two be separated. Hence the social relations are reflected in all the products of society (including the ideology of physics) as categories.

Physics is knowledge about reality, but it is abstract, generalized knowledge. The abstractions or generalizations are the reflections of the social relations by and through which the reality was made into conscious knowledge. Some of these categories are general to all society; but they appear in a special form in different societies, and evidently in the case of the crisis in bourgeois physics, it is the specifically bourgeois categories that are of vital interest, because of the way in which new knowledge, new practical content, is rending them asunder, and is itself crippled by the old form.

4. MATTER AND MECHANISM

The unconscious philosophy of the contemporary physicist

is mechanism. When the bourgeois considers matter as the object of cognition, he is unable to conceive of it except under the categories of mechanism. The categories of mechanism are: atomism, 'strict' causality, absolute time and space. Outside these categories, the object is unknowable to the bourgeois phillosopher: hence if like Kant he regards these categories as creations of the human mind, matter-in-itself becomes unknowable.

Matter is a name for the category of objective reality. The field of physics is objective reality in its most generalized form. Historically, as with Aristotle, the field of physics included all 'Nature'—i.e. all matter. But gradually certain qualities of matter were excluded from physics, e.g. those of biology and chemistry—and it became bourgeois physics.

The philosophy of physics is the philosophy of all bourgeois in relation to matter. It is mechanical materialism. The philosophy of all bourgeois philosophers in relation to matter is the same; but for various historical reasons bourgeois philosophers ceased to be interested in matter, and developed another part of bourgeois philosophy, that concerned with the mind or subjective reality. This they regarded as 'real' philosophy, distinct from physics. Hence what is called to-day, philosophy, is only a section of the true bourgeois philosophy or world-view.

It is equally true that the mechanism of physicists is only a part of their philosophy for they also accept the standard bourgeois world-view in regard to mind, that of idealism. But just as the 'philosopher' is not interested in matter, the physicist is not interested in mind.

In the main, therefore, physicists and philosophers share a general bourgeois world-view in which the physicists concentrate on developing one department, that of matter, or objective reality, and the philosophers that of mind, or subjective reality. The bourgeois philosophy of subjective reality cannot escape from the standpoint of idealism or conceptualism. Hence bourgeois ideology, in all fields, reveals this cleavage between subjective reality and objective reality as a struggle or contradiction between mechanism and idealism, matter and mind, causality and free will. This is the notorious subject-object relation, the most famous problem of bourgeois thought.

5. THE WORLD OF BOURGEOIS SOCIETY

Is it possible that this cleavage has any connection with the basic contradiction of capitalist economy, which secures its development and decline? Could it be that in the sphere of ideology a contradiction, reflecting the cleavage of the foundation, has first of all unfolded all the complexities of bourgeois ideology, and is now causing them to disintegrate in anarchy? In fact there is apparent a close connection between the two.

In feudal society man is subordinate to man. Serfs and land, the medieval means of production, are owned by the ruling class, which also exerts coercive rights (the feudal dues, monopolies and privileges) over the bourgeoisie.

The bourgeoisie secures the abrogation of all 'rights' of man over man, and substitutes for it merely a right to own and dispose freely of things, including one's own labour power. This involves the shattering of all feudal restrictions and the creation of the 'free market' for commodities. Formerly only a small surplus of the goods a man produced came on the market; the majority were for his own consumption. Now not only do all his products become commodities, but many things hitherto thought inalienable—his faith, his loyalty, and his truth—acquire a cash value too.

By this means social productivity is raised to a new high level. The social division of labour is carried to an unprecedented degree; and it involves of course a corresponding social organization of labour. The two are not exclusive, but are opposites which produce each other. Specialization involves integration. Where each commodity is produced from start to finish by one man in his home, no complex social organization of labour is necessary. When into the making of each product a complex chain of separate specialized processes has entered, including the making of machinery, transport, and central control, then a corresponding social organization of labour is necessary: the organization of the factory and the town.

The organization of the factory is conscious—planned and controlled from start to finish. But the sum of factories which constitutes society is not so controlled, but their working is controlled by 'laws' of supply and demand—that is, the free market. The free market was the condition for the establishment of bourgeois society.

What are the laws of the free market, which hold together the producers of a society based on commodity production?

'Every society based on commodity production has the peculiarity that in it the producers have lost control of their social relationships. Each produces for himself, with the means of production which happen to be at his disposal and in order to satisfy his individual needs through the medium of exchange. No one knows how much of the article he produces is coming on to the market, and how much demand there is for it; no one knows whether his individual product will meet a real need, whether he will cover his costs, or even be able to sell at all. Anarchy reigns in social production. But commodity production, like all other forms of production, has its own laws, which are inherent in and inseparable from it; and these laws assert themselves in spite of anarchy, in and through anarchy. These laws are manifested in the sole form of social relationship which continues to exist, in exchange, and enforce themselves on the individual producers as compulsory laws of competition. At first, therefore, they are unknown even to these producers, and have to be discovered by them gradually, only through long experience. They assert themselves therefore, apart from the producers and against the producers, as the natural laws of their form of production, working blindly. The product dominates the producers.'*

Evidently, therefore, there is a contradiction between the organized centres of production and the disorganization of social labour as a whole due to the interposition of the 'free' market. But this 'disorganization' is not a mere lack of organization, it is the specific form of society in a bourgeois economy. What stands between the organized centres of production are the rights of individual owners, whose life and freedom depend on their rights to extract a share of the value of the goods produced by the means of production owned by

* Engel's *Anti-Dühring*.

them. This share is not extracted immediately, when the goods are produced, but only when this value has been realized in the free market. Hence both the individual ownership and the free market are necessities for the existence of the bourgeoisie and of bourgeois economy, and their categories permeate all bourgeois society. The blindness in society as a disorganized whole is the inverse of the special status of the bourgeoisie.

The means of production must be worked by men, and since coercive ownership of men by men is abolished with feudal society, the bourgeois has no direct coercive ownership over men. But in fact men who own nothing can only live by bringing their labour power to the free market, because the means of producion, without which man in capitalist society cannot realize his labour power in products, are owned by the bourgeoisie. Hence the capitalist's coercive ownership of things in fact veils a coercive ownership of men; but in appearance bourgeois society is one in which man has not 'rights' over man, only over things—i.e. over Nature. His right over Nature which is also his freedom, is in bourgeois theory realized passively, as a simple property right. But man's right over Nature is in fact realized by the improved production technique, an increasing division of labour, which is also the source of the real conscious organization of society. This division of labour is not based on ideal categories or religious hierarchies, but on the laws of Nature as these are discovered; the stuff having to be treated in such and such a way, and to go through this and that process, to realize the end desired.

Hence certain complexes are formed in society which constitute its organization—machines, nests of machines and the men arranged round them in certain active relations. The exact structure of these organizations of men depends on the necessity of Nature.

Of course these complexes are called for by certain wants but these wants are uncontrollable in bourgeois society—they merely emerge from the blind market. Once emerged, their satisfaction is wholly dependent on the intrinsic properties of Nature—it is a technico-productive problem.

In fact man's desires are also subject to necessity. They

change with history, with the change of methods of production and corresponding alterations in the superstructure of society. Yesterday a Roman glutton; to-day an Egyptian hermit. But all this causation of desire in society is hidden by the basic form of modern society, in which desires emerge from the blind market.

Now society is the struggle of Man and Nature. In the more refined ideology of society this basic struggle appears as the basic problem of the subject-object relation. Man is the subject; Nature is the object. Therefore in bourgeois society, the object appears solely as 'things' over which man has rights, and whose laws or 'necessity' he discovers in order to satisfy his desires. These desires appear arbitrarily proposing an end for Nature to satisfy, and by exploring the necessity of Nature, they are satisfied.

Notice that these desires for products appear spontaneously, and the products, having been formed, disappear. The desires come out of the blind market, and vanish into it. And yet the market veils the desires of Man, his whole active relation to Nature, as a conative creature, and veils also the satisfaction of those desires, which take place behind the same screen. Hence the object is split off from the subject, and Nature appears as something wholly independent from Man. Nature is the object of determinism; she is the domain of Necessity.

Man desires certain things of her; and by making use of the known laws of her determinism, these desires are gratified. Man is subject to spontaneity.

Nature is always known as a passive object—as something not subject to man's activity nor the antagonist of his striving, but as something self-contained and shut in by its necessities. Hence Man's whole relation to Nature bears the stamp of the property relation, in which his right over it is the reward of his consciousness or cleverness—never of his activity.

The growth of the productive forces under bourgeois economy is an indication of the success of this conception of Nature. Nature's necessity becomes increasingly known. But this conception of Nature known by Man, is Nature known as a machine.

6. THE WORLD AS MACHINE

According to the bourgeois, the machine is a piece of Nature obeying deterministic laws so designed as to satisfy his wants and create use-value. It is as it were a self-contained piece of Nature which fulfils a 'plan.' The plan is his desire. This plan is to him something spontaneous and external to Nature.

Therefore the categories of objective reality in bourgeois philosophy are categories of the machine as it realizes itself in bourgeois society. The world is a machine—as machines seem to the bourgeoisie. It is the bourgeois himself who invented the term 'mechanism' and thus gave away the economic determination of his categories of objective reality. He had come to know Nature via the machine, hence the laws of Nature came to him to seem identical with the laws of the machine. He explored nature by means of the technical development embodied in the machine—whether the machine of the factory or the laboratory.

The point is, the machine is not just a piece of Nature. It is a piece of Nature associated in bourgeois society with human beings who work the machine. It is the kernel of a social complex which gives it its shape and significance. When the bourgeois sees Nature as a machine, therefore, he sees Nature stamped with all the special and transitory social categories which that complex bears when viewed from his special standpoint in society. Nature looks a little queer to the bourgeois because he has a peculiar standpoint in society from which the machine too looks a little queer, and yet it is only through the machine that Nature enters into the consciousness of society.

We are criticizing the bourgeois philosophy because its view of Nature is 'mechanism'. That does not mean we believe that Nature's laws are different in kind from those of a machine. In fact this would be an absurd suggestion; since a machine is constructed out of bits of Nature, according to natural laws, the laws of the machine cannot be wholly different in kind from those of Nature. Therefore what we are ultimately criticizing in the bourgeois philosophy of Nature is not the application of categories drawn from the machine to Nature, but the error in the bourgeois view of the machine. The bourgeois conception of the machine is at fault. That is why we say the categories of bourgeois scientific knowledge are economic categories, although it is knowledge about wild Nature.

The bourgeois theory of the machine is based on the part he plays in relation to the machine in concrete living. We have already seen that his role, and the relations of bourgeois economy, are such that man's desires emerge from the night of the market and are realized through the machine as products, which vanish again into the night. This is commodity-production, the basis of bourgeois economy in factory art and philosophy.

7. THE MACHINE AS SLAVE

Hence it seems as if Man's desires are altogether independent of the machine and that Man as it were stands outside Nature, like a visitor to the aquarium outside a tank. He observes the movements of the fishes. But the glass screen which cuts him off is a one-way screen. He can make his desires realized by the movement of the fishes, but the fishes' movements do not affect his desires. His relation to Nature is godlike. She serves his end like a slave. Nature, the machine, takes the place of the slave, servilely realizing the will of the master, with this difference, that the master must know her inner necessity.

The qualification, it must be admitted, marks an advance on earlier civilization. The slave obeyed the master's will, and because they were both men, it was not necessary for the master to know the slave's inner necessity, his capabilities and law, for these were crudely realized already by an inner instinctive sympathy. Like master, like man.

But even so, this godlike detachment of man from machine is an illusion. For this godlike survey of the machine overlooks the man who works the machine. Yet a machine without a man to work it is meaningless, since the machine is stamped through and through with operability. And as man's control over Nature by means of machines increases, so does the organization of society; and the lives of most of its units more and more dominatingly reflect the interpenetration of society by the machine. More and more men are organized by the necessities of struggling mechanically with Nature. Only the owning class escape from the bonds of this organization, and is so much the more ignorant in blood and bone of the nature of reality. Hence mechanism is an illusion peculiar to the ruling class. The men who work the machine realize that so far from its expressing a one-way relation of Man to Nature, it expresses an each-way determining relation of which they get the full brunt. The laws of machines of production determine their whole lives. These laws determine the complexes of organization which, taken as a whole, make up bourgeois society.

The machine as a visible entity is only the kernel of the factory-complex with all its outgrowths, but the organization it crystallizes, the natural necessary laws of production based on division of labour, shape the whole social hierarchy of the factory. It roughens their hands; determines their leisure; bows their backs; limits their horizon. Their very life depends on its activity; their relations to their fellows, to society; their freedom and their marriages and their friendships, are determined by the complex at whose heart is the machine.

Thus so far from the proletariat—the major part of society —standing in god-like isolation from the machine and Nature, their existence is determined by it; they are arranged about it like iron filings along the 'lines of force' round a magnet. For they *work* the machine; they form one producing complex with it. They cannot regard Nature as a passive shut-in-object of contemplation.

8. THE BOURGEOIS AS OWNER

But the bourgeois owns the machine. Ownership is a one-way relation in so far as it enters the consciousness of Man. The other relation, the ownership of a man by property, which stamps a man with its characteristics, is unconscious. Formally to own a thing means that it has every obligation to me, and I have none to it. Any obligations to it imposed on me by

208

law, custom or morality are regarded as so many limitations of ownership. Absolute ownership would exclude them.

Hence the bourgeois has in relation to the machine and the complex it produces that god-like isolation which is postulated in his theory of the machine. The wheel of the machine revolves, carrying round with it the proletariat who serve it and urge it forward; but it grinds out for its owner 'automatically' the freedom to gratify his desires in the market. He stands by; gives it perhaps an overseeing eye; or goes away for a holiday, knowing that it will continue to turn. Eventually he absents himself altogether; a chain of formalities, stocks and shares, veil even the turning machine from his vision.

But to suppose that any one-way relation between things is possible in reality is a fallacy. All relations are mutually determining; it is unthinkable that cause and effect should not mutually determine each other. I own the stick; I wield it; but there is a reaction on my hand. The stick is my property; I am equally a stick-owner.

But one determinism may be conscious; the other unconscious. The ownership is conscious; the being an owner is unconscious.

Thus the bourgeois is precisely aware of the way in which Nature, in the form of the machine, fulfils the desires emerging from the market and so gives him the means to fulfil his own desires. But he is unaware of the way in which the machine determines the movement of the desires of men.

9. CLASS AND WORLD-VIEW

The machine is a piece of humanized nature. It is composed of particles arranged according to a plan, the plan of a human desire. But the society which uses the machine, is a naturalized society. It is composed of men organized according to a plan, the plan of production. The organization of capitalist society, its factories, transport, and all the social grouping produced by this, is imposed upon it by 'the division of labour,' that is, by the necessities of Nature when these are operated upon by man to fulfil his desires.

But the bourgeois does not consciously plan the organization of society. It emerges blindly; it crystallizes out from the centres of production as the crystal of a super-saturated solution form on wires dipped into it. The warp and woof of the organized society of capitalist economy is spun blindy—by the growth of the machine under the blind laws of the market. Hence capitalist society presents the unique picture of disorganization amid organization.

Hence even the bourgeois is subject to the machine. But he is subject to it in a different way from the proletariat. The proletariat sees its subjection directly. The bourgeois owns the machine, and therefore the worker must sell his labour power to get into the factory and produce his means of subsistence. Once in the factory, his existence, his work, his co-operation with his fellows, are determined by the evident needs of machine operation.

Hence he has two relations to it not indissolubly connected; (a) a precarious and coerced relation to the machine due to the capitalist's ownership of it, (b) and the natural relation to it springing from the nature of machines. The first is obviously arbitrary and a matter of special social privileges. It is distinguishable from the latter, which is given in the very nature of life, since a machine is a machine, and must be greased, repaired and fed. Both these ways in which the machine determines the life of the proletariat directly are overt and conscious. One included all the weakness of capitalist society; its anarchy, slumps and mass unemployment; the other all its advances—its increased productivity and complex web of economy.

The bourgeois however is subject to the machine in an unconscious and veiled way. His suppressed determination by the machine is forced into the blindness of the market. The way in which production by its immanent laws determines the whole organization and movement of society is in bourgeois economy veiled by the market, and these laws do not appear as laws of the machine in relation to the bourgeois but as a totally new set of laws, the laws of supply and demand, and the laws of capitalist competition. But these laws are in fact lawless, since the capitalist never knows how much to produce or what will be the fate of the product. He never knows which way the market will turn, which is to say that he does not know the laws of the market. It is anarchic.

Yet in bourgeois economy the market is the only way in which human desires can appear as active forces realizing themselves, and dictating the machine process. Hence human desire appears to the bourgeois as 'spontaneous', that is, anarchic and undetermined or certainly not as determined by the machine, whose laws (as he thinks) he precisely knows. Hence the subject and object have become completely separated. On one side is the man, desirous, active and spontaneous, that is, subject to no law, emerging freely, and wholly undetermined by the machine. On the other side the object, Nature as known by Man, the machine, contemplated in splendid isolation, whose mere contemplation secures the subservience of Nature to him. This cleavage does not seem to the bourgeois odd; any other arrangement of it seems unconceivable. He cannot imagine himself being free if the spontaneity of human desires, or the independent mechanism of nature, were in any way infringed. And in this respect he is right, for these particular forms express the sole conditions which can secure the existence of the bourgeois class as a privileged class. If therefore they were abolished, the bourgeois class would cease to exist and there would be no more bourgeois freedom.

10. THE SHATTERING OF A WORLD-VIEW

The fact that this schematization of the subject-object relation contains a contradiction becomes increasingly evident. It is just the effort to resolve this contradiction which secures the development of bourgeois ideology in philosophy and physics, just as the same contradiction in the form of individual ownership and appropriation (spontaneous irresponsible desire) and organized social labour (the objective laws of Nature) brings about the development of bourgeois economy. Only finally the contradiction shatters its own categories and emerges in a synthesis: in economy, communism, in ideology, dialectical materialism.

The bourgeois feels the determining influence of the machine via the market in an increasingly coercive way. It appears as slumps, a general economic crisis, unemployment, currency chaos, over-production, a necessity driving him to war. And he gradually comes to feel that the 'machine has got out of control' and expresses this in vague desires for a close season for invention, limitation of plant, and rationalization. However he is not conscious of the precise way in which the machine determines his life as for example the proletariat is, because it determines it via the 'free' market and the 'free' market consists in its unconsciousness. His refusal to become conscious is not however merely wooden obstinacy, and pigheadedness. For consciousness is not a mere contemplation, it is the result of an active process, which in this case would imply active control of the market. But the market is merely the net result of the actions of individual producers for it. Hence active control of the market would involve active control of the whole process of production and therefore the extinction of his right of individual ownership, which is the condition of his existence as a bourgeois. Thus it is not mere obstinacy, but a life-and-death matter. For society to become conscious of the determining relations of the machine upon itself in their fullness, the bourgeoisie must cease to exist as a class. No wonder therefore that the subject-object relation is as insoluble by bourgeois philosophers as it was by philosophers of earlier class societies.

Therefore the categories of mechanism, which are the only categories the bourgeois philosopher is able to apply to nature, are categories of the machine in the special way it functions in bourgeois economy. He is unable to achieve any other categories, since even those of teleology, which is put forward as an alternative, are, as we shall presently show, precisely the same as those of mechanism.

11. THE SHARING OF MATTER

Physics is concerned with *objective* reality, with Nature, with matters behaving as a machine is supposed to behave. In physics nature is studied in a glass tank—the physicist merely wanders on and surveys the scene. Thus Nature in the struggle of man with nature appears as the object *in contemplation*, the object as it is in itself, measured in terms of its own necessity. Such an object is quantitative, bare of quality, and hence the Nature of bourgeois physics is bare of quality.

This stripping was a gradual process. Matter to Galileo and Bacon is still matter full of quality and sensuousness. But to realize 'matter as owned by the bourgeoisie', it is necessary to eliminate the observer. Since Nature is to be apprehended as it were by a kind of divine apprehension on the part of the observer, in which he stands in no mutually determining relation to Nature, it is necessary to strip matter of all the qualities in which the observer is concerned. Colour, for example. Here the colour involves a subjective element: it is not the thing in itself, but the thing as seen. At first matter is only stripped of colour, sound, 'pushiness', heat, which all prove to be modes of motion. Motion, length, mass and shape are however believed to be absolutely objective qualities, independent of the observer. However they prove one after the other to be relative to the observer. Thus matter is left finally with no real i.e. non-subjective qualities, except those of number. But number is ideal, and hence objective reality vanishes. Matter has become unknowable.

The categories of Time and Space, regarded as *absolute* categories, express this attempt to remove the bourgeois from active relation with the object. If the object, Nature, can be completely isolated from the subject, Man, it can be expressed in terms of itself—set in an absolute space-time. Man's relation to it is not, in that case, an umbilical cord of mutual dependence; the known Nature is not an active mutually-dependent relation between Man and the rest of reality, but known Nature is Nature absolute and yet in contemplation. This contradiction—a self-sufficient Nature, and yet one contemplated by Man—is the contradiction which drives on the development of physics. Since every quality of Nature is found to contain a subjective element which makes man dependent on something 'out there', just as it makes the quality dependent on something 'in man', this contradiction strips all Nature of quality. The most general objective qualities of Nature seem those of Time and Space. Space, the common likeness in phenomena and Time, the unlikeness, seem objective and intrinsic. Surely therefore they are completely qualities of reality-in-itself? Surely man is correct in hypotheticating an absolute framework of absolute Space and absolute Time?

In fact this is a demand that man, the subject, should live out of Time and Space. For if on the one hand we have mind, and on the other hand matter described in terms of itself, then we should have two worlds which do not have anything in common and would therefore be unknowable to each other. But the unknowable does not exist and therefore the closed world of mind and the closed world of physics cannot exist. The famous dualism of matter and mind is something artificially imposed by the special categories of the society which generated philosophy.

Yet this closed world is the aim of bourgeois physics. It is the inevitable presupposition of mechanism.

The characteristic of physics is supposed to be this; it is a world in which each entity is explained by another entity, until you arrive back at the first entity. In *The Nature of the Physical World*, Eddington gives a good picture of this closed world of physics. What is *matter*? Something explicable as a *stress*, which in turn is defined in terms of *potential*, which again is reduced to *interval*, which has to do with *scales*, which are composed of *matter*—and so we have performed the full circle. But, according to Eddington, at this point the reader interjects, 'Please do not explain any more. I happen to know what matter is.' Matter then is 'something that Mr. X knows', but for all that Mr. X. remains outside the carefully closed world of physics. Eddington here inserts a diagram of a closed polygon, with Mr. X. *outside* it, though forlornly attached to it.

But if Mr. X. were really outside the charmed circle, how could he come to know it? Mr. X. is in fact Mr. Bourgeois, and it is not his modesty, as might be thought, that keeps him outside, it is his pride. If he comes inside, if Mr. X. is in causal relation with matter, if he *is* matter, he is no longer human desire emerging spontaneously and realizing itself by a mere contemplative knowledge of the mechanical necessities of the object. Such a world must necessarily be a world of the Absolute, that is, of an Absolute excluding the human mind as an active part of it. The human mind just wanders on and surveys the frigid scene, without this process of knowing in any way altering it.

Such a world involves the following: There is an absolute Time and Space, independent of the human mind (the observer), in which particles follow absolute paths definable by the Hamiltonian Principle of Least Action. Laplace's divine calculator can now come on the scene, and after a lightning glance round in the course of which he grasps the relationship of everything to everything, he can predict the future and thus completely dominate the environment.

12. THE WILD WORLD

We now understand how it is that the Newtonian world presents such a strange likeness to bourgeois society *as the bourgeois envisages it*. It is atomistic. It is composed of individuals who merely proceed on their own right lines doing what the immanent force of each makes necessary. Each particle is spontaneously self-moving. It corresponds to the 'free' bourgeois producer as he imagines himself to be. Events consist of their collisions; and are the product of internal chance.

But a mysterious world force holds all these particles together in one system. Acting as a unifying regulating system, inexplicable and arbitrary, it adjusts, compensates, balances and produces the ordered circulation and self-regulating cycles of the sidereal and solar systems. This corresponds to the bourgeois 'free' market, the law of supply and demand, which holds all the bourgeois producers together, adjusts automatically their relations to each other, and acts as the grand unifying principle of society. It is no accident that this force of gravity is in Newton's mind closely associated with God. The same unconscious forces perturbing and regulating the anarchy of bourgeois society, drive the bourgeois again and again to the altar.

The Newtonian system is of its essence stable and oscillatory. It is like a pendulum. The laws of gravity, of absolute Time and Space, and of the conservation of matter, energy, and momenta, keep the system moving like a pendulum, eternally beating the same path.

But this is precisely true of the bourgeois economic system as the bourgeois economist sees it, in which the market, by virtue of the law of supply and demand, automatically adjusts production to consumption, and price to value, so that there is a perpetual equalization of the needs and production of society, a perpetual realization of the greatest possible happiness of the greatest possible number.

Yet we know that in fact the Universe is very different from the stable Universe of Newton. It is a Universe which develops. Solar systems come into being and decay; nebulae condense and grow cold. Life emerges, and grows insurgent and gives birth to consciousness. Mind is born. Hope and despair come into a world which does not know these qualities. The drama of qualified existence unrolls itself.

But by its very pre-suppositions, Newtonian physics is forced to deny the reality or relevance of these insurgent 'wild' qualities. They are qualities in which Mr. X. is concerned and therefore unreal. Physics makes a continuous and desperate effort to rid itself of these qualities, but only succeeds in ridding itself even of motion, time and space, its primary categories. Finally it ends up with Lemaitre's unstable exploding universe. Even such categories as distance are developing.

And exactly the same is true of bourgeois economics. So far from being a stable society, it is the most violently revolutionary society yet known, continually transforming its own basis and leading to a feverish development of social productivity:

'Constant revolutionizing of production, uninterrupted disturbance of all social conditions, everlasting uncertainty and agitation distinguish the bourgeois epoch from all earlier ones. All fixed, fast-frozen relations, with their train of ancient and venerable prejudices and opinions, are swept away, all new-formed ones become antiquated before they can ossify...'

Crises come with the violence and unexpecterness of earth-quakes. Bourgeois society is full of insurgent quality; yet the economists attempt to explain these disturbances, just as the physicist attempts to strip the Universe of quality, by branding them as deviations, as accidents, as malfunctioning, as unreal.

Thus in both cases we have two systems: the system as the bourgeois believes it to be, and as it really is. The first system, the ideal, is subject to the categories of mechanism, i.e. to the characteristics of the machine in society as the bourgeois believes it to be; the second, the real, is subject to the categories of dialectics, of the machine in society as it is known to the proletariat who form part of it.

But Newtonian physics, with its stable ordered world, is the philosophy of a bourgeois society still stable and not yet embarked on its revolutionary insurgence. It is a society of norms imposed from without; of compromise with the aristocracy. It is the era of manufacture. I have shown elsewhere how this era is reflected in literature of the English eighteenth century, and how it expresses the spirit of bourgeois economy where the market has not yet developed to a stage permitting the machine to become revolutionary, and continually transform its own basis. It is still the machine as hand manufacture, not as the steam-driven factory. It is the machine, only slowly passing out of the era of handicraft and still suffering from a shortage of labour and a restricted market. Presently it will grow insurgent and create the conditions for its own development. It will expropriate the petty bourgeois artisan in thousands and so create its proletariat; it will open up the markets of the world. But at the moment it needs for its slow growth the protection of laws, and labour regulations, which are accepted as norms given by eternal reason and producing a stable 'sensible' society. Hence the mechanistic categories of physics are categories of bourgeois economy in the era of manufacture.

But when the machine breaks loose, and begins to transform society, bourgeois science is also transformed. Other categories grow up beside the older mechanistic categories. The bourgeois class floats to power on the dynamic wave of the machine.

217

The Industrial Revolution has taken place. Man's view of Nature is impregnated with subjectivism, which in bourgeois society is idealism.

Now the bourgeois philosopher sees Nature through rapidly changing economic categories, and hence sees a changing Nature. He sees the change in Nature. Just as a film enables us to see motion in Nature, so does the Industrial Revolution, because of its rapid change of Nature and so of society. The interest of scientists is now directed to change in Nature, and the Darwinian theory emerges, which is a theory of change in Nature explained by the categories of the bourgeois society of the Industrial Revolution, with its *laisser-faire* policy.

Just as the early bourgeois conception of the machine, coupled with the stable categories of manufacturing society, led to the development of Newtonian physics, with its stable world and eternal oscillation of bare quantities, the Industrial Revolution, in which the machine produced an instability in society, led to the development of Darwinian biology, in which the categories of mechanism automatically give birth to a progressive evolution of species. The basic relation—the bourgeois separate from the machine—is still the same, but the transformation of society as a result of that relation has led the philosopher to direct his attention to a new field of quality, that of biology or Nature changing.

13. WORLD-VIEW AND SOCIAL CHANGE

And this indicates the way in which the economic categories of a society direct ideology into specific channels. Newtonian physics is not a reflection of bourgeois society; if it were it would not be knowledge about reality; and its practical success indicates its real content of positive knowledge.

Physics is necessarily the science of the most objective components of phenomena; it is the most generalized and formal aspect of matter. It is quantity as bare as possible of quality. As such it is an abstraction. The special circumstances of Newton's day, however, leading to a divorce of the object in con-

templation from the active spontaneous subject, made the philosopher imagine that physics was absolutely objective—and
thus produced the contradiction whose resolution led to its
development.

Thus the categories of bourgeois society directed interest
into physics and gave that physics, in addition to its pene-
trating development, a special distortion—the absolute separation of the object and the picture of a world which was a
macrocosm of mercantile bourgeois society.

In the same way society of the Industrial Revolution
directed interest into a field of objective quality subject to
rapid change; that of biology. It made Man look for change
everywhere, and began the development of all the evolutionary sciences: not merely biology, but also geology, cosmogony
and the like. This picture of evolution was also given a
characteristic distortion.

III

MAN AS IDEA

1. THE GENERATION OF IDEALISM

The Newtonian flourishing of physics was succeeded by the Darwinian growth of evolutionary science. The way for evolutionary theory had already been paved by the development of idealism. Idealism appears in bourgeois philosophy to oppose itself to mechanism, and in a certain sense it does. But if we look into concrete living, we see that both are generated simultaneously. For on the one hand the object, Nature, emerges as the self-contained machine; and on the other hand, as a quite separate phenomenon, Man's desires, his whole activity in so far as this is valued, appears spontaneously, out of the night, and appears to develop of its own, as an independent subject.

Mechanism stripped Nature, the object, of all qualities which had in them any tincture of the subjective, and which therefore made Man dependent on nature. This set free all sensuous active quality as Man's exclusive possession, the attributes of Mind. All the active sensuousness of reality was developed as part of the non-natural science of knowledge. It became a question of thought and thus its development fell to the lot of 'philosophy'—i.e. that part of bourgeois philosophy which, because it is cut off from the object—i.e. from experimental test—is regarded as the queen of thought and is set above science. It was the peculiar result of the cleavage between subject and object produced by bourgeois economy that the sensuous active element in concrete living was developed separately from science as idealism.

Berkeley, Hume, Kant, Fichte, Schelling and Hegel represent the stages by which the subject is cut completely free from the object. I do not propose to deal in detail with these stages here, as they will be familiar to the student of philosophy and to non-students would be too technical for brief explanation. The point is that this was a process in which man or mind, figuring as active, sensuous subjectivity, was stripped of all those qualities which had an objective component in them. But since no quality emerging as a phenomenon is absolutely objective or subjective, no quality is situated in an absolute self-sufficient Space and Time, nor does any quality exist completely out of Space or Time. The stripping from subjectivity of all qualities containing objective components left it as bare as matter when it was stripped of all subjective quality. Matter was left with nothing but mathematics existing in the human head. Subjectivity was left with nothing but the Idea; and obviously this could not be the idea in the material human brain, for this would tie the Idea to matter. Hence this final reality was the Idea existing out of the human brain— the Hegelian Absolute Idea.

Not only has subjectivity by then been stripped of activity and sucked of sensuous blood, but it has in fact become objectivity, for the Idea existing apart from the brain is objective reality and therefore enters the category of matter. Idealism has become materialism, just as mechanical materialism, when it ended as mathematics, had become idealism. Mechanism and idealism, although they seem irreconcilable opposites, are only so in the sense that they are different sides of the same penny. They are produced by the cleavage of subject and object which results from the special conditions of bourgeois economy.

2. THE ADVANCE TO DIALECTICS

It therefore fell to bourgeois philosophy to develop in a classic way the active sensuous side of existence. Now what is active is changing and thus the development of subjectivity was the development of an evolutionary philosophy. This became evident with the emergence of the Hegelian Dialectic, which is an evolutionary theory of subjectivity. The categories of mind here generate each other in an evolutionary way. Thought has become full of history and time.

But we saw that this was a subjectivity carefully pruned

of the objective component. Hence it was a subjectivity whose activity was an activity on nothing real—on 'appearance'—which is how the object figures in the realm of mere experience. Hence subjectivity in the form of bourgeois philosophy lacks the essential test of practice, and experiment. It lacks activity upon the object which of course can only be realized in practice. Yet in fact all subjectivity, even mere knowing, is activity though objects. Hence subjectivity strangles itself.

None the less subjectivity, by gathering into itself all the sensuous active qualities of existence, does, even when robbed of the object, contain the impress of material reality, like bark stripped from a tree. By comparing these unanchored qualities among themselves, it is possible in a confused way to extract the most general laws of activity and change, just as by comparing the categories of objectivity among themselves one gets the confused but general physical laws of mechanism. These laws of subjectivity are laws of logic. It is not formal logic, but the Hegelian logic of dialectics.

Dialectics, as developed by Hegel, does not therefore merely express the laws of 'thought'. Because the 'thought' of Hegel is really subjectivity or active sensuous existence, in the widest sense, Hegelian dialectics attempts to realize the most general law of change. It grasps at the emerging of the unlike, the birth of quality, the movement of evolution, the passing of history, the process of real Time. In this it proves the opposite of mechanism. Mechanism is concerned with the persistence of matter, the conditions of stability, the survival of the like, the shuffling of quantity, of the substance below change, the isotropic framework of space.

But dialectics can only be filled with content by activity upon the object—that is, by practice and experiment. Since the object did not exist for Hegel, his dialectic could never be filled with realistic content, and remained a beautiful and intricate mill grinding the air of theory and producing nothing but his prejudices and aspirations.

3. THE EXPLOSION OF THEORY

The failure of Hegel was inevitable. Because of the bourgeois conception of the machine and of the general make-up of society, human desires include all the blood-warm valued qualities of existence and emerge spontaneously on the scene— their past history is veiled in the shadow of the free market. It is not possible to see the process by which they were originally determined through the 'production complex' at whose heart lies the machine. Hence mind seems undetermined—that is, spontaneous and 'free.'

But this reflected separation of theory from practice and of desire from object is a reflex of a cleavage of classes which is fundamental to society. On the one hand there is the bourgeoisie, in whose heads the theory of society is concentrated, by virtue of the class division which has given to the bourgeoisie the task of the conscious supervision of the labour process. On the other hand there is the proletariat who actually deal with the object, Nature, but to whom theory is a 'reserved' item, a privilege of their betters. The philosophy of the bourgeoisie sunders theory from practice because they are sundered in the concrete living of society.

The study of the object becomes the study of the object *in contemplation* and therefore lacks the dynamic reality of struggle. The effect of this is to make science too mechanistic and rob it of living theory. That is not to say science has no theory: it is impossible to have any practice without a theory, but science's theory is the minimum theory possible, a theory which is empiricist and opportunist because it springs directly from practice. It is not a theory which has been evolved to meet the needs of a man's whole life in society—including his scientific speculation. It is a specialized theory designed only to meet the needs of a man as a scientist and not as a man with blood in his veins who must eat, labour, marry and die. This limitation is pointed out with pride by modern scientists. It leaves room for God, they explain.

Take the case of physics. There is first the general theory or philosophy of mechanism, which the bourgeois scientist adopts unconsciously. He has no idea it is a metaphysics: he imagines it to be the only way of looking at things scientifically—i.e. objectively. He supposes that the object as it appears in bourgeois economy is the only way in which Nature can appear to men. This philosophy is common to all sciences.

In addition there is the specialized theory springing directly from the practice of physics, which from time to time contradicts this theory and leads to its improvement.

All goes well till a point is reached where practice with its specialized theory has in each department so contradicted the general unformulated theory of science as a whole that in fact the whole philosophy of mechanism explodes. Biology, physics, psychology, anthropology, and chemistry, find their empirical discoveries too great a strain for the general unconscious theory of science, and science dissolves into fragments. Scientists despair of a general theory of science and take refuge in empiricism, in which all attempt at a general world view is given up; or in eclecticism, in which all the specialized theories are lumped together to make a patchwork world-view without an attempt to integrate them, or in specialization, in which all the world is reduced to the particular specialized theory of the science with which the theorist is practically concerned. In any case, science dissolves in anarchy; and man for the first time despairs of gaining from it any positive knowledge of reality.

This is the state of bourgeois science at the present day, and the crisis in physics is only a special expression of it. And of course it is only a still wider version of the general movement of bourgeois economy into anarchy; the productive forces at all points have expanded and burst the confines of the production relations. Humanized nature seems to be escaping, like a Frankenstein monster, from the meshes of naturalized men. The machine is getting out of control of the mechanic. This points the way forward. The disintegrating old contains the developing new. A new set of production relations; a new society; new ideological categories; a new or wider world view.

4. REALITY AS APPEARANCE

But the effect of this disruption of the old bourgeois worldview on scientists is to throw them back, for an explanation of reality, upon those qualities, in all their active sensuousness, which they had successively abandoned to subjectivity. We saw that the development of subjectivity fell to the lot of so-called philosophers.* I say so-called, for while they were certainly philosophers, their claim to regard their field, subjectivity, as all philosophy, is untenable. Philosophy can only mean the most general theory of practices, and therefore it must include the theory of science. But philosophy merely concerned itself with subjectivity which excluded even mind regarded as an object (i.e. experimental psychology). It was an important moment for so-called philosophy when psychology slipped out of its grasp into the camp of the experimentalists, for this finally exposed the completely anchorless state of its ship. It was subjective activity, *active upon nothing at all.*

Hence the feature of the present crisis in physics, is that the 'scientists turn to philosophy'. What in fact this really means is that they find their philosophy of mechanism shattered beyond repair by the progress of science and turn to the other side of the medal, to the erstwhile schismatics of subjectivity, to fill the breach. Scientists now seek in the 'laws of thought' a certitude which they cannot find in the laws of the object.

But we saw that the subjectivist had in the interim developed on the same lines as the mechanist. He had stripped the subject of all objective qualities until nothing was left but the absolute Idea—the Idea existing objectively out of the brains of men. But in doing this he had stripped subjectivity of the subject—man. Hence when the mechanist turned to the subjectivist for assistance he found that the subject had vanished. The object had for the mechanist become unknowable, or a thing-in-itself, or had ceased to exist—these are all different ways of putting the same discovery—and now he found that exactly the same has happened to the subject.

What then could exist, *philosophically,* for the scientist? Only phenomena—that is, appearance—the conscious field regarded as independent of subject and object. The subject-object relations is regarded as existing apart from its terms. This has some resemblance to the absolute idealism of Hegel, but because the scientist regards even subjectivity mechanically, he cannot accept the dialectic logic of Hegel. Hegel's dialectics ostensibly draws its validity from the power of reason.

* Also artists, but this is another story.

225

It rests on the inward and unquestionable witness of the 'I' which thus, in the alienation of the Absolute Idea, appeals to itself to deny itself. But the scientist, by his training and experience, cannot accept the 'I' as the criterion of validity. He is born in practice. Hence he cannot accept the subjective authority of the Hegelian dialectic. He can only accept phenomena as they come. This is positivism.

But in fact phenomena emerge from the concrete living of society, and this is an active struggle of Man and Nature. If Man and Nature are ruled out as unreal and non-existent, phenomena all have absolutely equal validity: hallucination and real perception, scientific theory and barbarous logic, there is no means of choosing between them. Truth is meaningless. We are in fact—if positivism is carried out logically—back at the subjective idealism of Berkeley and the scepticism of Hume. Positivism is solipsism. Nothing exists but my experience.

But in fact the positivist will not face up to his premises. He continually smuggles in some co-ordinating principle which in fact presupposes the existence of the very things he cannot prove. For example, he includes in phenomena 'other people's phenomena' and so accepts the findings of science and other organized knowledge. Yet in fact he has no right to accept other people's perceptions except by admitting the link, his human brain and other human brains, which means admitting the subject, Man, and the object, the matter of which brains are composed. He smuggles in 'principles of economy' which are simply logical laws admitting therefore the validity of the subject; and 'laws of efficiency' which admit the existence of the object through the test of the practice.

Mechanism sacrifices theory to practice. Subjectivism sacrifices practice to theory. Positivism denies the validity of both, but in fact is always driven to smuggle one or other in by a back-door, because the very reason for its existence is that theory has been whittled away by mechanism and practice by subjectivism. Hence positivism is always a confused, amateurish and dishonest philosophy. It makes a degradation of bourgeois thought as compared to the simple grandeur of

Newtonian physics and the world-dominating insurgence of Hegelian dialectics. This confusion is very clear in the writings of the older positivists, Mach and Pearson, and the newer positivists, Eddington and Jeans. Their writing is full of contradictions, they shift from one premise to another without realizing it: their writing is a mesh of excluded middles and *non sequiturs,* directly it deals with philosophical questions.

5. THE SCREEN OF PHENOMENA

'Sensation is nothing but a direct connection of the mind with the external world; it is the transformation of energy of external excitation into a mental state ... the sophistry of idealist philosophy consists in that it takes sensation, not as a connection of the mind with the other world, but as a screen, as a wall which separates the mind from the outer world.' (Lenin)

Consciousness (phenomena) is a relation between Man and Nature, but positivism attempts to take the relation without the terms. This in itself is a result of the splitting of the terms in concrete living.

So split, consciousness, part of the subject-object (the theory of it) ceases to be active. It is impossible to have real activity without two terms, without a contradiction, and a unity of opposites whose activity springs from their interpenetration. Hence consciousness becomes a mere passive 'reflection' of the world; its function becomes merely to be a pale copy of existing practice. The relation of knowing ceases to be an active and mutually determining relation, and becomes a godlike apprehension separate from material reality. But directly it is cut off in this way, it loses its real content.

Hence ideology in bourgeois society becomes distorted to a mere symbol or code-word for reality. Reality knocks on the nerve endings and these are 'interpreted' as consciousness by the subject. This theory of consciousness as mere reflection leads to a regretful admission that it is a 'misleading' reflection. For since all the known subjective qualities (colour, scent, shape, mass, pushiness, beauty) are merely symbolic ciphers for the thing in itself, the 'reality' codified is a queer grotesque spectre, built vaguely out of the most objective qualities obtainable. Thus according to Eddington, the real table is a swarm of molecules buzzing hither and thither, and is totally different from the table we see. The table we see is a mere fiction, a symbol of the real thing. Consciousness here has become a screen. Hence the severance of the subject and object, of Man's natural desires from nature as known by Man, leads to a splitting of consciousnesses. The consciousness of the bourgeois philosopher is torn into two. One half of it flies to the objective pole, to become a bare 'copy' of practice on the object and so eventually come to a stage where the object seems unknowable by consciousness.

Moreover, because practice advances on different fronts, this theory splits into several theories adhering to different practices (biology, physics, psychology, etc.) The other half flies to the subjective pole, to become a 'spontaneous' undetermined desire. This emerges as mysticism and religion, with a subject as unknowable as the object. This double decadence into positivism and mysticism is clearly shown in the following quotations from Eddington:

'In regard to our experience of the physical world, we have very much misunderstood the meaning of our sensations. It has been the task of science to discover that things are very different from what they seem. But we do not pluck our eyes out because they persist in deluding us with fanciful colourings instead of giving us the plain truth about wave-length. It is in the midst of such misrepresentations of environment (if you must call them so) that we have to live. . . . In our scientific chapters we have seen how the mind must be regarded as dictating the course of world-building; without it there is but formless chaos. It is the aim of physical science, so far as its scope extends, to lay bare the fundamental structure underlying the world; but science has also to explain if it can, or else humbly to accept, the fact that from this world have arisen minds capable of transmitting the bare structure into the richness of our experience. It is not misrepresentation but rather achievement—the result perhaps of long ages of biological evolution—that we should have fashioned a familiar world out of the crude basis. It is a fulfilment of the purpose of man's nature. If likewise the spiritual world has been transmuted by a religious colour beyond anything implied in its bare external qualities, it may be allowable to assert with equal conviction that this is not misrepresentation but the achievement of a divine element in man's nature....

'... We have to build the spiritual world out of symbols taken from our own personality, as we build the scientific world out of the metrical symbols of the mathematician.'

'... The idea of a universal mind or Logos would be, I think, a fairly plausible inference from the present state of scientific theory; at least it is in harmony with it....'

'... The materialist who is convinced that all phenomena arise from electrons and quanta and the like controlled by mathematical formulae, must presumably hold the belief that his wife is a rather elaborate differential equation; but he is probably tactful enough not to obtrude this opinion in domestic life. If this kind of scientific dissection is felt to be inadequate and irrelevant in ordinary personal relationships, it is surely out of place in the most personal relationship of all—that of the human soul to the divine spirit.'

'... The physicist is not conscious of any disloyalty to truth on occasions when his sense of proportion tells him to regard a plank as continuous material, well knowing that it is "really" empty space containing sparsely scattered electric charges. And the deepest philosophical researches as to the nature of Deity may give a conception equally out of proportion for daily life; so that we should rather employ a conception that was unfolded nearly two thousand years ago.'

'... Starting from aether, electron sand other physical machinery we cannot reach conscious man and render count of what is apprehended in his consciousness. ...'

'... If those who hold that there must be a physical basis for everything hold that these mystical views are nonsense, we may ask—what then is the physical basis of nonsense?'

'... We have associated consciousness with a background untouched in the physical survey of the world and have given the physicist a domain where he can go round in cycles without ever encountering anything to bring a blush to his cheek.'

'... The conclusion to be drawn from these arguments is, that religion first became possible for a reasonable scientific man about the year 1927.'

'Heaven is nowhere in space, but it is in time. ... Science and theology can make what mistakes they please, provided that they make them *in their own territory*; they cannot quarrel if they keep to their own. ...'

These quotations, taken at random from the final chapters of Eddington's book, indicate the extraordinary confusion and helplessness of the scientists of to-day, faced with the break-up of the old bourgeois world-view. On the one hand objectivity, Nature, has become a game, a symbolism, a separate domain where the physicist can go round in circles without encountering anything real. Nature has become unknowable.

And Man, the subject, dragging with him all the rich qualities of interesting life, has entered the arid regions of *theology*. Could reaction go farther? Because physics has made of Nature something no one can believe as real (a swarm of sparsely distributed electric charges) it is no longer necessary to believe in the refined 'unitarianism' of modern Broad Churchmen—we can go right back to the Virgin Birth, the miracles of the loaves and fishes, and the 'simplicities' of the New Testament narrative. The wild Elizabethan human desires set free by the bourgeois market have become pious. The machine planned by the bourgeois to satisfy his wants has become unknowable; it has slipped out of his grasp down into the night of the proletariat.

6. THE RE-DISCOVERY OF THE OBJECT

For, in fact, this is where Nature has disappeared. The severance of subject from object by the development of a class cleavage in society, has resulted in that part of society which groups itself round the machine, becoming increasingly organized Man—Man organized by Nature. It follows the grain of objective reality and enters increasingly into the production complex of humanized nature. This group in practical contact with Nature is increasingly *proletarian* society—society debarred from consciousness by the conditions of its existence. It is active of Nature in a blind way—but it is active. It is true that in the experiments of physics for example the bourgeois is in active contact with Nature, but only on a small front. Even that contact is enough, as we have seen, to produce a disintegration of his whole world-view.

But in the main the most important part of objective activity is handled by the proletariat. The most elaborate and intricate organizations produced by the incursion of Nature into society and the humanization of Nature as a result of the division of labour are organizations of the lives of the proletariat. The dizzy unfolding of Nature within society which is modern civilization takes place within the boundary of the proletariat. The bourgeoisie rides on top of this terrific pregnancy, unorganized except in the old State forms and these forms become increasingly arbitrary, increasingly the product of the apparently blind desires of the bourgeoisie.

They stand in a coercive one way *owning* relation to the forces wielded by the proletariat, and therefore seem all the more free of the object, and masters of Nature. But in fact the object has now retired completely into the night of the exploited class. The bourgeois ignorance of the object, and of the determining relation it has over their lives, makes them its slaves, tossed hither and thither by slump and boom. By cutting finally the cord that binds their desires to the necessity of the object, and making desire and subjectivity a matter of faith and theology, the bourgeoisie prepare the ground for their ejection from power. The pregnancy of the proletariat with the humanized object is a pregnancy which can only issue in revolution.

We saw that practice must inevitably carry with it some theory, however partial and specialized—a theory perhaps distorting and negating the general world-view of the practician. Thus the practice of the physicist carries with it a limited and bloodless theory which conflicts with the older bourgeois world-view and produces a helpless dualism or anarchy. In the same way the actual experience of the proletariat produces a special theory of its own, the theory which springs from the practice of trade union organization.

This limited theory is directly contradictory to the whole theory of bourgeois society, in which freedom lies in absence of restraints, and in a completely free market for labour-power and wages. Trade union organization, with its restrictions and limitations on labour, negates this basic consciousness of bourgeois society, but it is forced on the proletariat by the necessities of concrete living. Hence it has a shattering effect on such portions of bourgeois consciousness and world-view as have been implanted into the proletariat.

None the less the plentitude of freedom and therefore of consciousness still remains in the sphere of the bourgeoisie. The proletariat, alone, cannot rise beyond trade union consciousness. This consciousness, although it sees freedom to be the outcome of restrictions of the market and thus denies bourgeois ideology, yet proposes a freedom which is dependent upon the existence of a bourgeoisie, a freedom within the pores of bourgeois society. It is thus a consciousness limited on every side by bourgeois consciousness and unable to make itself independent, unable to advance to the status of a new world-view.

But the progress of capitalism transforms its own basis and creates conditions of unfreedom even for its own bourgeoisie. The big bourgeoisie grows and expropriates the smaller, who is forcibly proletarianized; or else the big bourgeois forms an alliance with the feudal aristocracy to prevent the advance of the other section. Thus a section of the bourgeoisie is driven to ally itself with the proletariat. Part of this section has no other aim than to use the power of the proletariat to wring concessions from the big bourgeoisie and bring back the old conditions of existence more favourable to petty bourgeois ideals, conditions of existence in which a petty bourgeois could flourish without danger from monopoly capital. This gives rise to the movements of anarchism and reformist social-democracy, which remain within the categories of the bourgeois world view and try to drag the proletariat into it.

But 'when the class struggle nears its decisive hour, the process of dissolution going on within the ruling class, in fact within the whole range of old society, assumes such a violent, glaring character that a small section of the ruling class cuts itself adrift and joins the revolutionary class, the class that holds the future in its hands ... a portion of the bourgeoisie goes over to the proletariat, and, in particular, a portion of the bourgeois ideologists, who have raised themselves to the level of comprehending theoretically the historical movement as a whole. ...'

This small portion joins the proletariat. It does not attempt to use it as a tool to fulfil its own desires because it has been forced in practice to comprehend the historical movement as a whole—i.e. the victory of the proletariat and the impossibility of a return to petty bourgeois ideals. It does not however shed its bourgeois consciousness but drags this with it into the proletariat. The object has already slipped out of the grasp of the bourgeoisie as part of its world-view. The subject has however developed to reach its climax as the Hegelian dialectic. This is a moving dialectic, and it is within the framework of the Hegelian dialectic that this section of the bourgeoisie comprehends the historical movement as a whole at the same time as material causes drive it to a revolt against the existing system and an alliance with the proletariat.

We have already seen that the object, Nature, in its full development by capitalist society, had disappeared into the concrete living of the proletariat. This class was pregnant with Nature as increasingly realized in society by the division of labour. Hence when bourgeois subjectivity in the shape of its most advanced development, dialectics, is driven by material conditions into the bosom of the proletariat it once more encounters the object, and the object is now a result of technological advance, in its most highly humanized form. We saw that dialectics, in spite of its logical rigour and world-embracing grandeur, became mere mystical mumbo-jumbo because it was subjectivity active upon nothing, upon mere appearance and remaining therefore unfounded. But in the heart of the proletariat it encounters the object.

It must not be thought that this is a kind of marriage of long-separate twin souls who suddenly embrace. It is not a case for example of bourgeois mechanism (objectivity) being fused with bourgeois idealism (subjectivity). For mechanism loses the object ultimately without developing the subject, and dialectics ultimately loses the subject without developing the object. Materialism becomes idealism and idealism materialism. Their fusion therefore produces only positivism—the relation without the terms. This was bound to happen because one started with a *contemplated* object and the other with a *spontaneous* subject. Hegelian dialectics cannot marry the object, wrapped in the proletarian night, in the world of theory, for the object is not yet conscious. The object is wrapped in night, and subject and object live in different worlds. Before the marriage can take place, the object must be made conscious by activity, by practice upon it in a world-changing way. It is not a mere case of 'fitting' the results of science into the categories of dialectics.

Dialectics must become active upon the object in real life; only in this way can dialectics become full of content. And since the object is at first entirely concrete and unconscious, this abstraction must begin in the least abstract and most practical way, by making the proletariat conscious of its most general class interests and goal, and by developing the theory of the proletariat from that primary and fundamental activity.

For this reason dialectics became with Marx and Engels a practical revolutionary theory, and it is in this way, as the result of practice, that it becomes dialectical *materialism*. From this most concrete basis, dialectical materialism can then proceed to draw in the ideological products of society—the sciences, ethics, art—and reform them within the new categories.

Can dialectical materialism escape in its development the limitations of bourgeois society, in which the subject became separated from the object? The class of which it has become the world-view, the proletariat, is pregnant with the object and this has produced an increasing organization, a revolutionary expansion, which will continue until the proletariat has become a whole and thus has realized a classless society. As this expansion takes place the revolutionary class, pregnant with the object, sucks more and more of the subjectivity, the consciousness of society, into its sphere. And thus as it actively expands, as scientists, artists, and 'philosophers' desert the

bourgeois class and enter it, its world-view, dialectical materialism, synthesizes more and more of the genuine but anarchic
and dispersed elements of bourgeois consciousness. But this
new consciousness is not one in which active subject is parted
from contemplated object, and the real activity of society
sinks into the night of an unconscious class. In dialectical materialism subject is restored to object because in the society
which generates it, consciousness is restored to activity and
theory to practice.

IV

THE DISTORTION OF PHILOSOPHY

1. THE MONOPOLY OF CONSCIOUSNESS

The essence of the distortion of ideology by a class society is this: a class society consists of a ruling class and and exploited class, and the consciousness of society is the consciousness of the ruling class. This follows from the very mechanism of class formation. At a certain stage division of labour demands that certain men stand to social production in the relation of supervisors, managers and overseers of labour. Only by this means can productivity advance to a higher stage.

Chosen in the first place by tribal society for innate qualities of intelligence, the process of development changes them from overseers or custodians of the means of production on behalf of the community, to owners of them in their own right. But the higher consciousness necessary for the supervisory role persists with this class in their development, and thus the whole consciousness of society gathers at the pole of the owning class.

As the obligation of supervision becomes more and more an absolute right of ownership, the practice passes more and more out of the orbit of the ruling class, who handle increasingly only the theory of society. They stand outside the main organic complex in which Man struggles with Nature. Practice, divorced from theory, yet secretes, as it must, a theory in its pores which represents only a limited and objective consciousness, contrasting with the formal and unanchored consciousness which is the seat of privilege.

The former is a practical but departmentalized theory, split into hundreds of units. The latter is generalized, but is theoretical and stamped through and through with class illusions.

Hence in a class society, the consciousness developed by society receives a characteristic distortion due to the fact that theory is sundered from practice in a special way, and only a part of concrete living falls within its scope. The rest passes out into the night of the other class and returns again transformed—no one knows exactly how.

This is not to say that a classless society is in possession of absolute truth. The classlessness of primitive tribal communism is very far from being the recipe for absolute truth. On the contrary the conscious theory of such a society is primitive, poor in content, and undifferentiated, consonant with the primitive state of society. For Truth—i.e. the living theory of a society—is not an absolute good dropped from heaven; it is an economic product. It is a specific penetration of Nature by Man, and Man by Nature which, as by a mutual reflexing movement, has given rise to an image of each in the terms of the other. In the theory of consciousness, Man interprets Nature in images of himself. In the practice of production Nature is minted in human metal. But science, art and ethics— the vehicles of theory about society—are generated by the development of society itself. The glittering superstructure can only rise upon the foundations of economic production on which it acts and re-acts. It is this action and reaction which produces the continual modification of the superstructure by the base, like the nourishment of a flower by its root. There is a rising and a falling current of sap. Theory is negated by practice, and modified accordingly; the new theory opens the way for a more effective practice.

In a class society however there is a characteristic splitting between theory and practice which isolates the superstructure to an increasing extent. At the same time this distortion of the superstructure is the result of a growth and rearrangement of the root system, which makes for a more efficient economic production and hence—at first—for an elaboration of the superstructure. It becomes specialized, and blossoms. It is only when the specialization and root development pass a certain stage that the life of the whole organic structure is affected.

2. PRIMITIVE MATERIALISM

In this respect therefore a distinction must be made between the special *distortion* of ideology by a class structure in society and the limitations imposed on ideology by a given system of production. These two factors do not necessarily work together and a specific distortion, by overcoming the limitations of production, may give rise to a luxuriant though one-sided growth.

Primitive ideology conceives reality free from the distortions of a class society. It is materialistic in its outlook. Animism is primitive materialism. Class society completely separates mind from matter, and the activity of the Universe from the stuff which is active. It separates growth and change, as an immanent force, from that which grows and changes. It analyses motion into space, the most generalized form of the persistent object, and time, the most abstract form of phenomenal activity. Theory lies apart from practice.

When idealism finds that the savage makes no such distinction, but observes a world in which things move because of an immanent power, and change by virtue of inner activity, not being changed or impelled by forces outside the Universe, it at once imagines that the savage has first separated mind, subjectivity, from objects and then thrown them back again into the objects in the form of Mana, Oronda, spirit, or power. But of course the savage has never been through this prior stage. The savage sees the world (or rather objects, he does not yet see a Universe) as self-changing and self-developing things. He himself is a self-changing, self-developing thing and therefore he makes the mistake of supposing that the activity of objects is to them what subjectively his own is to him. He attributes to them will, feeling and desire, as he knows these things. Perhaps to this degree he is guilty of 'animism'. But he is by no means guilty of the animism ascribed to him by class society, that of throwing back into nature all the categories of subjectivity, of spirit, sucked from it by a class ideology.

To this degree dialectical materialism is a return to primitive materialism just as communism is a return to primitive communism.

It returns to reality, the life that has been extracted from it by the class distortion of ideology. But it is materialism gathering up into itself all the richness of ideological history which has taken place as a result of the economic development which this cleavage made possible.

It synthesizes mechanism—the bourgeois development of objectivity and practice—with its sundered pole of subjective theory. And in exactly the same way, on the economic level, it gathers up into itself, and resolves the contradictions, between the organization made necessary by the division of labour and the personal freedom made possible by the plenty which is the result of division of labour.

Primitive materialism is materialist because it gives to substance an inner activity and capacity for history which is abstracted from it by class society. Of course it is a crude self-moving power—that of Mana. In the same way primitive materialism is monist—it ascribes to all things a sympathetic influence on others, like the universal law of gravity of Newton. This 'sympathy' is also crude and subjective—that of magic.

3. THE COSMIC MARKET

Bourgeois practice also gives objects a certain self-moving power, under the abstract guise of force, and a certain monism under the guise of gravity or the space-time continuum. In this unity of pluralism and monism it is still materialist. But already ideology has been robbed of all the sensuous and qualitied richness which is present in reality in however crude a form in primitive materialism. These have been delivered over to theory for a separate development.

The abstraction of bourgeois objectivity is due to a similar abstraction in society. The growth of the market equates all commodities to a common denominator—exchange-value. Even men are reduced to a common labour-power. This ruthless stripping of all qualities to an abstract commonness reaches in the era of manufacture a limit which gives us on the one hand the abstract 'economic' Man, the producer, the common unit of labour power, and on the other hand the common regulating principle, the market.

This is reflected in Newtonian physics. The particles, independent and self-sufficient, travelling on ideal right lines at equal speeds (except for their collisions) are equivalent to the abstract producers, the units of society. And the law of gravity represents the regulative principle of the market.

How impossible it is for bourgeois man to escape at that period from this conception of objectivity is shown by the contemporary conception of Leibniz, superficially different from Newtonianism but in fact the same in essence. The self-moving particles are the monads. The regulating principle of the market is the God to which all the monads open their windows.

The law of gravity, God, and the 'free' regulative market are conceptions that fit in with bourgeois society like hand in glove. The abstract God of bourgeois deism is a God peculiar to a society which has reduced the mysterious unknowable element in society to the market which equates everything to a common term, exchange-value. God is always humanity's name for its confused perception of the past of society which is hidden from it. To the primitive the divine element is above all magic and magic is 'sympathy.' It is the mysterious but undifferentiated instinct which binds together a tribe. It is the herd instinct realized in an economic shape. As such it is one category of the interconnection or determinism which everywhere secretly unites phenomena and makes the Universe one. The primitive projects his subjective experience of this interconnectedness, which is nothing but tribal solidarity, into the object, and sees Nature as united by magic—a 'feeling' between things. And as division of labour occurs and individuals realize themselves in the tribe as elders, chiefs and kings, he sees this magic wielded by individuals, who presently acquire the status of gods.

Bourgeois practice becomes stripped of quality and human warm-bloodedness. Magic now changes into determinism, in which the possibilities of man's active charge of matter are generalized in a framework of causality. Because this is free from the savage's subjectivity, it is real scientific causality and not the 'feeling' of magic. But this very abstraction from subjectivity has robbed determinism of all quality. God becomes a kind of self-moving necessity. Hence bourgeois man's confused notion of what unites society appears as the bourgeois God, the monotheistic principle of existence.

4. GOD-MAKING

But by reducing quality and use-value to exchange-value, bourgeois society could not make quality disappear. It could only prise quality loose from the object to float round as subjectivity, as 'spontaneous' human desire. Although this subjectivity is developed separately, it also is a confused perception of society but of the opposite face; it is also attached to God. Thus the God of bourgeois society is a compound God, playing a dual role. On the one hand he is God the colourless abstract principle of theology, source of necessity and law, the God of Malebranche's and Descartes' philosophies. Such a God is unappetizing. He is a symbol for man's faith in practice which, because it is torn apart from theory, is a faith *in* practice and not a theory of practice. On the other hand he is God the focus of subjectivity and quality, the God of the mystic, the God of the Trinity; the personal God: the God to whom it is possible to ascribe the Virgin Birth, the Crucifixion, anger, and an interest in the individual. Here we have an appetizing God who is the same as the other. He is a *human* God, just as the other is a natural God. This confounding of Gods is the source of all the contradictions of religion—why does a kind God allow us to become lepers, and children to be hurt, for example? The God full of human values who is yet forced to permit evil because he is caught in the wheel of his own infinite justice and respect for law is a reflection of human desires trapped by natural ncessity because the interplay of the two is not yet understood.

But it is wrong to suppose that these two different Gods could have been fused—that theology and mysticism could have come to terms. For their fusion would mean the reunion of theory and practice and therefore the disappearance of the confusion which led to God. The divine principle of the savage, the unifying magic which is also causality, does not suffer from this cleavage because it is a causality full of feeling and warm blood. They fly apart in a class society and it is precisely their flying apart which develops on the one hand causality and on the other hand subjectivity.

The theological God represents as it were the back parts or wounded stub of objectivity or practice. Theory appears to be ripped from practice and objectivity is cut off from subjectivity in consciousness, because the shadow of the night of the exploited class lies over their connections and makes them secret. The personal God is the mutilated end of subjectivity. Yet if they could be fused, if the underground connections between objectivity and subjectivity could be dragged to light (because the exploited class has come into the possession of consciousness) then everything would be plain, and there would be no need to give the mysterious name God to a clearly revealed process of society.

This separation of theory from practice in society, which gave rise to the God of class society with his special dual role of abstract monistic law and human quality, reflected a division of labour which was a necessary stage of evolution if productivity was to advance. It was therefore the means of advancing scientific thought and human feeling. Logic, as with the schoolmen, and poetry, as with the Greek tragedians, were tied to complexes of thought whose lineaments, bathed in the penumbra of a class, were the scaffolding of an undeveloped consciousness.

This dual role of Deity is not peculiar to bourgeois philosophy. It is general for all class society, in which a cleavage between theory and practice must necessarily take place. In all the developed religions we see a monistic abstract tendency which is monotheism in embryo. Even in the most fantastically pluralistic pantheons of Egypt or India, this abstract God appears as necessity, or the Divine Principle, as Brahma, Karma. It is the Law, to which even the Gods themselves are subject: and it is expressed also in the thought that all the Gods are aspects of one personality. In this way man expresses his confused perception of science. He has a formal hypothesis for his nascent understanding of the interconnection of everything, as this interconnection is coming to light in the practical exploration of Nature by society.

But this interconnectedness is denied by the cleavage in society, which wrests subjectivity from objectivity. Hence subjectivity appears in the manifold guise of the Gods with all their rich personalities and endearing or formidable traits. Man thus exercises an aesthetic function which has been confused by his role in society. This is the realm of mythology as opposed to art. Man exhibits capacity for making false concrete images which yet express real subjective truths.

This twin division has sprung from magic for which the world is full of interconnectedness and self-motion but only as qualities of *feeling* and therefore correspondingly crude and simple.

Bourgeois philosophy expresses this contrast between monotheism and pluralism in the sharpest way. On the one hand the refined theological concepts of Hegelian philosophy, in which God becomes a depersonalized Idea like that of gravity; on the other hand the preservation of all the barbarous mythology of early Christianity because of its warm human quality. These myths lose the fluidity of legend and become fixed, like a piece of journalism. But what signals that this marks the *final* stage of religion, and the oncoming of a classless society in which these penumbras will not be cast, is that both abstract and personal Gods are fossil Gods. In the bourgeois era religion loses its artistic myth-creating power and merely preserves the myths and hagiography of the classical and medieval eras: and equally theology cannot escape from musty Platonism and scholastic reasoning. The life has gone out of both, and this life reappears elsewhere as science and art of an unprecedented luxuriance, even though both the science and art are still distorted by the necessities of appearing in a class society, and cast a shadow in which mysticism is bred.

5. NATURE AND THE SLAVE-OWNER

The distortion of the world-view by its generation in a class society varies with the basis on which class divisions rest. In bourgeois society the freedom from social 'restraints' which is its form produces on the one hand an active but 'spontaneous' subjectivity, and on the other hand, a merely contemplated necessity.

In Aristotelian society, however, the distortion is of a different form. There is no longer a cosmos of self-moving particles whose movements are automatically regulated on a universal scale by a mysterious force of gravity; nor does subjectivity appear as something completely alien and spontaneous; for the free commodity market, of which such a world-view is the reflection, is not fully developed in such a society. Pre-bourgeois class society is a slave-owning or serf-owning society, and hence its philosophy of objective reality is one of coercion or will; coercion is not veiled in such society, for production is openly determined by the will of the slave-owner. True, coercion is the moving principle of bourgeois society, but it is veiled and not conscious, and men see reality through a glass coloured by their subjective relation to society. But coercion is conscious in earlier class society. There is no free market into which the exploited toiler can bring his labour-power on a spurious basis of equality with the owners of the means of production; nor does the social will emerge from the market in a spontaneous abstract way like a force of Nature. Social will is the lord's will—the slave produces directly for him—and the relation is simple and coercive. The master proposes an end and the slave fulfils it as a matter of coercion. Thus the physical world viewed by the ruling class of such a society is a world of ends and purposes—it is teleological instead of mechanist. Or rather it is mechanistic in a slave-owning way. It still obeys the categories of mechanism for these are merely the categories of objectivity but now the machine is a slave-owning machine and not a capitalist machine.

The conscious relation of the ruling class to men engaged in changing Nature to meet social desire is different, therefore Nature looks different to them. They explore it with a different microscope. The object is seen through the instrument of a slave class and not of a proletariat.

In a slave-owning society the productive complex at whose kernel is the machine is still undeveloped. The machine is a mere tool, an outgrowth or auxiliary. Hence the supervision of the slave is not a matter of knowing the inner determinism of nature in a detailed fashion, but mainly a matter of conveying one's purpose to the slave, who fulfils it to the best of his ability. He is a human being; it is sufficient to give him a command. One sets before him an aim. The organization of labour does not reflect as deeply as in bourgeois society the social division of labour. There are slave gangs—masses of men on whom the master's will is imposed with a lash—there is none of the elaborately differentiated organization of a factory staff springing from the necessities of the stuff handled and the machinery used.

Hence the movement of objective reality, Nature, can be satisfactorily expressed in terms of purposes, or ends. Fire rises because its destined place is above; heavy material falls for the same reason: it too seeks its 'appointed' sphere. The whole Universe is satisfactorily explained as a theatre of Will. Determinism or the interconnectedness of phenomena, which is the most general category of objective reality in all societies, must in slave-owning society take the form of a pre-willed Fate. The Universe is a complete arrangement determined by some divine consciousness in a Universal Plan. In the same way accident is merely Divine necessity. As with Oedipus, accident is one will thwarting another; God interfering in the plans of man; or Moira in the plans of God. And because no market exists to cut man from Nature by a chasm and give the machine-complex an apparently self-moving power, the causality which is cosmic Will has to be perpetually *sustained*. The planets are urged on by spirits; the moving object perpetually needs force to overcome a resistance; there is a Prime Mover, God, who does not merely act as a universal co-ordinating force, but who actively pushes things on. This activity is not the laborious activity of a slave, directed physically upon an object, but the activity of will of a slave-owner, active upon nothing but the coerced mind of the slave. God, the master, must always stand over slavish Nature, lash in hand. Hence teleology is not opposed to mechanism, it is mechanism as it emerges in a slave-owning society, just as mechanism is teleology as it emerges in a bourgeois society. But the higher degree of interpenetration of Nature and Man which takes place in bourgeois society ensures that mechanism is a richer, more complex, more accurate picture of objective reality than teleology. However, teleology contains more warm human qualities, it is less torn away from subjectivity, than mechanism; and even in bourgeois science it reappears in the spheres of change and higher quality.

Science in society is nature as it emerges in theory, but it can only emerge to theory in practice: it therefore rises through the producing class—the class that mingles actively with Nature. Hence the categories of science or 'things seen' *always reflect in a class society the particular conditions of functioning of the working class as seen by the ruling class.*

But the categories of mind, or 'things felt', emerge directly from the consciousness of the ruling class. Just as it the ruled class which wrestles with Nature, it is the ruling class which is conscious. Therefore the categories of mind—of philosophy, art, and mystical religion—*always reflect in a class society the particular conditions of functioning of the ruling class as* felt by them. Hence in a bourgeois society subjectivity is spontaneous and appears mysteriously containing its own inner sanction just as social desires appear spontaneously out of the free market. Its form shares the independence and irresponsibility as well as the ignorance of causation which is the inevitable atmosphere of the capitalist producer.

Of course bourgeois production is in the first place centred round dead stuff, and does not to any large extent handle living matter in a fashion which would make categories of life important. Agriculture is not mechanized. However, the later development of science leads to the study of biology. Thus biology keeps the categories of slave-owning teleology longer than physics.

Moreover teleology can reappear in biology in a specifically bourgeois form, which it would not be appropriate to discuss here as it would take us too far from our subject. All that need be said here is that bourgeois teleology, when applied to Nature, is by no means the opposite of mechanism, but reflects the categories of capitalist machine production in a different way, owing to the later stage of evolution of capitalism.

V

THE COLLAPSE OF DETERMINISM

1. THE PROBLEM OF FREEWILL

It is a remarkable feature of the present crisis in physics that it raises as central problems difficulties which have always been supposed to be the concern of philosophy. Against their inclinations scientists are driven to be philosophers: that is, they are driven to question the assumptions they had inherited unquestioningly from science; and now this has become a questioning of the very foundations of their world-view.

We have already dealt with the way in which the problem of the subject-object relation began to reveal itself in physics. And now another basic philosophical problem, that of determinism, is recognized by most physicists as requiring restatement in the light of new developments in physics.

If the development of macroscopic or relativity physics raised the whole subject-object problem anew, it was the progress of quantum or atomic physics which forced reconsideration of the problem of causality. Not only have both these problems yet to be solved within the limits of their special fields, but something like a Bohr's correspondence principle in philosophy is required to correlate the two fields.

In the nineteenth century it seemed as if the philosophical basis of determinism had been settled for science in the seventeenth century. Descartes, Locke, Leibniz, Malebranche, Spinoza, Hobbes and even Hume came substantially to the same agreement, in spite of the apparently wide differences between for example the materialism of Hobbes, the spiritualism of Leibniz, the scepticism of Hume, and the theology of Malebranche. Moreover in their philosophy they only gave a systematic basis to the empirical principles of Galileo and Bacon.

Physics developed on this apparently firm basis for three

centuries, and it is only to-day that the whole theoretical basis appears to be shifting, at the same time as the foundations of bourgeois society itself are crumbling away. Here too then it must be that the categories implicit in bourgeois society are inadequate to the new content. The bourgeois world-view is becoming chaotic.

What exactly is it that is contradicting the old solution of the problem of determinism in Nature, and of its associated problem that of freewill in Man, and of yet another problem, often confused with the first, that of causality?

The concept of strict determinism which is at the root of bourgeois physics is most simply expressed by Laplace, who imagined a calculator provided with accurate figures of the precise velocity, mass, and position of every particle in the universe at a given moment. From this he could predict the whole future course of the Universe.

2. THE PRINCIPLE OF INDETERMINISM

This view has been undermined by Heisenberg's Principle of Uncertainty. This principle has proved of great value in experimental quantum physics. It states that the position and velocity of an electron or elementary particle can never be both exactly known. Only an approximate figure can be obtained if both are to be calculated, although either separately can be known to any required degree of precision. The more precisely the velocity or the position is measured, the less precisely the position or the velocity can be ascertained. The connection between them is the extremely small quantum of action—Planck's constant. This quantum connects position and velocity in such a way that the precise location of the electron, or the precise estimation of its velocity, involves a possible error in the other factor, of an extent determined by Planck's constant.

The importance of the principle is that it states an absolute or intrinsic uncertainty as a law of nature. This has been interpreted by many well-known physicists as meaning that indeterminism is a law of Nature.

The principle itself is the result of the development of the quantum theory, the basis of modern atomic research. This theory presumes a fundamental discontinuity in nature which hitherto had always been supposed to be continuous. The differential calculus and Cantor's definition of continuity are both irreconcilable with the quantum. It is now believed that all transactions between atoms are quantized—that is, that the 'action' involved must always be an exact quantum or integral multiple of quanta. Action is energy, or mass, multiplied by time. The quantum of action is excessively minute ($6.55 \cdot 10^{-27}$ erg seconds) which is why this discontinuity in nature had not been observed before. The theory has received a body of experimental confirmation: Nature proceeds by jumps.

How do physicists account for the success of theories such as Newton's and Einstein's, which presume a basic continuity in phenomena and in practice seem to give an accurate picture of reality? This is accounted for by Bohr's Correspondence Principle, which states that in proportion as the number of atoms involved increases, quantum laws approach more nearly to the classical laws of Newton and Einstein. The sort of objects observed by classical physicists, such as earths and billiard balls, contain so many billions of atoms that the difference between quantum laws and classical laws is not measurable. The innumerable discontinuities overlap so to speak and become continuous. It will be noticed that this is only a probability. The discontinuities might coincide and be perceptible. But the odds against this are so enormous that the possibility can be neglected in the ordinary way.

Thus the old 'immutable' laws of classical physics are now held by physicists to be only statistical or 'probability' laws. They are only very likely to apply to mass phenomena, such as those of billiard balls and suns. In this they are like certain laws which had long been familiar to physicists, the laws of thermodynamics. According to these laws, heat and pressure in a gas are due to molecular movement. The molecules bounce and jostle each other like flying billiard balls. It is obvious that at any moment these billiard balls may all find themselves flying away from a surface simultaneously, and then there would be the 'miracle' of a gas without pressure. Gas pressure rises with an increase of heat because the molecules move faster.

Again, when hot and cold bodies are in contact, the faster moving (hot) molecules hit the slower moving (cold) molecules and speed up the slow molecules, themselves slowing up as a result. However, a number of collisions are likely to take place in which the slow molecule strikes the fast molecule in such a way that the fast molecule is still further speeded up and the slow molecule still further slowed. If by chance, in any one instance, all the collisions, or the greater number of them, were to be of this character, there would be the 'miracle' of a hot body gaining heat from a colder body. The nature of the circumstances however makes this unlikely. The more molecules, the greater the probability. This probability approaches certainty with ordinary objects; and so the scientist confidently predicts that the kettle of water will not turn to ice if placed on the fire.

However the classical laws of motion, such as Einstein's and Newton's, were supposed to be of a higher character than the laws of thermodynamics. It had always been supposed that the probability laws of thermodynamics could ultimately be reduced to certainty laws. Just as the insurance company's 'expectation of life' in the case of middle-aged men can be reduced to certainty in the case of a particular middle-aged man whom you happen to see being run over by a bus. For example, if we throw a die, we may say it is only a five to one *chance* which number turns up but it would appear that if we knew the exact position of the centre of gravity of the die, and the minute irregularities of the surface of the die, the table, and the interior of the dice-box, and the exact path and velocity of the hand as it moved in the throw, and the mass and specific gravity of the die and box, and the times involved, and the density and temperature of the air, and so forth, then we could, according to Hamilton's classical Law of Least Action, compute with absolute certainty what the number would be. In the same way it was felt that if we knew the life history of every molecule involved in a heat exchange we could estimate its behaviour and by summing the life history of all the molecules concerned arrive at an exact law, certain in its operation, which would however be so like the probability law in the case of visible objects that the certainty would not be worth the extra trouble.

Heisenberg's Principle of Uncertainty shatters this hope. The individual life history of the molecule depends on that of its constituent atoms, these in turn depend on that of its constituent electrons, and the life history of these according to Heisenberg's Principle can never be exactly known.

How did Heisenberg arrive at this conclusion? In this way: if a quantum of action is involved in all electronic trans- actions, as now securely established, any observation of a particle must involve the release or addition of a quantum of action to the particle observed. This will affect the particle correspondingly, like the recoil from a gun. Observation in- volves interference (the emission or reception of light, for example) and the quantum sets a minmum to this inter- ference. The quantum of energy is a product of both position and velocity. The sharper we make the position the more we alter the velocity; the more exactly we observe the velocity the vaguer the position.

According to various physicists such as Jeans and Edding- ton, the conclusion to be drawn from this is that causality and determinism are no longer principles of physics, and it is possible to understand how the human will can be free.

3. THE SANCTION OF DETERMINISM

It is important to note that to the bourgeois determinism, causality, and free will have specific meanings which are by no means general to philosophy but suck their significance from the soil of bourgeois culture.

Determinism is to the bourgeois a characteristic of the world of Nature. It implies a necessary connection between events of such a character that the whole universe of events can be regarded as unrolled from the beginning according to inevitable laws. This predeterminism (as it in fact is) is sym- bolized by Laplace's calculator to whom the progress of the

Universe can be exactly predicted once any section of it is known. He could of course with equal certainty move back into the past. Thus the whole of being from beginning to end is necessarily determined by any one sector.

Evidently the doctrine of absolute determinism cannot be proved in practice, for to do so requires the unrolling of the whole of being. It is a principle. Nor can its sanction in the form stated be found in reason. How then did the seventeenth-century philosophers and scientists who laid the foundations of determinism justify their principle?

It was justified by an appeal to God's omnipotence and omniscience. Since God knew all that would come about, it was impossible that what would come about could be otherwise than as God foresaw it in His infinite reason. There was then a necessary connection between events, which could not be otherwise. Hence natural laws were laws of God and also of reason.

The precise expression of this principle took various forms. With Malebranche and Descartes substance (matter) was so inert that it required creation anew for each moment of time. Conservation and change were the same. Hence Matter was from instant to instant suspended in God who therefore supplied a necessary connection between instants of existence.

To Descartes God was also the primary cause of motion. He put in a given quantity of motions, as well as of matter, and the Laws of Conservation of Motion thus expressed a Divine determinism as a lack of active interference by God in the Universe He had made.

Hobbes quite simply grounded determinism on the omniscience of God. God knew everything: hence everything was already settled in its minutest details: the details could not be otherwise than they would be.

Spinoza, in spite of the monism of his Universe, was also a 'strict' determinist. Contingency, efficiency, and freedom are to him only 'apparent'; they are aspects of the divine substance, which is completely determined. True, the aspects of this substance are accidental. The existence of anything whose essence does not involve existence cannot be conceived as necessary, reasons Spinoza, and therefore must be accidental.

None the less these things whose essence does not involve existence are treated by Spinoza as merely apparent; they are little better than illusions. The underlying basis of all phenomena is a substance, God, which is completely determined.

Leibniz, in spite of his idealist approach, equally bases his system on absolute determinism. Although his monads are windowless, they appear to act and react on each other according to causal laws, because all has been arranged by God beforehand according to a pre-established harmony. This harmony is therefore an overriding necessity; it is absolute determinism. It is true that Leibniz attempts to introduce 'pure possibles' and a distinction between hypothetical necessity and absolute nesessity. But the object of this seems to be as follows. At each stage the monad has before it various 'pure possibles' in the form of a choice of acts, of which it chooses one. Thus it is free. God however foresaw that it would choose this 'pure possible' and therefore there is a pre-established harmony. Obviously the only purpose of this qualification is to give a meaning to the conception of freedom and to prevent God from being Himself predetermined by the monads. It in no way interferes with the absolute predeterminism of the Universe.

Newton, although not an expert philosopher, accepted unquestioningly this method of approach. To him dead matter was inert, and all the transactions of matter were effected by spirit.

'We might add something concerning a certain most subtle spirit which pervades and lies hid in all gross bodies by the force and action of which spirit the particles of bodies attract one another at near distances, and cohere, if contiguous; and electric bodies operate to greater distances, as well repelling as attracting neightbouring corpuscles; and light is emitted, reflected, refracted, inflected, and heat, bodies, and all sensation is excited. . . .' (Gen. Schol., *Principia* III, p. 547.)

When the same kind of spirit is used to explain the force of gravity, it becomes the Divine Spirit—God. Thus in Newton's Universe too the particles are suspended in God, and derive the necessary connection of the events in which they participate from Him.

Hume is generally supposed to deny causality. Yet in spite of his scepticism he brings to his study of phenomena a naïve conviction of absolute determinism, and finds a justification for it in a principle of 'uniformity.' He denies causality; but bourgeois causality is in any case not the same as bourgeois determinism. The 'invincible uniformities' of Hume are therefore a subjective and individualistic form of strict determinism.

In the older theological form these uniformities had a sterner cast. Since the uniformity was a necessary connection mediated by God, one might look for laws of Nature, like those of gravity, of a divine simplicity. In Hume's sceptical approach, there seemed no reason for such a faith; it is a mere individualistic foible. Hence Hume was the first positivist. With positivsits, as with Cartesians or Newtonians, there is an initial presumption of absolute determinism in Nature. The former however make it a theological rule; the latter smuggle it in as a principle of economy or (in this case) uniformity. Hume is therefore a mechanist, but a confused one, as he imagines that by being sceptical of causality and freedom he is being sceptical of mechanism. But as we shall presently see, causality is not the same as determinism.

Kant carries this confusion of Hume's somewhat farther. Hume unconsciously sought for determinism and uniformity in natural phenomena and having found them believed them to be primary because of his mechanistic bias. He might as easily have sought indeterminism and diversity and when he found them—as he could—insisted on accepting them as primary. It would have been equally valid. But Kant *consciously* seeks for 'causality' (i.e. determinism) in Nature; or rather he says that the mind necessarily imposes a deterministic scheme on phenomena. How the mind can do this unless the phenomena are of a character which makes this possible—i.e. already have necessary connections of some kind—is not discussed satisfactorily by Kant. Kant thus substitutes for a necessary connection between phenomena a necessity of the mind to see connections between phenomena. The mind takes the place of God in earlier philosophers. But the net effect is the same. All knowable phenomena—all that exist for us—are determined as absolutely as in the Cartesian scheme.

Berkeley adopts a similar view: all phenomena are 'caused' by a spiritual substance which is in fact God. Hence all events are grounded in God, just as they are by Newton or Malebranche, and this suspension of inert matter in God provides, because of God's omniscience, an absolutely deterministic framework. There is a necessary connection, *which could not be otherwise* than it is, between all events. It is true that from Newton to Berkeley there has been a change from corpuscles to phenomena (*esse est percipi*) as the basis of events, but this merely represents the divorce of the philosophy from experimental physics. Interest has swung from activity upon objects to enjoyment of objects. It is also true that from Hobbes to Kant there has been a progress from the omniscience of God to causality as a category of Mind. But in both cases an absolutely deterministic framework of events is sanctioned, and the change shown by Laplace, whose divine calculator was really only an exceptionally clever mathematician. God has already become a mere scaffolding for an hypothesis—the principle of determinism—and a scaffolding for which there no longer seemed much need.

4. FROM GOD TO MAN

The eighteenth-century materialists adopted the seventeenth-century principle of absolute determinism. But they did not regard this principle as sanctioned by God; on the contrary it was a hypothesis about Nature, quite independent of the omniscience of God. Hypothesis is hardly the right word. Since they did not admit the possibility of its being modified by experience, it was a dogma. But it was a dogma in its own right. But it was not a dogma for which they advanced the sanction of an omnipotent God. Hence Lamettrie accused Descartes of bringing in God merely 'to please the priests,' to indicate that his system was consistent with God.

We have already mentioned the cleavage between the theological God of mechanism and the subjective God to whom a variety of personal characters is attached. In the age of the dogmatic materialists, the personal characters attached to God bore a close resemblance to those of Louis XIV and the *ancien régime*, and it was for this reason more than any other that the encyclopaedists rejected God as a hypothesis for which they had no use.

Hence the dogmatic materialists are not so different from those seventeenth-century philosophers who give their physics a spiritual tinge. All share a belief in absolute determinism as universally applicable to matter (or objective reality). Indeed this is equally true of Berkeley and Kant. Hegel makes some distinction as to the spheres of Nature in which mechanism is applicable; but fundamentally he accepts the same view. This dogmatic mechanism is aside from the question whether they are materialists or idealists. They are materialists if, like d'Holbach and Diderot, they regard the stuff to which these categories apply as being the sole objective reality; they are idealists if they believe like Berkeley that the stuff to which these categories apply is God. Or again they may be Kantians and believe that objective reality is unknowable in itself and that its deterministic categories are imposed on phenomena by the mind, or they may be dualists like Descartes and believe that substance is bound by God's determinism and yet that in some way mind is free. They may be monists like Spinoza, and believe that matter and mind are aspects of a Divine substance who obeys his own laws; or monadologists like Leibniz and believe that the particles are mindlike and exist according to a pre-established harmony, matter being only a confused perception of mind. They may be positivists like Hume and see matter as a stream of phenomena of which a principle of uniformity is the only organizing factor. It is evident that the connecting link in all these diverse philosophies is a belief in the validity of absolute determinism as applied to natural phenomena. It is therefore by no means the case that mechanism is the distinguishing feature of dogmatic materialism as modern philosophers hold. Russell for example suggests that materialism as a philosophy is characterized by (*a*) The sole reality of matter; (*b*) The universal reign of law. Point (*b*) in the light of point (*a*) means that the essence of dogmatic materialism is 'The universal reign of law in natural phenomena', and we have seen that this belief was common to Descartes, Berkeley, and Kant, who are by no means materialists.

It is true that Lamettrie, for example, is a dogmatic materialist in his assertion of the universal reign of a particular type of law in phenomena, but Hobbes, in deducing determinism from the omnipotence of God, and Kant, in deducing it from the character of the mind which fits all phenomena into such a scheme, are equally dogmatic as to the universal reign of determinism in natural phenomena.

The precise way God or mind enters the scheme therefore is a question of the particular relation of God to social development. In the time of Newton, the bourgeoisie advanced against feudalism by backing a protestant God against a Catholic one. As Marx said, the case of Charles I, and the success of the Puritans, showed how divine inspiration from above could be countered by divine inspiration from below. Hence the God of this period is a God who expresses the expansive and practical relation of the bourgeoisie to Nature. He is a God who does not discourage experiment and speculation. It is precisely by experiment with Nature, by its command over the object, that the bourgeoisie at this period advances.

Half of religion is confused science—a muddled perception of objective reality. The perception of objective reality involved in bourgeois society is a deterministic one, and therefore at this stage the bourgeois confuses determinism or necessary connection with God. The theological God is simply the bourgeois name for abstract qualities of real matter, just as the personal God is a name for the abstract qualities of human society.

5. THE TRANSITION TO IDEALISM

Towards the latter half of the eighteenth century religion had become a reactionary force, and had allied itself with the landed aristocracy and finance capital. It was the enemy of the small bourgeois. Hence on the one hand we have the spokesman of the reactionary church, Berkeley, making God syno-

nymous with matter itself, and not merely its necessary connection, and robbing science of its sanction in practice. On the
other hand revolutionaries such as Voltaire and Lamettrie
strip matter of as much of God as possible, and become Theists
or atheists. With both schools matter is all which is not-mind,
but with Berkeley not-mind is God, with Lamettrie not-mind
is not-God, who, being neither matter nor mind, does not
exist. Kant and Hume represent still other positions; with
them the determinism is drawn out of the flux of experience.
By Hume it is drawn out of this flux considered as outside the
mind—from the far side of the flux, as it were. With Kant it
is drawn from the mind's side of the flux. In both cases the
mind of the individual replaces God.

Hence we have four possible derivatives of mechanism in
an individual philosophy: (*a*) The nature of God—matter's
behaviour explained in terms of God. (*b*) The nature of Nature 'matters' behaviour explained in terms of matter (*c*) The
nature of phenomena, matter's behaviour explained in terms
of personal experience. (*d*) The nature of mind, matter's behaviour explained in terms of the perceiving mind.

It is obvious that all these have as their foundation a
dogmatic predisposition towards seeing mechanism in Nature.
This is so fundamental that it must be drawn from the very
categories of bourgeois society. True there are differences in
the whole trend of the philosophy. Newton's philosophy is
one resolutely turned towards the object—Nature—and seeking to explore it—it is a world-grasping experimental philosophy. Berkeley and Kant are concerned primarily with the
subject and with theory and therefore cut themselves off from
the object and from experiment. The positivists go even farther in this direction, since in consistent positivism we can
find no 'real' principle in phenomena, not even, as with Kant,
a principle of the mind. We can only find principles of
'economy', etc.

But this difference in the trends of these philosophies represents the difference between progressive and reactionary
classes. As capitalism develops, theory becomes sundered from
practice, subjectivity becomes the special province of philosophy and objectivity that of science. Local reactions within

the general development appear as special solutions of the problem. All agree on the attribution of mechanism to Nature: the only quarrel is how large a field is embraced by Nature, and this is a matter of how much is demanded by mind, which again is a reflection of how far theory has grown away from practice. It is only when bourgeois society as a whole is doomed, that the bourgeois categories of mechanism began to break down even for the special field of mechanism, the science of physics.

We have already explained how mechanism becomes the world-view of the bourgeoisie in regard to Nature; how it is no accident that capitalist society, which so developed the machine, sees Nature as a machine; and that when its theories of the machine are negated by capitalist crisis so its theories of Nature as a machine must at the same time also prove their contradictoriness. Strict determinism is a characteristic of bourgeois mechanism. It must be sharply distinguished from fatalism, which makes no distinction between Nature and man, whereas absolute determinism, by making determinism a characteristic of Nature, gives man an apparently divine power over Nature. Fatalism is appropriate to a class society based on open coercion of class by class, and hence is an ingredient in all pre-bourgeois religions; it is based on necessity conceived as will. Determinism is however based on necessity inherent in the objects as contemplated; it is appropriate to a society in which coercion is veiled and is achieved though an administration only of objects, men being apparently entirely free. Man stands apart from the object and controls it because of his knowledge of its inherent necessity.

Strict determinism is not the sole characteristic of mechanism. With mechanism there necessarily goes a special distortion of the subject-object relation, in which the subject is torn from the object in a particular kind of way. We have already dealt fully with this.

The conception of strict determinism is also bound up with the problems of causality and freewill, and of probability, accident and necessity. These conceptions too are given in bourgeois society a special interpretation. They are all of a piece with the world-view of the bourgeoisie.

Selected Name Index

Errata

This edition has been photographically reproduced from the 1965 edition printed abroad and contains the following misprints:

page	line			page	line		
7	16	*for* Heisenburg *read* Heisenberg		82	12	*for* un *read* an
12	28	*for* and *read* an			36	*for* recogniced *read* recognised
14	39	*for* mnemenic *read* mnemonic		95	9	*for* intinct *read* instinct
17	19	*for* is is *read* it is			15	*for* ntaure *read* nature
		for expresion *read* expression		120	15	*for* daulism *read* dualism
18	6	*for* culure *read* culture		121	31	*for* in *read* it
	10	*for* setn *read* seen		122	29	*for* These *read* There
22	34	*for* mnemenic *read* mnemonic			31	*for* prision *read* prison
31	24	*for* homogenous *read* homogeneous		126	30	*for* harnesed *read* harnessed
52	14	*for* inellectuals *read* intellectuals			39	*for* results *read* result
61	10	*for* thereapy *read* therapy		127	16	*for* conciousnesses *read*
64	21	*for* lenhgth *read* length				consciousnesses
65	20	*for* woud *read* would		259	8	*for* began *read* begin
79	5	*for* abstrated *read* abstracted				